Colonial Entrepreneurs

Colonial Entrepreneurs

*Families and Business
in Bourbon Mexico City*

John E. Kicza

University of New Mexico Press
Albuquerque

Library of Congress Cataloging in Publication Data

Kicza, John E., 1947–
  Colonial entrepreneurs, families and business in Bourbon Mexico
City.

  Revision of thesis (Ph.D.)
  Bibliography: p.
  Includes index.
    1. Mexico City (Mexico)—Commerce—History.   2. Mexico City
(Mexico)—Manufactures—History.   3. Elite (Social sciences)—
Mexico—Mexico City—History.   4. Businessmen—Mexico—
Mexico City—History.   I. Title.
HF3240.M5K52   1983   305.5'54'097253   82-21962
ISBN 0-8263-0655-1 (v. 1)

Substantial portions of Chapters 2 and 5 have appeared in different
formats in "The Great Families of Mexico: Elite Maintenance and
Business Practices in Late Colonial Mexico City," *Hispanic American
Historical Review*, 62:3 (August 1982) and "The Pulque Trade of Late
Colonial Mexico City," *The Americas*, 37:2 (October 1980) respectively.

To Diane

Contents

Illustrations   viii
Tables   viii
Preface   xiii
1   Introduction   1

Part One: Elite Composition   11
2   The Elite   13

Part Two: Commerce   43
3   International Trade   45
4   Provincial Trade   77
5   Retail Trade in the Capital   101
6   Patterns of Advancement
    in the Commercial World   135
7   Consolidation of Position   155

Part Three: Manufacturing   185
8   Manufacturers   187
9   Artisans   207
10   Conclusion   227

Appendix   245
Abbreviations   253
Notes   255
Glossary   275
Bibliography   277
Index   293

Illustrations

Diego García Conde map   x
Map of late colonial Mexico City   7
following page 154
Drawings of five *pulquerías* in Mexico City
Eighteenth-century apartment house, plan for main
   floor
Second floor of the apartment house
Main floor plan, family mansion of the Conde de
   Santiago de Calimaya
The House of Tiles, family mansion of the Conde del
   Valle de Orizaba
Conde de Heras Soto's family mansion
Marqués de Jaral de Berrio's interior patio
The Parián and Cabildo building, main plaza of
   Mexico City
Dress of a regidor c. 1800
José de Cevallos
José Mariano de la Cotera, Marqués de Rivas Cacho
Servando Gómez de la Cortina, Conde de la Cortina
Miguel González Calderón
Gabriel Gutiérrez de Terán
Francisca Javiera Tomasa Mier y Terán
Domingo de Rábago, Conde de Rábago
Juana María Romero
Francisco Antonio Sánchez de Tagle
Manuel Antonio Valdés
Mariano José de Zúñiga y Ontiveros

Tables

1 The Population of Mexico City in the Late Colonial
   Period   2
2 Ethnic Composition of Mexico City in 1790 and 1805   3
3 Marital Status of the Mexico City Population in 1790   3
4 Types of Stores in the 1816 Commercial Survey   8
5 Creole Presence in the Mexico City Consulado,
   1780–1820   26
6 Untitled Great Families of Mexico City in 1750–1821   33
7 Established Elite Families in the Mexico City Cabildo
   in 1780–1810   35

8 Peso Value of Silver and Gold Produced in Eighteenth-
   Century New Spain   48
9 Spanish Ships Docking in Veracruz 1728–1739 and
   1784–1795   49
10 Voting Membership in the Consulado of New Spain,
   1809–1826   53
11 Commercial Loans made by the Firm of
   Peredo y Cevallos   58
12 Some Commercial Loans of Cofradías   59
13 Cacao Received in Mexico in 1758 and 1759   68
14 Retail Prices for Cacao in Mexico City   69
15 Merchants Dealing in Cacao in 1758 or 1759   70
16 Cochineal and Sugar sent from Veracruz to Spain in
   1796–1810   72
17 Annual Profits Earned by Juan Reyes as Managing
   Partner of a General Store   80
18 Sales to Provincial Clients by José Gómez Campos in
   1785–1789   83
19 Mexico City Merchants Who Were Shareholders in the
   Real de Bolaños in 1788   89
20 Total Value of Different Categories of Stores   112
21 Merchandise on Sale in a Mexico City Pulpería   115
22 Financial Summaries of Five General Stores in
   Mexico City   117
23 Financial Summaries of Four Vinaterías in Mexico City 119
24 Pulquerías of Mexico City in 1784   122
25 Salaries of Commercial Employees   138
26 Select Genealogy of the González Calderón Family   156
27 Select Genealogy of the Icaza and Iraeta Family   156
28 Wife's Dowry and Husband's Capital in Merchants'
   Marriages   163
29 Age Differences Between Peninsular Merchants and
   Their Creole Wives   166
30 Ranks and Honors Received by Merchants, 1770–1826   174
31 Listed Values of Panaderías at Sale or Inventory   189
32 Listed Values of Tocinerías at Sale or Inventory   199
33 Membership in the Craft Guilds of Mexico City in 1788 209
34 Membership of the Guild of Cotton Weavers in 1796   224

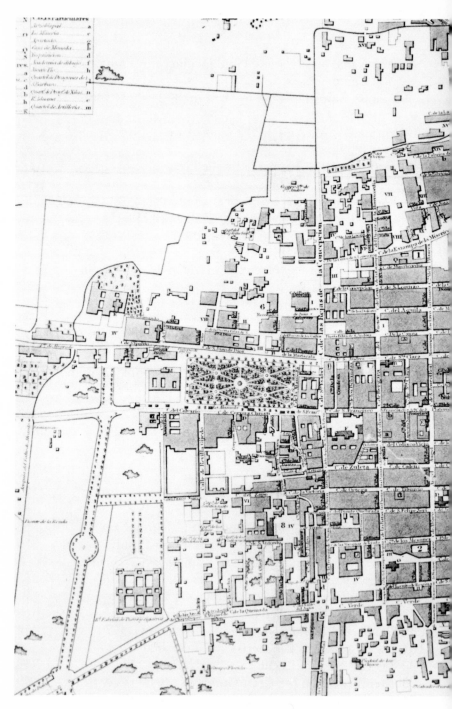

Portion of map of Mexico City in 1793 prepared by Diego Garcia Conde.

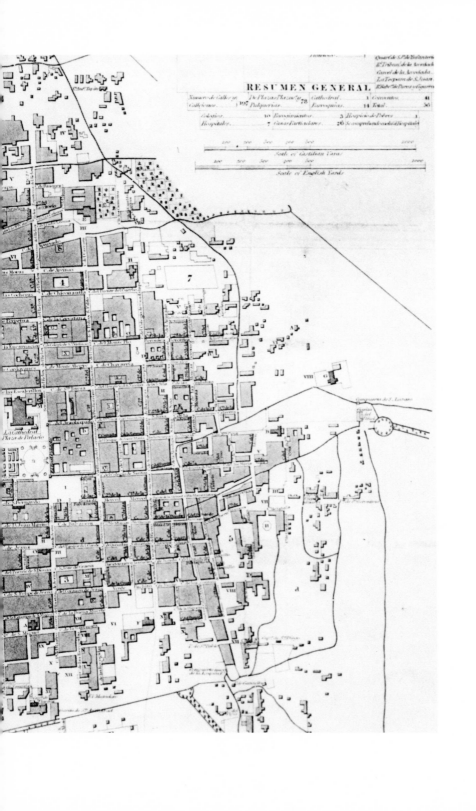

Preface

Mexico City was the headquarters of colonial government and ecclesiastical administration, the dominant commercial center of Middle America, an important manufacturing site, by far the largest city in the Americas at the time, and the residence of the greatest part of New Spain's elite. In the last half-century before the achievement of independence, it dwarfed all other cities in the Americas in the completeness and intricacy of its social composition and in the scale and diversity of its business institutions. Despite these facts, Mexico City itself has been little studied by historians. Occasional publications have examined certain groups and institutions located in the capital, but none to date have described systematically the composition and life patterns of the broad spectrum of social groups in this urban world and how these elements interrelated. In addition, while scholars have long recognized that the capital in certain regards conditioned the development of regional centers from the earliest days of the colony—through its roles as the colony's leading trading entrepot, as the locus of consumption for many domestically produced items, as the bureaucratic center for both church and state, and as a magnet attracting many of the elite and considerable wealth from the provinces— they have not delineated the specific mechanisms by which this was done.

The present study offers a consideration of those mechanisms during the late colonial period, that is, the years between roughly 1770 and 1821. The emphasis throughout is on the business life as opposed to the economic aspects of the personnel in the major occupational and nonoccupational groups found in the city. In other words, attention is given to the structure, procedures, and organization of business rather than to the precise profitability of individual transactions or enterprises or to yearly fluctuations. Thus this work does not purport to present a comprehensive portrait of all forms of economic activity or of every person and group in this urban society. It does, nonetheless, cover many aspects of the lives of people from a wide range of social groups. It attempts to define the primary patterns of behavior in both business and society (for they are inextricably intertwined) of persons active in a gamut of professions, to point out the range of options available to those in each of them, to outline how they made their careers, and to describe how they interrelated with others both within their professions and without.

The entire study will be published in two volumes. This, the first volume, is divided into three sections, not counting the introduction and conclusion. The brief introductory chapter (Chapter 1) supplies some important background material on the demographic and ethnic makeup of the city at the end of the colonial era. The first section consists of just one chapter (Chapter 2) which examines the composition and social and business behavior of the highest elite of the colony, a group I have termed "the Great Families."

The second section, containing five chapters, treats the world of commerce in Mexico City. It begins (Chapter 3) with a consideration of the organization, scope, and practices of the international traders, a small but crucial group within the mercantile community, and then moves on (Chapter 4) to the role played by these and other merchants of the capital in provincial trade. A panoply of social types, from small shopkeepers to owners of chains of specialty shops to owners of large general stores, participated in retail trade (the topic of Chapter 5) along with the great wholesalers, who never thought any enterprise too small if it could yield a profit. A chapter on advancement within the commercial world (Chapter 6) reveals the diversity of career paths open to people in this sphere of the economy and how many individuals dropped out at different points for varying reasons. The final chapter in the section (Chapter 7) embraces a number of different topics concerning the culmination of a mercantile career, that is, the social and economic behavior of the most successful merchants.

The third section considers the many persons active at different levels of the considerable manufacturing and processing and the number of crafts which based themselves in the city. The first of the section's two chapters (Chapter 8) discusses the personnel and operations of a variety of large-scale productive establishments, including slaughterhouses, mills, bakeries, and *obrajes*. The second (Chapter 9) treats the artisans, those thousands of men (and some women) who were employed in scores of crafts and hundreds of shops throughout the capital and its environs. The concluding chapter (Chapter 10) offers both a summary of major themes in the preceding chapters and an overview of patterns and topics which cut across the entire study.

The second volume will consist of two major sections. The first will look at professionals. Individual chapters will investigate lawyers, clerics, government officials and notaries, and other professional groups, specifically medical men, pharmacists, architects, artists, and school teachers. The second section will examine nonoccupational groups present in Mexico City who are not embraced by any of the previous chapters. These include women, foreigners (nonhispanic Europeans), blacks, and Indians.

A comment on chapter subheadings and on chapter order might be useful. The many subheadings are intended to assist the reader by offering a quick introduction to each subject covered and by enabling him to locate readily any subsections which may be of particular interest. The order in which chapters are presented is not intended as a statement about the relative social rank of the differing occupations in the late colonial period; many persons in later chapters had both greater wealth and higher social standing than those in some of the preceding ones. By and large, the occupations cannot be arranged into a hierarchy. Any attempt to do so must ignore such important considerations as social and economic differentiation within each occupation, the role of the family in ascribing both position and function to its members, and the frequency with which persons pursued multiple occupations (or were at least economically active outside of their specific professions).

In this work, chapter order is designed to be heuristic, with the hope that each chapter will help in the understanding of those subsequent.

This study makes an effort to bring out aspects of Mexico City's business and social history which are characteristic of cities throughout Mexico and, to some extent, throughout Spanish America. Certainly, this urban center was distinctive in its size, wealth, and the volume of its commerce and production. But once these factors are recognized, they can be pointed out and dealt with, thereby enabling us to discern the commonalities of life and behavior across communities.

Since at least the mid-1960s, scholars have endeavored to illuminate the history of colonial Latin America through closer examination of society itself rather than through the prism of juridical and governmental edicts, utopian schemes, or the self-serving pronouncements of interested persons and institutions. To date, social historians who have concentrated on Mexico have generally chosen to examine a single hacienda, set of haciendas, or at most a province, in the last case usually emphasizing the regional center, with rather less attention to surrounding neighborhoods and villages. Some of the best studies in the latter category have been distilled and presented in a book entitled *Provinces of Early Mexico.*[1] These articles and the larger works from which they derived often stress the uniqueness of the local society under investigation and downplay thematic comparison with other areas. In addition, many of them recognize the impact, large or small, that Mexico City had on the society and economy irrespective of the time period, but because of the focus on a single province or municipio cannot describe the dynamics of domination by the capital or the extent to which the specific form of domination was either unique to a single region or general to the larger colony.

The present study, then, is complementary to the provincial studies that have preceded it. By looking from the center out to a number of different provinces and communities, it will fill in many of the areas left vague by these earlier studies and illustrate what in a region's relationship with Mexico City was distinctive to it and what was shared with the colony as a whole. In that sense, this work is national in scope, referring with frequency to businesses, dealings, persons, and institutions in many different parts of the country.

In the course of completing a long-term project such as the present one, a person receives a great deal of assistance, both financial and intellectual, from a number of parties. The research for this work, conducted in Mexico City during the academic year 1975–76, was financed by a Research Training Fellowship from the Organization of American States.

Much of this study appeared originally in the form of a doctoral dissertation conducted under the guidance of James Lockhart. Conversations in Mexico and in the United States with friends and colleagues, including Leslie Lewis, Paul Ganster, Linda Arnold, John F. Schwaller, Stanley Hordes, Matt Meier, and Michael Vail, both clarified specific points and influenced the overall perspective of this work.

My work in Mexico City was greatly assisted by the expertise and courtesy of the staff of the Archivo General de la Nación, then headed by Jorge Ignacio Rubio Mañé. Ignacio González-Polo and Leonor Hernández García of the research staff of the Biblioteca Nacional were most helpful in sharing their knowledge and in their efforts to secure material for me.

The efforts, affability, and ability of David V. Holtby, my editor, and of Jenel Virden, my typist, have greatly facilitated the completion of this project. Washington State University generously financed the typing of the final draft.

I wish to express my deepest appreciation to my parents for the resolute support, manifested in so many ways, which made this work possible. A special thanks is owed to Diane, my wife, for the backing and understanding she has always offered, even when this project took away from time we should rightfully have spent together. Finally, I remain personally responsible for all shortcomings in style and substance which the reader might encounter in this book.

Colonial Entrepreneurs

1 Introduction

A systematic examination of the composition of Mexico City's population, including its size, ethnic makeup, and residential patterns, would be manifestly useful by way of introduction to a treatment of the city's business life. Unfortunately, given the nature and length of this study and the great amount of research and space that comprehensive coverage of the above matters would require, I can offer here only a skeletal treatment of these topics, attempting to provide the reader with at least a certain amount of basic information to make the following chapters more readily meaningful. Similarly, a discussion of the workings of the municipal government and the physical layout and provisioning of the city would simply demand too many pages. The reader is therefore referred to several articles which are devoted in whole or in part to such topics.[1]

The Size and Ethnicity of the City's Population

Mexico City was without question the most populous city in the Americas (and not just Spanish America) through the entire colonial period. The only cities which could rival it during these centuries were Lima, Peru and Bahia, Brazil, both of which were always smaller by some tens of thousands of persons. The population of Mexico City would not be surpassed in the western hemisphere until the rapid growth of New York City in the middle decades of the nineteenth century. Table 1 presents a list of population figures for the city from 1772 through 1820.[2] Table 2

1

Table 1.   The Population of Mexico City in the Late Colonial Period

Year	Population
1772	112,462
1790	113,240[a]
1793	130,602
1803	137,000
1805	128,218
1811	168,846
1820	179,830

[a]The figure for the 1790 census is usually given as 112,926, but that appears to derive from the incorrect addition performed by the person who originally added up the final figures. My own calculation of subtotals gives the above figure.

   Sources: (Given in order of the population figures.): "Noticias de Nueva España en 1805" in Enrique Florescano and Isabel Gil, eds., *Descripciones económicas generales de Nueva España, 1784–1817*, (Mexico: SEPINAH, 1973), p. 180; BN, ms. 458 (1395), f. 16, "Estado reducido de los habitantes de México empadronados en el año de 1790"; Richard E. Boyer and Keith A. Davies, *Urbanization in 19th Century Latin America: Statistics and Sources*, (Los Angeles: UCLA Latin American Center, 1973), p. 41; Alejandro de Humboldt, *Ensayo político sobre el reino de la Nueva España*, (Mexico: Editorial Porrúa, 1973), p. 129; "Noticias" in Florescano and Gil, *Descripciones*, p. 180; DM, Jan. 20, 1812; Boyer and Davies, *Urbanization*, p. 41.

describes the ethnic composition of the city in percentage terms for two of these years, and Table 3 offers a broad view of marital patterns in the city in 1790. It appears that the 1805 computation forwarded by the Mexico City Consulado found in Table 2 is little more than a restatement of the 1790 figures with a few of the categories rearranged. Let us therefore concentrate on the 1790 breakdown, as it provides the more sophisticated data.

   Starting at the top of the list of ethnic groups in Table 2, we see that the two thousand plus peninsulars (*europeos*) were overwhelmingly male. Furthermore, though the total number is very small when compared with the enormous size of the locally born Spanish population, let alone the total, it is nonetheless large enough to support the argument developed at length in this work: that only a relatively small fraction of peninsulars ascended to even moderately prominent places in Mexico City society. Even if every wholesale merchant in the capital was a peninsular (which

Table 2. Ethnic Composition of the Mexico City Population in 1790 and 1805

Ethnic Group	1790[a] Male	Female	Total	% of Total	1805 % of Total
Europeos	2,185	174	2,359	2.25	2.25
Españoles	20,925	28,662	49,587	47.25	48.00
Mestizos	4,255	8,287	12,542	12.00	—
Indians	10,643	13,100	23,743	22.60	24.00
Mulattoes	2,816	4,161	6,977	6.60	—
Negroes	112	157	269	.30	—
Pardos	—	—	—	—	6.75
Castas	3,836	5,622	9,458	9.00	19.00

[a]The total for 1790 is 104,935; missing are the 8,305 persons both lay and ecclesiastical employed in religious and educational institutions in the city. They were listed separately.
Sources: BN, ms. 458 (1395), f. 16, "Estado reducido"; "Noticias" in Florescano and Gil, *Descripciones*, p. 180.

Table 3. Marital Status of the Mexico City Population in 1790

Men Age Group	Single	% Single	Married	Widowed
0–7	8,716			
8–16	7,373		75	207
17–25	4,492	53.7	3,485	381
26–40	2,285	20.4	7,966	976
41–50	846	18.1	2,945	888
51 and up	693	16.7	2,407	1,038

Women Age Group	Single	% Single	Married	Widowed
0–7	9,980			
8–16	8,793	42.0	350	269
17–25	5,642	20.0	6,781	1,002
26–40	2,993	20.0	9,462	4,696
41–50	899	16.5	2,061	2,484
51 and up	653	13.6	1,479	2,659

Source: BN, ms. 458 (1395), f. 16, "Estado reducido."

was most certainly not the case), they would total less than 200, and if every member of the colonial government in the capital was a peninsular (actually less than 50% were), they would total only about 500. Thus, even in an optimum situation that was never approximated, more than two-thirds of all immigrants from Spain (and remember they were nearly all male) had no opportunity to use the commercial and governmental channels of social ascent, and as we shall see in subsequent chapters, no other channels were generally available to them.

Creoles (*españoles*)—that is, those who were born in America and were called Spanish by their own society—constituted nearly half of the capital's population, and they appeared to make up an even larger proportion than that, since most hispanics lived in the central city while a great number of Indians and *castas* resided in outlying barrios. Of course, it is now well recognized that the "Spanish" designation was cultural rather than genetic in nature and that individuals could both advance into it and descend from it as their fortunes and lifestyles changed. That being the case, it is not surprising that virtually every person in the business world (with the exception of artisans) who was studied in this project was regarded by society as Spaniard. The very fact that one had advanced high enough to be part of the business community would have brought about the transformation from casta to hispanic.

In its most inclusive sense, the classification "castas" embraced all ethnic groups, including blacks, intermediate between Spaniards and Indians. In fact, some of these groups were of sufficient size and so readily identifiable—mestizos and mulattoes for example—that they were commonly designated separately (see Table 2). However, in the body of this work, the term "castas" will refer to all ethnic groups except Spaniards and Indians.

It is difficult to comment on the mestizo and Indian designations. All evidence indicates that by the end of the colonial period, even those Indians and castas located on the edges of the capital lived a highly urbanized existence, many of them earning wages in the hispanic sector of the economy, wearing European-style clothes, able to speak Spanish, and consumers of European goods, when affordable. The Indian and mestizo classifications then probably reflect mainly the individual's degree of acculturation, self-perception, and occupation.

The city had few blacks and very few slaves. What slaves there were worked as personal servants in some of the great houses. There is no evidence that they were still status symbols as in earlier times; some members of the highest elite listed no slaves or blacks among their servants. The mulatto population was significant; many were employed as artisans, in construction, and in some of the most arduous (but not necessarily lowest-status) occupations in the city.

Reference to the Mexican social structure as a caste system is misleading, for people were able to move readily from one classification to another depending on their occupation, wealth, and lifestyle.[3] An individual could change designation within his own lifetime, and his children could make pretensions to other categories, if they had the cultural attributes that were associated with them. In sum then, these ethnic terms were used to delineate a certain spectrum of social types; they hardly served to limit the individual's choice of occupation, residence, or companion. At any given moment, every person in the society was a member of one or another of the categories, but was able to move from it, in some cases with considerable ease, through his or her own actions.

Residential Patterns

A valuable article by María Dolores Morales presents extensive information about the ownership of real estate in the city in 1813 and also some material about residence patterns.[4] Various church agencies, including monasteries, convents, and cofradías, owned (reckoning by value) 47 percent of the property in the city. Virtually all of it was rented out to private individuals for the standard yearly rental of 5 percent of the total value of the structure. (Priests as individuals owned very little real estate in Mexico City.) A small group of private persons held 43.9 percent of the urban real estate. A mere 1.7 percent of the city's population owned urban lots and structures, and three-quarters of these proprietors had only a single house. Only 1,655 small private proprietors owned their own homes. The vast majority of the citizenry lived in roominghouses (casas de vecindad) owned by landlords who normally did not dwell on the premises.

Church organizations owned great numbers of these rooming-houses. The colonial elite tended to invest instead in private homes, starting, of course, with their own great houses valued in the tens of thousands, where they lived with their retinues. They might also possess one or more other houses of considerable value, which they would rent out. If they owned yet others, they usually rented out very small single-family dwellings of little value in out-lying sections of the city.

Overall, there seems to have been little speculation in urban real estate and only infrequent transfers of ownership. The colonial elite and the agencies of the church rarely sold their holdings. Most other houses were small single-family structures (though the families themselves might have been large and somewhat extended) which were passed down to the next generation.

The Distribution of Retail Stores

Retail stores proliferated throughout the city. There was not a block within the eight cuarteles that composed the city proper which did not have at least one. More commonly there were several, and it was not unusual in the central city for a single building (often the residence of a prominent family) to contain five to seven on its ground floor.[5] The greatest concentration of stores, without doubt, was in the area stretching for two blocks from the central plaza in all four directions. The Parián—reputedly so called after the retail business district controlled by the Chinese in Manila— was a collection of cajones (large stores selling primarily imported merchandise) in a rambling single-story structure located in the southwest quarter of the central plaza. In 1816 it contained 180 separate stores, none of which were small operations.[6] Constructed after the 1692 tumulto, the Parián endured until Santa Anna ordered its demolition in 1843.

Immediately to the west of this building ran the Portal de Mercaderes, a walkway containing nothing but retail stores; again most of them were cajones. To the south of the Parián and extending along the entire eastern boundary of the plaza was the Portal de

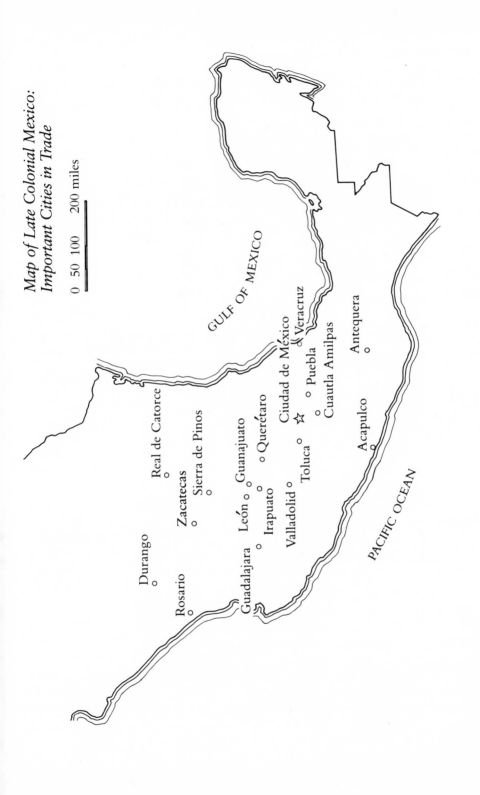

Map of Late Colonial Mexico:
Important Cities in Trade

0 50 100   200 miles

GULF OF MEXICO

Durango
Rosario
Zacatecas
Real de Catorce
Sierra de Pinos
Guadalajara
León
Guanajuato
Irapuato
Querétaro
Valladolid
Toluca
Ciudad de México
Puebla
Cuautla Amilpas
Veracruz
Antequera
Acapulco

PACIFIC OCEAN

Flores (so named after the Indian woman who sold flowers at that spot). This major arcade contained similar stores and also served as the main dock for the canoes which came up the canal from Chalco to deliver fresh produce to the capital. Even in late colonial times the canal was open all the way to the Portal, and commodities were unloaded there to be sold from mats and cloths on the ground by Indian and mulatto women scattered across the open expanse of the plaza. The building housing the Mexico City cabildo stood on the southwest corner; the viceregal palace occupied the entire eastern side of the plaza and the cathedral the northern. The Monte de Piedad took up the northwest part.

The Calle de los Plateros was the major avenue leading from the

Table 4.   List of the Number of Stores Within Each Category Found in the 1816 Survey of Commercial Establishments in the Eight Cuarteles of Mexico City

Type of Store	Number
Almacén (Imported-Merchandise Warehouse)	30
Cajón (Imported-Merchandise Retailer)	188
Tienda[a] (Neighborhood Grocery Stores)	208
Vinatería (Liquor Store)	170
Cerería (Wax Store)	9
Locería (Pottery Store)	2
Sedería (Silk Store)	7
Librería (Book Store)	6
Azucarería (Sugar Store)	5
Velería (Candle Store)	2
Alacena (Small Store Selling Used Items)	6
Tlapalería (Paint Store)	6
Mercería (Dry-Goods Store)	2
Semillería (Seed Store)	5
Puesto (Small Grocery Store)	3
Vidrería (Glass Store)	1
Maderería (Wood-Products Store)	1
Unspecified	28
Total	679

[a] Includes Pulperías and Tiendas Mestizas.
Source: AGN, AHH, leg. 426, exp. 16.

plaza to the west. It extended to the Alameda and contained, besides many silversmith shops, a number of both general merchandise and specialty stores, along with fondas where people could eat and the omnipresent vinaterías, where both sexes could drink liquor or buy it to take with them. North of the cathedral were streets of family residences, including some of great opulence, and a multitude of stores catering to their occupants. East of the plaza, behind the viceregal palace, was a less wealthy neighborhood with large numbers of artisans and Indians. Many stores were still in evidence, though they were not as valuable as those located on the other three sides. Here also, reflecting the distinct class differences in alcoholic consumption, pulquerías outnumbered vinaterías. To the south and southwest of the plaza were located many of the great houses of the capital, and in them, at street level, were situated a great variety of retail establishments which served the Spanish population predominant in these districts. Many of these houses, the residences of leading wholesale merchants, contained the warehouses and primary retail outlets of their owners.[7] Table 4 lists the numbers of different types of retail stores identified within Mexico City in 1816. It includes no artisan shops or other places of manufacture. Likewise missing are the stands of the tobacco monopoly, pulquerías, and restaurants and taverns of every sort.

PART ONE
Elite Composition

Defined by their economic and social achievements, the elite of
late colonial Mexico City emerged from a variety of business
backgrounds. But once having attained membership in the highest
social rank, these people modified many of their practices and began to follow broadly similar paths of action in order to secure the
longevity of their families at this exalted level. The following
chapter describes the spectrum of their behavioral patterns and the
reasons behind their preferences.

2   The Elite

The issue of the composition of the elite in the late colonial period, its mode of recruitment and replacement, and its business and marriage patterns is vital to an understanding of the social, economic, and political processes of Latin America in this era. In this chapter, I will describe the social and business behavior of the pinnacle of Mexico City's society in the era 1750–1821, a group which I term "the Great Families" so as to differentiate them from other well-to-do and respectable families of the city who, though members of a broader elite, could not normally compete with or marry into this exalted segment of society. The criteria which separated the Great Families from the other elements of the upper class in Mexico City were their unparalleled wealth, the diversity of their holdings and investments, the success of their business practices, the honors that they received, their ability to place their children in the upper ranks of the civil and ecclesiastical administrations, their close alliances with other leading political and clerical figures, their choice of marriage partners, and, as a culmination of all of these other factors, their longevity at the summit of the social hierarchy. There was no corporate or institutional structure to the Great Families; they did not all belong to a single organization nor did they collectively enjoy a specific title, form of address, or profession which distinguished them. They were defined by their social and economic behavior, their business and personal associations, and their success. The above characteristics constitute the factors which differentiate this group from the others in this society, but they should not be applied inflexibly, for not every member fulfilled all of them simultaneously.[1]

Ethnicity and Elite Status

Being identified by the society as a Spaniard, whether creole or peninsular, was in no way sufficient to locate a person in the ranks of the elite in the large and expanding population of late colonial Mexico City. In 1790, when the city contained roughly 110,000 people, approximately one half of them were considered to be of Spanish descent.[2] The degree of race mixture which had taken place over the previous two and a half centuries and the willingness of the society to reclassify people of different ethnicities according to their individual accomplishments, marriage patterns, and cultural behavior caused the Spanish sector of the population to expand rapidly.[3] The mere fact of becoming a store owner or a master craftsman—that is, ownership of nonresidential property or possession of a remunerative skill—was often sufficient to elevate someone into the ranks of those the society regarded as Spanish. The fact that race mixture by itself did not diminish a family's stature or eliminate it from inclusion in the highest elite is shown in Doris Ladd's study of the Mexican nobility, which reveals that several late colonial noble families had definite strains of Indian or Negro blood in their ancestry, a fact well known in the society at large.[4]

Nor were the Spanish, whether creole or peninsular, able to enjoy high-status and well-paying employment by the mere fact of their ethnicity. Significant numbers worked at manual tasks. In a very real sense the Spanish sector of Mexico City society in the eighteenth century was occupationally complete, with members to be found at every level of society, including many at the lower. This occupational distribution is demonstrated in both the 1753 and 1811 censuses of the city. Spaniards worked as unskilled laborers and house servants. The 1753 census reports peninsulars employed as weavers, carpenters, and tailors, among other nonprestigious occupations, while some were totally without employment. The *Diario de México* often carried advertisements by jobless Spanish immigrants soliciting any sort of low-level supervisory post, whether in the city or the countryside.[5]

Terms of Address and Titles

Nor could the terms of address commonly used by the people identify the elite in the late colonial period as they had in the first century after the conquest. Usage of the terms "don" and "doña" had been broadened to the extent that virtually every male in the city who was a master artisan or a small shopkeeper was so addressed, while women who were indigent and sometimes not even Spanish might still be referred to with the feminine equivalent.[6] In general, in the business world any person not serving as a clerk or performing manual labor under the direction of another person could lay claim to use of this term. Thus any attempt to define the elite through ethnicity or use of "don" would embrace perhaps one third of the adult male population of the city. Such a broad definition of elite is unserviceable, certainly when we are trying to identify the very highest social element.

Military and academic titles are equally poor guides to the pinnacle of colonial Mexican society. While it has been established that officer rank in the various militia units created in the eighteenth century was attractive to many of the provincial elite, the vast majority of the male members of the capital's elite did not pursue or receive such designations.[7] Perhaps the reason was that they did not have the opportunity, for Mexico City already had a regiment traditionally maintained and staffed by its Consulado and did not seek any new militia units. But more likely, while officer status offered the provincial elites an honor and title that they hungered after, the Great Families of the capital, secure in their positions in society and already enjoying a variety of real and honorary titles and positions, felt no such status deprivation and thus did not chase after available openings. As for academic titles, a university education was normally pursued by a person planning to enter one of the traditional professions, and as we shall see later on, few among the dominant elite of the capital sought to enter these occupations.

Mexico City as a Unique Locus of Wealth

Wealth, enormous wealth, was an absolute prerequisite for a berth among the Great Families. No genteel poverty was tolerated within this group; to lose your money or a good part of it was to lose your status and your ability to marry with the remaining members. While a family in decline could continue to have considerable wealth relative to most others in the society, it would still not be eligible for inclusion in the highest elite. Possession of immense wealth differentiated the Great Families of Mexico City from the lesser elites of the capital and from virtually all the provincial elites of the colony and laid the necessary base for the acquisition of the honors, posts, and personal connections which collectively composed the ideal of this exalted segment of society. To belong to the Great Families required wealth of over a million pesos or a figure very near to it. About one hundred families in late colonial Mexico City had that kind of money. Only about a dozen families in the remainder of the colony could match their wealth.[8]

The entire colony south of the capital, though it rendered products of considerable value such as cacao and cochineal, channeled its wealth through the businessmen of Mexico City and Veracruz and was therefore incapable of maintaining an elite of the stature of that of the capital.[9] East of the capital, Puebla was a prosperous provincial center whose textile obrajes and fertile lands supported a comfortable regional elite. But this area neither produced a major profit-yielding resource nor marketed any domestic or imported items on a scale large enough to render the income necessary to make its leading families rivals of the colony's most prominent.[10] Veracruz was emerging as a commercial power of some standing in this era, but the rising merchants of this community had to look to long-distance trade with the interior for their markets, for the tropical lowlands around the city were sparsely populated and did not turn out a major marketable commodity.[11] The port city itself remained small and unhealthful, with most of its elite situating themselves elsewhere and only entering the city when required by business.

Only the north, and more specifically a few of the mining cities of the North, yielded enough profit on a regular basis to support millionaire families across generations. But many of the miners of this region chose to locate themselves and their business operations in the capital. Exceptions to this rule were found only in Guanajuato and Guadalajara. The few millionaire families based in these regional centers amply demonstrate the restricted scale of business operations in even a thriving province when compared to the scope and prosperity regularly enjoyed by the enterprises of Mexico City. D. A. Brading's examination of Guanajuato in the early 1790s has shown that only four or five families had fortunes which exceeded or approximated a million pesos.[12] Nor was this local elite able to dominate its mining investments without interference from interests centered in Mexico City, for some members of the Guanajuato elite chose to move to the capital or to marry into its elite, thus routing yet more of this city's mining wealth to the capital.

Guadalajara was the other city in Mexico besides Veracruz to gain a consulado in the late colonial era, but the scale of operations of both its merchants and estate owners and their reach into the hinterland were seriously limited by the size of the local market and did not approach the colony-wide economic interests which characterized the Mexico City elite. Guadalajara had only two families at this time which had wealth equal to that of the Great Families of the capital. The other members of this provincial elite had estates worth at best 300,000 pesos, while the wealthiest merchants of Guadalajara ran businesses valued at no more than 100,000 pesos.[13] The wholesale merchants of Mexico City commonly had fortunes of 500,000 pesos or more; a good number of large shopkeepers in the capital had enterprises worth at least as much as the best-off importers of Guadalajara. Finally, while Guadalajara could draw on the wealth of only the Bolaños silver mine, Mexico City attracted great amounts of revenue from mines located throughout the country.

Late eighteenth-century Mexico City contained perhaps 400 families whose total wealth exceeded 100,000 pesos. Besides the approximately 100 Great Families already cited, this figure includes a substantial lower elite composed of the wholesale merchants and large retail shopkeepers situated in the capital plus a number of families whose prosperity was based on some combination of estate ownership, proprietorship of a mill or obraje, mine ownership, government service, and the professions. The most successful artisans might have fortunes valued in the tens of thousands of pesos, but no evidence unearthed to date has revealed any with a personal estate greater than that. The central district of the capital—the main plaza and the streets extending perhaps three blocks from its sides—embraced a complex of great houses, government buildings, artisan shops, and, most especially, retail stores and commercial warehouses. Virtually all of the nearly 200 members of the Mexico City Consulado had their operations there. In addition, most of the major outlets of imported goods were located in this area. These included not only the retail establishments customarily maintained by the trading houses but also a number of independent stores, commonly termed cajones, which dispensed these items on a retail basis. The Parián—a walled marketplace in the main plaza owned by the cabildo—by itself had dozens of these businesses, and many of them had values of over 70,000 pesos. More cajones and a number of specialty shops were located in nearby streets. Often a single family owned several of these stores. Nor did these proprietors restrict their economic activities to retail commerce. A select few ascended into the ranks of the import wholesalers, but far more invested their earnings in agricultural estates, artisan shops, mills, and yet other commercial operations.[14] In like manner, the other members of this lower elite, whether based in estate ownership or the professions, regularly invested in the various levels of commerce, in artisan shops, and in other business enterprises involving mining, milling, or agriculture. Hence, while these individuals and families based their fortunes on one field of enterprise or profession, they all sought to broaden their holdings and investments in other spheres of business whenever possible.

The Great Families of Mexico City lived in mansions, some of which took up a fourth of a city block, clustered around the center of the city. The censuses of 1753 and 1811 show that the heads of these families lived surrounded by other family members, many of whom were married, and a number of retainers who might be prominent members of the business and professional communities in their own right, and were attended by perhaps fifteen or twenty servants, who might be Spanish, black, Indian, or casta and who themselves were often married and with children who were raised in the mansion.[15]

Estate Ownership and Elite Maintenance

No matter how a person accumulated the considerable wealth necessary to elevate himself and his kin to Great Family status, he invariably acquired landed estates as soon as possible in his career and in as many different ecological zones as he could in order to use his control over these agrarian resources to maintain his family's position in the elite over the long run.

The Great Families who invested heavily in estates were outstandingly successful in maintaining their high social rank, so the evidence would indicate. There is no indication from the 1750s on to the end of the colonial period that more than a few of these families descended in status or faced a declining economic situation.[16] In fact, what is remarkable is the number of elite families from the sixteenth century who maintained their wealth and station through the entire colonial period. Several of them gained noble titles early on, most notably the Condado de Santiago, Marquesado de Aguayo, Marquesado de Salinas, and Condado del Valle de Orizaba. And other landed families established in the sixteenth century who chose not to acquire titles of nobility likewise enjoyed exalted social rank at the end of the colonial period. These include the Cervantes y Padilla, the Teruel, and the Luyando clans.[17]

The attractions of estate ownership were several. Throughout its colonial history the Mexican economy suffered from a severe shortage of circulating medium; as a result, the entire economy—from petty retail transactions to purchases of entire businesses—was dominated by credit transactions. To operate successfully in this setting an individual required a strong line of credit in order to contract loans and to buy on time. All parties which let out money and goods demanded guarantees; as a rule the only collateral which agencies of the church—among the major lenders in the society—and private parties would accept was land. Not uncultivated land, which at this time was virtually worthless, but rather developed land, haciendas, which were worth a great deal exactly because of their physical improvements and productive capacity. For this reason, every merchant who had the capital to do so acquired at least one estate as early in his career as he could. If he could not buy one, he might marry into a family with rural properties and gain an estate in that manner. Even the great international wholesalers of the colony followed this tactic and for the same reason. These people valued liquidity—so necessary for overseas transactions—probably more than any other group in the society, but they also appreciated that estate ownership was absolutely vital to prolonged success in this credit-based economy.[18]

Those businessmen who did not have landholdings were required to turn to persons who did in order to secure the debts they contracted. In other words, those dealings not guaranteed by pledges of real property were covered by bondsmen (fiadores) who themselves had estates with which to ensure the debt. An examination of bondsmen shows that whatever their declared occupations, they were normally property owners whose real estate could be seized if the contract were not fulfilled.

Methods of Promoting Agricultural Profitability

Although every businessman on the rise sought to purchase an estate, only the Great Families owned hacienda complexes located throughout the country. The wealthy elite of Mexico City alone could afford to operate holdings in the far corners of the colony. Though some members of the provincial elites also had large estates, theirs typically were situated near to the regional centers where they were based. That is, while provincial centers had marketing and supply regions which were strictly delimited, Mexico City alone had the capacity to draw from the entire colony. The sheep which supplied the capital came from estates in the far North, from which they were driven in yearly migrations.[19] The Bajío supplied a variety of grains and livestock, but the growth of Central Mexico was causing ranching to move farther northward as ever more land was devoted to agriculture. Nearer to the capital, the Chalco region produced much of the maize consumed in the city.[20] To the northeast of the city, in rather arid land, enormous pulque ranchos dominated production of the intoxicant for the capital.[21]

The Great Families of the capital frequently had major holdings devoted to various branches of agriculture in different ecological zones. We now know that the classic Great Estate of Mexico was often a complex of holdings of different sizes and capabilities which might not even be contiguous. The owners not uncommonly grew several different crops in just one complex, calculating that possible losses or market failures in one branch would be compensated for in another. The Great Families did the same thing on a countrywide basis, specializing in the production of a single crop in any one area, but raising a variety of products on their properties throughout the colony. They expected that in the best of times the commodities would earn considerable profits, while in the worst of times, one or another of the crops would yield sufficient income to insulate the family from financial disaster.

The diversity of agricultural estates held by the elite across the country and the specialization characteristic of each one, when combined with the considerable attention, capitalization, and manpower devoted to each enterprise, rewarded the elite with economic security and, periodically, enormous profits. It is no accident that the agricultural investments of the Great Families were concentrated in exactly those branches of farming which were the most profitable and that their estates were best situated to supply the major markets—the capital and the mining centers—which had the largest number of consumers with disposable incomes.

Because the elite clans could concentrate their rural investments in large hacienda complexes which produced the most lucrative commodities—wheat, sugar, pulque, and sheep—on the best land and could sell the produce in important urban centers, they typically earned a dependable profit and derived enormous economic stability from their estates. The large-scale agricultural production of the Great Families enabled them to affect commodity prices.[22] Their wealth meant that they could hold their harvests off the market until they could secure the highest price possible for their crops. Their attention to market forces and to profits guaranteed that they would emphasize production of those commodities which would yield the best return. Smaller producers who did not enjoy the same resources or markets as the Great Families and who could not compete against them often had to turn to less profitable crops and, as a consequence, were far more susceptible to bankruptcy.

The structure of pulque production for Mexico City in the late colonial period well illustrates the way in which elite families were able to control the most lucrative branches of agriculture and sometimes even the marketing of the product. Pulque rendered a steady and profitable return which at least equalled that of any other commodity. The abundant cash-paying public of the capital assured a continual demand for the beverage, while the costs of transportation and the threat of rapid spoilage limited the sphere of production to the semi-arid region immediately northeast of the city. The Great Families of Mexico City not only owned the vast majority of pulque ranchos but also owned a number of the pulquerías which dispensed the drink in and around the capital. Normally, the elite leased these outlets to other parties who were required to buy pulque from the proprietor's estates.[23]

Estate ownership offered yet another hedge against bad economic times: leasing. An estate owner who thought that profits were doubtful or who lacked the funds to make necessary improvements could choose to lease out all or parts of his property to other individuals.[24] Even proprietors of very profitable haciendas sometimes leased out portions of their land in order to gain a regular income to cover operating expenses until the sale of the harvest yielded its substantial revenue. Certain branches of agriculture were so lucrative at times that investors chose to lease rather than purchase estates, figuring that the land would yield an income greater than the lease price. In his study of the landholding patterns of the elite of Guadalajara in the late colonial period, Richard Lindley found that sometimes merchants who leased an estate were actually offering up capital needed to improve the property immediately prior to acquiring it.[25] There is no evidence of this practice among the elite families of Mexico City.

If ownership of extensive rural properties offered the Great Families a steady return on their investments together with occasional enormous profits, it provided yet another advantage to families concerned with transferring their wealth intact across generations. Of all major business enterprises, only estates could be easily subdivided and passed on to a person's survivors. This was facilitated by the number of individual properties commonly included in the complex called the family hacienda. Further on, we shall see that though subdivision of landed properties could with time threaten the economic power and financial stability of a family, there existed common patterns of social and business behavior designed to overcome this potential problem. On the other hand, mines were typically composed of a single system of tunnels, and while a mine's profits could be easily divided up, ownership of the actual diggings could not be, as the individual shafts varied greatly in quality. In like fashion, the international trading houses of Mexico City could not be simply divided up or even transferred, for the entire enterprise was based on the twin axes of the existence of large amounts of liquid capital combined with an extended and very intricate web of correspondence accounts and commercial understandings which existed between the colonial wholesaler, his overseas suppliers, and the retailers of the capital and the provinces. These personal relationships were not readily transmitted; hence merchant houses were normally passed on to a single descendent, either a creole son or an immigrant nephew, who had been trained for years in the business, often with extended assignments overseas and sojourns throughout the hinterland of the colony.

The Vertical Integration of Businesses

To say that particular individuals or families were estate owners is not to state that they dedicated themselves exclusively to the productive end of the business. Rather, one of the most distinctive aspects of agriculture as practiced by the Great Families is the vertical integration of the production, processing, and distribution of commodities, a goal which was desired but usually not achieved by other sectors of the society. While the higher profits available to the family which was able to eliminate middlemen and thereby handle all phases of production and distribution certainly reinforced this preference, the more central reason for this practice was the security of supplies and markets that it ensured. Hence, as related earlier, a family which produced great amounts of pulque normally owned one or more pulquerías in the capital that were leased out for fairly low payments, but with the stipulation that the renter buy a stated amount of pulque from the proprietor. Such agreements freed the families from the demands and harassments of retail distribution and provided them with a steady income while guaranteeing that they would not be deprived of a market by the actions of competitors.

In like manner, some of the Great Families owned large flour mills in the Valley of Mexico and textile mills which processed and distributed the wheat from their farms and the wool from their sheep ranches.[26] Ownership of these enterprises was profitable in its own right. The González Calderón family owned the largest flour mill in the colony and some years ground a full third of the wheat marketed in Mexico City.

Large Estate Owners and Commerce

The wealthiest clans stationed permanent marketing agents in the city to represent their interests, while also operating general stores on their rural estates. These separate acts addressed themselves to the same goal: control of the commerce of both locally produced commodities and imported finished goods in the regions dominated by the estates of this elite. Owners of large haciendas used their economic power to serve as commodity traders not only for their own properties but also for the smaller haciendas and ranchos that neighbored them. Smaller producers realized that the wealthier proprietors had the capacity to transport produce more inexpensively and that their ability to sell the harvest of the region's estates as an entity rather than as competing interests meant higher income for all. So being unable to compete against the economic power of the dominant owners, they marketed through them and thereby passed on to them the higher profits available to the merchant with major supplies of grain.[27]

The most powerful hacendados also exploited their commercial connections, their access to capital, their marketing capabilities, and their preeminence in rural regions to establish themselves as major retailers. Independent storekeepers were often unable to compete with these landlords because of the low population density and relative lack of money and consumers in the countryside; proprietors of large estates thus enjoyed a commercial monopoly over an extended area. They had the capacity to extend credit for prolonged periods without suffering economically, and the debts owed them by the smaller agriculturalists only bonded these producers more tightly to the landed elite.[28]

While ownership of a complex of estates which were agriculturally diversified and vertically integrated was a vital component of the financial portfolio of the Great Families, these kin groups did not abandon commerce when they undertook large-scale rural investments. Many of them had used careers in international commerce as the route to elite status and recognized that the two economic fields were compatible and, in fact, enhanced each other. We have previously seen that the landed elite exploited their rural preeminence to dominate both commodity trading and commerce in manufacturing items in the countryside. But they were not satisfied with just intracolonial trade. To maintain the wealth necessary to remain in the highest social stratum of colonial society demanded that the security and range of investments available in agriculture be coupled with the risk-taking and consequent higher profits identified with international commerce. For this reason, many of the Great Families, no matter how ancient their prominence, maintained members, typically creole sons or immigrant nephews, in the Mexico City Consulado operating the family's overseas trading house. Both titled and untitled elite clans regularly followed this practice. As a result, while peninsulars made up the majority of the membership of the Mexico City Consulado in the late colonial period, the creole elite comprised a significant presence, with an influence even greater than their numbers through their sponsorship of other, less powerful, members of the guild, who might be from the same clan or an affiliate of it.[29] Table 5 lists titled and untitled creole elite families definitely represented in the Consulado in the period 1780 to 1820.

These creole wholesalers were sometimes trained by being stationed in Spain for a period of years in order to develop the personal connections so vital to the efficient· operation of overseas trade at this time.[30] At other times they worked directly under the tutelage of their fathers or uncles in the Mexico City trading houses or were encouraged to undertake their own commercial ventures in the provinces or the capital itself.[31] Regardless, once they had established their credentials, they were elevated to Consulado membership and there represented their family's interests.[32]

But elite creole families did not invariably turn to their own children to manage their overseas commerce. Sometimes a nephew was brought over from Spain and then trained in the business over a number of years before he too was installed in the Consulado. To

Table 5.   Creole Presence in the Mexico City Consulado, 1780–1820

Titled Families Represented by Creole Members:

Condado de Heras Soto
Marquesado de Guardiola
Marquesado del Apartado
Condado de Regla
Marquesado de Vivanco
Condado de Jala
Condado del Peñasco
Marquesado de Rivas Cacho
Marquesado de Castañiza

Untitled Families Represented by Creole Members:

Ibarrola
Sánchez Hidaldo
Maniau y Torquemada
Sánchez de Espinosa
González Calderón
González Guerra
González Vértiz
Iturbe
Icaza (2 members)

bind his interests yet more tightly to those of the larger creole clan, it was often arranged for him to marry one of his colonial cousins. Thus, his interests and those of his offspring became inextricably linked with those of the larger Mexican kin group.

Patterns of Business Diversification

The level of economic development in late colonial Mexico was still too low to permit specialization in a single field of the economy for any prolonged period. Though the internal market was growing, transportation was so costly and inefficient and markets so limited that any big businessman who concentrated his investments in just one financial sphere was courting disaster. Great swings in the volume and profitability of production could be expected periodically in each field of the economy, and as the volume of goods and the types of business arrangements were still quite limited, diversification of a family's investments was crucial to long-term prosperity. And this was more true in mining and commerce than in other undertakings, as these were especially susceptible to the frequent interruptions in overseas shipping which characterized the late colonial period. When leading families of the capital were threatened by ruin, it was more often from their overseas trading operations than from their rural investments.[33]

Because of the enormous capital required to invest in silver mining, international merchants—noted for their liquidity and their reliance on steady supplies of specie—were far more prone to invest funds in this field of enterprise than were elite families which already had much of their money tied up in landed estates. But D. A. Brading has shown that a number of creole families made their original fortunes from mining.[34] They had financed their enterprises by drawing together family funds, by borrowing, and by accepting large advances from the merchants who supplied their mines and their communities. Families which made their original fortunes from mining, whether creole or peninsular, often consolidated their wealth through investments in agriculture.[35] Once again, this form of investment was complementary to their prior specialty, for mining required massive inputs of animals and grains to keep functioning, and estate ownership provided the miner with guaranteed supplies. Thus, what occurred was diversification rather than abandonment of mining.

Ownership of obrajes or mills by itself did not provide enough wealth to lift any family into the highest ranks of society. The markets for the goods produced and the profit margin possible on them were both too small to turn out the level of income necessary. Furthermore, proprietors of mills and obrajes who did not own rural estates periodically had to make enormous capital outlays to acquire vital raw materials; the result, all too often, was that a pall of heavy debt hung over these enterprises. But while the character of the colonial economy did not make these businesses a promising route to elite status, later investment in mills and obrajes was attractive to the established landed elite as secure markets for their agricultural production. Ownership of processing plants gave the Great Families the vertical integration of businesses that they craved. As a consequence, elite families, whether titled or not, purchased and operated such establishments over many years without considering their possession a threat to their social stature or reputation.

The Elite and Professional Careers

Careers in the law and in the church were not prime avenues of advancement to the highest stratum of colonial society. Nor, for that matter, did many children of the Great Families enter the professions. But when they did, the prominence of their families virtually assured them a quick ascent to the highest posts in the profession. Examination of the lawyers and clerics present in Mexico City in the late colonial period shows that the vast majority came from respectable, comfortably well-off families from the provinces and the capital, that is, from the lower elite and the significant middle sector of the society.[36] Only a distinct minority of the Great Families sent even one child into the professions. In fact, probably as many or more children of the highest elite went into wholesale commerce as went into any single profession. These families already enjoyed such stature that they did not need the social luster provided by academic degrees or careers in the liberal professions. Likewise, as we shall see further on, they already had valuable connections with the high officials in both the government and the church and therefore had no immediate need for the access to these administrations which careers in the professions might open up. In general, children of the Great Families preferred to stay in the larger family business, directing one aspect or enterprise within it and perhaps someday the entire operation, rather than to get a university education. They certainly did not need the money that a professional could earn, which though not insignificant, could not approach the wealth already attained by these families. So the professions were normally occupied by members of the lower elite who could benefit from the income, the status, and the connections that such careers could provide.[37]

Children of the Great Families who did opt for professional careers rose rapidly in the respective hierarchies. Those who practiced law became the legal representatives of important corporate bodies, rectors of the Lawyers' Guild (Colegio de Abogados), or high-ranking officials in the colonial government. Licenciado Luis

Gonzaga de Ibarrola was the son of a member of the Consulado and the brother of two other members. Exploiting his family's position, he served an extended term as head notary of the Merchants' Guild and was later elected and reelected rector of the Lawyers' Guild. He culminated his career by becoming a familiar of the Inquisition and honorary secretary to the viceroy.[38] Those elite offspring who entered the church quickly ascended to the Mexico City cathedral chapter or at least to prized assignments in the parishes of the capital or the university, while at least one became a bishop.[39]

It is not surprising, however, that some families put far more stress on participation in the professions and the government than did others. Hence we can refer to a subsection of the Great Families as the "professional elite." Unquestionably the most prominent family in this category was the Beye de Cisneros. In the eighteenth century, members of this family served as lawyers, priests, academics, and government officials. Three brothers at mid-century became lawyers; two of them also became priests. One founded the Colegio de Abogados and served four times as its rector. Another occupied a chair in the legal faculty of the university and was later named agente fiscal de lo civil for the Audiencia.[40] The following generation also excelled in the professions. Four brothers all became lawyers, priests, or both. Three entered the cathedral chapter of the Colegiata of Guadalupe, and one of them twice served as rector of the College of Lawyers, while another was the colony's representative to the Spanish Cortes in 1811. The fourth brother also became a lawyer, served as a subdelegado, and succeeded his uncle as a regidor of the capital.[41]

The Beye de Cisneros family was not unique, just the most successful. Several other clans rivaled its achievements in the professions; yet other clans sent one or two members into the professions. But these professional families were all alike in having considerable personal wealth other than income from their formal professions. The Beye de Cisneros family owned a complex of estates, as did a number of other such families.

While several families rose into the ranks of the highest elite through government service, especially as officers in the mint and the treasury, they were exceptional. In general, those government

officials of stature on a par with that of the Great Families eventually would move on to service in Spain itself. Some creole elite
families owned important permanent posts in the colonial government which were handed down through the generations as part
of the family patrimony. Government service was prized not for
the money associated with it, though many posts could be ma-
nipulated to yield a substantial return, but for the status that it
conferred. In seeking out high-level government positions, the
Mexico City elite was endeavoring to reenforce its economic
power with political power and to serve in posts that the society
deemed proper for its leading families.[42]

An Overview of the Elite's Business Practices

In the characteristic organization and management of their businesses, the Great Families of Mexico City sought to institute
diversification of their holdings, vertical integration of their enterprises, and patriarchal control over all economic operations of the
family. Other elements of the society sought to do many of the
same things for similar reasons. Most levels of society operated
in a common economic climate and had the same need for good
business practices, but only the elite had the scale of wealth and
property which enabled them to use these procedures to their
maximum advantage.

Fortunes made originally in commerce, mining, and agriculture
were best secured through diversification on a massive scale into
other fields of the economy. Such large-scale diversification not
only helped guard against financial collapse brought about by a
downturn in any one economic sphere, but was also regarded as
complementary to the other business enterprises. People of this
time saw no contradiction in participating in different areas of the
economy at the same time. Agriculture helped to supply mining;
commerce offered a valuable assist to agriculture; mining could
support further commercial activity. The cycle went on and on
and in every direction.

An examination of the economic activities and investment patterns of both the Great Families and other lower-elite groups dem-
onstrates the limited utility of occupational designations in this
society. Lawyers could serve as marketing agents, priests as mer-

chants, and everyone might own landed estates. Businessmen pursued diversification vigorously. Most people who were prominent in a profession had major investments in other fields of the economy as well. And those who did not were still usually operating within a family business in which they were handling one or another of the family enterprises.

Vertical integration of businesses also made good business sense. It provided the family with both a guaranteed source of supply and secure markets, while at the same time eliminating division of profits with middlemen. Hence the international wholesalers also operated stores both in the capital and in the provinces, while wheat farmers owned mills, sheep ranchers had obrajes, pulque processors had pulquerías, and silver miners had refineries and rural estates.

The typical business of the late colonial period was not headed by an individual specialist but rather constituted part of an extended family's diversified economic empire. The family sought to man all important managerial and supervisory positions with persons related to it by blood or marriage. Outsiders who became indispensable to the business were normally made spouses of family members.

Patriarchalism

To consolidate its holdings—and thus increase its economic power—and to promote a sense of family unity and identity, an elite family normally sought to organize all of its business operations around a single patriarch (or matriarch). This person would oversee the total operation and make the ultimate decisions, often not just over economic concerns but also over such matters as marriage partners and careers for other family members. Organization around a patriarch prevented a family from competing against itself and mobilized all of its resources for its own long-term betterment and stability. Most members of the family usually recognized the benefit of this approach and were willing to subordinate themselves and their immediate personal interests. Ultimate identification and status came from the family name, while the long-term prosperity of the family ensured prestige and comfort for all of its members.

The position of patriarch was so crucial that competition for the post was sometimes the source of bitter rivalry. This was perhaps the biggest threat to the family's solidarity and economic position. Some kin groups were periodically shattered by internecine struggle and jealousy over the choice of patriarch. Members might withdraw completely from involvement in family business. But despite the pitfalls associated with selecting a patriarch, most Great Families still did so because of the obvious advantages it gave to the family's economic investments and the unity and direction it gave to the larger clan. Once again, occupation is not a flawless guide. While many patriarchs were merchants or had the largest estate holdings in their name, others followed different pursuits.

Transferral and Distribution of Family Wealth

Marriage and death offered perhaps the greatest threats to the continuance of a family fortune. To marry the offspring of a generation to their various partners meant probably to transfer significant parts of the family estate along with them. Likewise, the death of one of the leading members of the family often entailed the division of much of the property among a number of heirs.[43] But the colonial elite was not helpless before these potential problems. It was vital that some units of the family fortune—especially trading houses and mines—be retained as integral bodies while others could be more easily divided up. Hence, one heir might gain an entire commercial firm or mine, while the others would get substantial mills and estates but would retain an interest in the merchant house or mine. Consequently, one person would control all of the major commercial activities but would be responsible for supporting other members of the family from the profits.

Nor was this the only devise. Marriage within the clan, usually between cousins or between the widow and a nephew, helped to consolidate the holdings of the family. Just as effective was the common practice of heirs granting their power of attorney to the new family patriarch. No transfer of ownership was involved, but this act greatly consolidated the value and economic power of the family's property. And, of course, some families chose to entail all or the better part of their properties. However, a surprising number never utilized this mechanism, perhaps because of its inflexibility.

Honors and Titles Among the Elite

Having once gained enormous wealth, families pursued honors and recognition which would bestow rank and glory on the entire clan and thereby certify its rightful place among the recognized elite of this society. Many chose therefore to acquire noble titles. There were approximately fifty titled families in Mexico at the outbreak of the independence movement; the vast majority of them resided in large mansions in the center of Mexico City.[44] But to say that titled families were among the highest elite of the capital is not to say that they were the exclusive members or even that they dominated the top social rank of the city. They constituted somewhat less than half of the Great Families of the capital.

Purchase of a title was not the only means to gain social recognition or to institutionalize a family's elite status. Table 6 provides a partial list of untitled Great Families in this period. Some untitled elite families chose to promote one of their members as a knight in one of the military or honorary orders, ancient or newly founded,

Table 6. Some Untitled Members of the Great Families of Mexico City in the Period 1750–1821

Adalid	Ibarrola
Barberi	Icaza
Beye de Cisneros	Iraeta
Cervantes y Padilla	Lugo de Terreros
Cuevas y Aguirre	Luyando
Fernández de Córdoba	Maniau y Torquemada
Fernández de Madrid	Mimiaga
Foncerrada	Obando
Gómez de Cervantes	Puyade
González Calderón	Rodríguez de Velasco
González Castañeda	Sánchez de Tagle
González Guerra	Sánchez de Espinosa
González Maldonado	Sánchez Hidalgo
González Vértiz	Teruel
Gorráez	Velázquez de la Cadena
Guerrero	Villaurrutia

of Spain; specifically those of Santiago, Alcántara, Calatrava, Montesa, or Carlos III. These and all other high honors certified the blood purity and worthiness of the entire family over generations and hence served the vital purpose of validating the larger kin group and its ancestry and not just the individual who received the formal title. Also, membership could be maintained generation after generation, if good reputation and high social rank could be preserved. The rigid qualifications required for membership and the consequently small number of persons accepted made entrance into any one of these orders a distinct honor, even for a long-established family.[45]

Acceptance as a familiar of the Inquisition was another honor bestowed on very few in this society. It also glorified the ancestry of the entire family of the successful applicant. In theory, these people assisted the Holy Office in tracking down heretics and nonbelievers; in reality, the designation ratified the blood purity of the clan and helped to protect it from the threat of investigation. Thus achievement of this status cited the worthiness of a family which had risen through the ranks of the business world.[46]

The cabildo of Mexico City, while not the exclusive preserve of the highest elite, nonetheless contained a substantial number of representatives from the leading families, and there is no question that membership on the municipal council was actively pursued by both established and newly emergent elites because it conferred considerable prestige and not a little power. All the regidores who were not from the Great Families came from lineages of proven respectability and wealth in the city, often of very long duration. Table 7 lists the representatives of the Great Families found in the cabildo between 1780 and 1810. Titled families had their members, as did ancient untitled elite families, plus new elite families drawn from the ranks of international merchants, and even some recently established professional elites. Reforms instituted by the crown in the 1770s were intended to open up the cabildo to a broader section of the population, especially the peninsular merchants. They were, however, at best a partial success, for the cabildo itself determined the membership of both alcaldes and honorary regidores. As a result, the international merchants appointed to these posts were joined by a large number of estab-

Table 7.   Members of Established Elite Families Represented on the
Cabildo of Mexico City in the Period 1780–1810

	Regidor Perpetuo	Regidor Honorario	Alcalde Ordinario
Miguel Francisco de Lugo y Terreros	1780–1786		
Luis María de Luyando	1780–1786		
José González Castañeda	1780–1786		
Ignacio Tomás de Mimiaga	1780–1788		
Manuel de Prado y Zúñiga	1780–1788		
Antonio Rodríguez de Velasco	1780–1810		
Luis Gonzaga González Maldonado	1780–1797		
Felipe Antonio de Teruel	1789–1799	1782–1783	1798–1799
Manuel de Luyando	1789–1799	1783–1784	
José Mariano de Mimiaga	1787–1794		
Marqués de Uluapa	1789–1810		1788–1789
Ignacio Beye de Cisneros	1789–1805		
Manuel Monroy Guerrero y Luyando	1794–1810		1803–1804
Juan Manuel Velázquez de la Cadena	1799–1810	1795–1797	
Francisco Manuel Sánchez de Tagle	1806–1808		
José Rodríguez de Velasco		1780–1782	
Conde del Valle de Orizaba		1782–1784	
Isidro Antonio de Icaza		1783–1784	
José Adalid		1784–1785	
José Juan de Fagoaga		1794–1795 and 1798	1807–1808
Marqués de Salinas		1798–1801	
Conde de la Presa de Jalpa		1798–1799	
Francisco Maniau y Torquemada		1801–1802 and 1810	
Conde de Miravalle		1802–1803	
José Joaquín Sánchez Hidalgo		1802–1804	1808
Marqués de Santa Cruz de Inguanzo		1806–1808	1805
Marqués del Jaral del Berrio		1805–1806	
Joaquín Sánchez de Espinosa		1805–1806	

Table 7.   (continued)

	Regidor Perpetuo	Regidor Honorario	Alcalde Ordinario
Juan María de Cervantes y Padilla		1809–1810	1806
Ignacio Leonel Gómez de Cervantes			1789–1790
José Mariano de Fagoaga			1796–1797
Marqués de Selva Nevada			1800–1801
José Mariano Sánchez de Espinosa			1805
Mariscal de Castilla			1806

Source: BN, *Manual y Guía de Forasteros*, 1780–1810.

lished elite members who now received a chance to participate in the municipal council after having been shut out previously because of its very restrictive policies and the lifelong tenure usual to its members. Table 6 also lists the alcaldes and honorary regidores from this same period who were representatives of the Great Families, including those permanent regidores who simultaneously served as alcaldes, a very common practice. Note that some persons who began as honorary regidores later gained permanent posts.

The Elite and the Colonial Government

The creole elite of Mexico City was able to secure high government positions for some of its offspring, to purchase and hold important and prestigious offices over generations, to affiliate itself intimately with important judicial and financial officers through intermarriage, and to absorb into its midst yet other top-rank government officials from abroad who settled permanently in the colony. The close relationship that the Great Families maintained with the highest functionaries of the government distinguished them from other members of the society. The officials were attracted to the enormous wealth, power, and webs of kinship affiliations which this local elite could mobilize on its behalf. On the other hand, the elite respected the power and prestige which the top officials enjoyed from their positions and from their identification with the king. Furthermore, if the officials were promoted to posts in Spain itself, this would cast even greater luster on the people associated with them.

Even in the era of the Bourbon Reforms, which had the explicit aim of diminishing the political power of local colonial elites, the leading families of Mexico regularly placed their offspring in important posts in the government and saw them rise steadily in the royal bureaucracy. Francisco Ignacio González Maldonado was elevated to the rank of oidor of the Audiencia of New Spain at the same time that his brother Luis Gonzaga sat on the municipal council of the capital city. Similarly, Tomás González Calderón was transferred from the Audiencia of Peru to that of New Spain and there rose to become regent during the time that his family held both a slot in the Mexico City Consulado and a complex of agricultural estates. In this same era, Francisco Javier de Gamboa, who was educated in Mexico City and began his legal career as the Consulado's agent in Spain, and Baltasar Ladrón de Guevara, who also was educated in the capital and who spent his entire career holding government posts there, ascended into the Audiencia. They were joined by several other judges who were either born in the colony or had come there as youths to make their careers, fortunes, and marriages. The oidor Diego Fernández de Madrid himself controlled a complex of large estates in northern Mexico which had come to him through marriage and were managed by his brother.[47] The Villaurrutia family, which occupied important judicial and ecclesiastical positions in Mexico and other colonies over two generations, was related through marriage to the powerful Fagoaga and Sánchez de Tagle clans of Mexico.[48]

The colonial elite not only placed its offspring in important judgeships with regularity, it also attracted the allegiance of oidores born elsewhere, including Spain, by offering its daughters to them in marriage. Three peninsular-born oidores of New Spain married daughters of titled creole families in the years after 1770. Two of them were later ennobled and eventually appointed to the Council of the Indies, while the third became a regent of the Audiencia of New Spain. Nor did the elite restrict marriages just to high-court judges. One of the fiscales of the Audiencia wed the daughter of the Marqués de Aguayo. Antonio Mora, the Intendant of Oaxaca, himself married a daughter of the Marquesa de Jaral de Berrio, while his daughter did the same with Antonio Iraeta e Icaza, a creole member of the Consulado and the head of a clan with extensive commercial and agricultural interests. Directors of the treasury and the royal mint were also attractive spouses. Domingo de Rábago, later to become the conde of the same name, wed the daughter of the director of the royal mint, while at the same time, the Marquesa de San Román wed the superintendent of the mint. Finally, in what was perhaps the most prestigious match made by any citizen of Mexico in the late colonial period, María Rafaela Gutiérrez de Terán, the daughter of a powerful merchant family related through marriage to the González Calderón clan, wed the Conde de Casa Flores, the son of a former viceroy of Mexico.

Government service itself occasionally provided an avenue into the colonial elite. Some families were able to use their government positions to assemble the wealth, honors, and prestige which were necessary. The creole Miguel de Berrio y Saldívar was able to translate his tenure as dean of the accounting office of the royal treasury into a knighthood in the Order of Santiago and in 1774 into acquisition of the title Marqués de Jaral de Berrio. Two years later, the title Conde de Medina was gained by the creole Juan María de Medina y Torres, the treasurer of the mint.[49] A couple of local titled families purchased important and prestigious posts in the government which they regularly passed down to their descendents. The Marqués del Valle de la Colina owned the Notaryship of the Royal Audiencia, while the Conde del Valle de Orizaba had that of Government and War.

Marriage Patterns Among the Elite

As marriage remained a prime mechanism for both acquiring and maintaining wealth and status in this society, a person's choice of marriage partners was crucial. An examination of the nuptial patterns of an entire generation of specific elite clans reveals several recurrent tendencies. The number of marriage partners suitable for the highest elite was severely limited. As the members of a family at this rank had few peers, any wedding to a person of lower station was potentially threatening to the status of an elite member and his or her clan. Thus as a general rule, offspring of the Great Families intermarried with other members of the same social stratum, either with persons from different clans or with their own relatives up to the proximity of first cousins. The result of this process over generations was that the great creole clans were often related to each other by marriage or by blood. This naturally promoted a sense of common identity and political unity within this exalted social level.[50] To date, the best illustrations of these marital patterns among the elite are available in the genealogical tables provided in books by Brading and Ladd.[51]

The extent to which family patriarchs were able to direct the marriages of their siblings and offspring is not totally clear. Some well-known family disputes and strategic alliances show that they often played some role. And, as most people identified strongly with their families and viewed marriage as primarily a financial and political undertaking to promote family wellbeing, they were willing to accept such arrangements. But the exceptions are notable. Some sons of the elite lived openly with their mixed-blood mistresses or even wed them, while other sons and daughters who went along with the patriarch's choice of marriage partner experienced insufferable domestic lives and sometimes became embittered as a consequence. In fact, when economic fragmentation afflicted elite families, it seems to have resulted as much from the actions taken by family members alienated for this reason as from any other.

A significant minority of elite offspring, both male and female, chose not to marry. Perhaps they could not locate a suitable mate among the limited number of socially appropriate candidates or the family could not afford the transfer of funds and properties which such a union might require, especially when there was a large number of children in a family. It was not in the best interests of either side in such a match to have the other subdivide its holdings to the extent that they would be insufficient to maintain the new couple's elite status. Very few unmarried adults at this social level chose to enter the church. In this period the number of bachelors and spinsters of elite station outnumbered by several times those who donned ecclesiastical garb. Neither the norms of the society nor the demands of the family required unmarried individuals of either sex to become ecclesiastics. Very few unmarried persons lived out on their own, but then very few wanted to; to remain in the family mansion surrounded by relatives, friends, and retainers was a very attractive option.[52] Appropriate to the wealth and station of their families, those offspring who did enter the church are very noticeable, because the males were likely to sit on the cathedral chapters or head up the university or some major ecclesiastical agency, while the females were likely to found a convent or to become the abbess of one already established.

Those offspring who did not marry into the established creole elite wed either high government officials as previously mentioned or the most successful of the international merchants and commercial farmers. While overseas commerce still afforded the primary means by which to assemble a fortune sufficient to enable an individual to enter the highest stratum of colonial society, the enormous growth in the urban market in the eighteenth century increased demand for products such as sugar and pulque to such an extent that they too could yield great wealth. The constituents of these two groups ardently pursued absorption into the established creole elite. If they were unable to marry into this social stratum, they were unlikely to marry at all (for that would mean marrying beneath them and thus limiting their social ascent) or they would wait until fairly late in their lives, when they had finally accumulated the wealth and honors required, and wed a woman of the elite who was typically far younger than they.[53]

International Merchants and Elite Membership

The subject of the status held by international merchants in late colonial Mexico is undoubtedly controversial, but several things have become clear in recent writings.[54] International commerce was a risky but potentially very profitable business. Many of the Great Families continued to participate in it even after their fortunes were made. Nonetheless, the majority of international traders emerged from the ranks of peninsular immigrants, especially from those related to established Mexican families. Only a very small minority of the immigrant population actually rose to the rank of international merchant, and of these, even fewer accumulated wealth to rival that of the creole elite. Most wholesale traders acquired landed estates as early in their careers as possible. And finally, most of the very successful merchants married into elite families of the colony, whether the family itself was ancient or recently established. Thus the individual merchant was absorbed into the larger, firmly based family, subsuming his personal interests to its own, adding his offspring to its population, and receiving in return the honors, prestige, connections, and certification of elite status that only membership itself could provide.

An examination of the Mexico City Consulado in the late colonial period indicates that only a minority of its membership had wealth equal to that of the most important creole families. In addition, many members remained subordinate to a smaller cohort of traders in the guild who maintained the largest commercial networks, received most of the wealth, and gained most of the honors and important positions bestowed on merchants by the colonial and municipal governments, by the church, and by the Consulado itself.[55] It was these men who were accepted as suitable marriage partners by the creole elite, some of whose members had themselves recently entered thanks to their mercantile success and to whom the merchant might already have a blood tie.

Certainly these enormously successful entrepreneurs could bring a fresh infusion of capital and business expertise into an elite clan, but in return they received not only the status and honors which came only to these families but also the real property, the diversified investments, the web of prominent and powerful relatives, and the connections in the local and colonial governments and the church. Experience had taught these very pragmatic people that this constituted the indispensable base on which any long-term family fortunes must be constructed.

In an overall view then, while a significant prosperous and socially mobile middle sector flourished in late colonial Mexico City, the wealthy extended creole families, the true pinnacle of this society, were very successful in maintaining their elite station through astute business and social practices. These clans were rarely supplanted by rapidly rising entrepreneurs but rather absorbed them into their midst, usually through marriage. The level of wealth, diversity of holdings, business operations, honors, and connections enjoyed by the Great Families were emulated by other elements of the society, but none of them were able to muster the combination of ingredients which made these clans so successful over the long term.

The strategy for maintaining wealth and status in the late colonial world was far different from that necessary for gaining them in the first place. Government service, overseas trade, mining, and commercial agriculture afforded the main avenues of social ascent, with marriage into an established elite family, purchase of a complex of rural estates, or acquisition of a noble title or some other honor for the family normally serving as the ratification of success. Very few of those who rose in business ever achieved all that was required to ascend to this heady level. The occupational specialization so necessary to the up-and-coming businessman became a potential threat once elite status was reached. At this point, the wise individual diversified his holdings while simultaneously integrating his financial empire as much as possible, all the while without abandoning his original occupation.

PART TWO
Commerce

The five chapters of this section explore the organization and operation of trade emanating from Mexico City in the late colonial period. International, provincial, and retail commerce are discussed in separate chapters. In addition, this section examines the career patterns of merchants of different rank, especially their business and social relations with other individuals, both within and outside of their occupations. Attention is also given to the considerable participation in commerce undertaken by many persons who were not merchants by actual profession.

3 International Trade

The truly great merchants of late colonial Mexico City were the almaceneros (wholesale traders), who imported manufactured goods from Europe, Oriental fineries from Manila, and cacao from several parts of Spanish America, and who in this period were expanding the exportation of primary products—especially sugar and cochineal—abroad. To succeed, these men had to innovate and to alter their trade patterns in an era when the organization of international commerce was being transformed by the coming of the Industrial Revolution and by the maritime disruptions brought about by Spain's wars with other nations of Europe.

The Atlantic Setting

The commercial world of late colonial Mexico City can only be understood within an international context. During the eighteenth century, until the Seven Years War and the nearly concurrent demise of the fleet system, most European goods bound for Mexico were shipped from Cádiz, though the goods themselves were largely products of other countries, especially England, and were merely transshipped through Spanish commercial firms by British merchants, who—along with the manufacturers—reaped most of the profits. England, having achieved a takeover of Atlantic trade in the seventeenth century that would pave the way for its Industrial Revolution, had made progressive incursions into the trade between Spain and its colonies. (It enjoyed the same success in that between Portugal and Brazil.) English merchant houses gained their promi-

45

nence in Spanish colonial commerce through the use of three devices: they employed Spanish merchants as front men for their activities in Cádiz; they invested directly in ownership of the port's
merchant houses; and they sold goods directly to Spanish wholesale
traders. All these approaches contributed to the structure of maritime trade in the time preceding the Industrial Revolution.

But by the 1760s, England's tremendous industrial growth and
its consequent need for new and expanded markets transformed the
character of transatlantic trade. English firms were no longer willing to accept the heavy long-term capital investments and extended
delays in reimbursement entailed in the Spanish fleet system and
now pursued both higher rates of profit and a more rapid exchange
of goods based on their ability to assemble greater financial resources and to exploit technological and maritime superiorities.[1]

Having abandoned the restrictive convoy system, the English
began to rely more on interlopers, who sailed their cargo ships
individually into colonial ports and there sold their freight with
the tacit approval of officials (who themselves profited from this
trade). Also, beginning in 1766, English interests benefited from
the free port system, which encouraged colonial merchants to
send their own ships to ports in the British West Indies. These new
commercial patterns were predicated on the existence of colonial
traders independent of Spanish merchant houses who were able to
pay for English finished goods. And indeed they did exist, and in
great numbers.

Spain itself was anxious to move away from the old fleet system
but was unable to do so before the dramatic increase in international commerce brought about by the Industrial Revolution. Earlier Bourbon kings failed to implement reforms in navigation and
commerce which their ministers recommended, but the government of Charles III finally did take steps against England's domination of Spanish colonial trade and access to bullion before its arrival in the peninsula. Spain attempted to implement a mercantilist
policy within the empire by gradually opening up direct shipping
between all the ports of the home country and those of its colonies. Simultaneously, having come to the realization that England
enjoyed its commercial preeminence more because of financial and
technological advantages than because of treaty concessions, Spain

took efforts to stimulate its own industries by offering them gener-
ous subsidies and artificial monopolies. Not surprisingly, these
efforts, occurring as they did in response to a growing English
economic superiority, failed to stimulate Spanish entrepreneurs or
reverse prevailing trends. Few of these attempted industries and
trading companies prospered or played any significant role in the
arena of international commerce.[2]

In sum, by the late colonial period the character of transatlantic
trade was being transformed by the Industrial Revolution then
emerging in England. Vestiges of older maritime patterns combined with a wide variety of new arrangements. The advantage
now lay with the innovator, on either side of the ocean, who recognized the changed conditions and marshalled the resources necessary to exploit them. In this context, Spanish merchant houses,
though able to make their presence felt, consistently acted in response to external stimuli and remained incapable of establishing
control over colonial overseas trade.

The Mexican Setting

The years from about 1770 to the onset of the Independence struggle without doubt constituted an era of demographic and economic
expansion in New Spain which, although periodically disrupted,
was never curtailed by Spain's economic woes. The first census
for the colony with some claim to reliability, conducted in 1793,
showed a total population of 4,483,469, including estimates for
some provinces where no actual count was taken. In 1810 Fernando Navarro y Noriega, benefiting from more recent population counts in some regions, reported a population of 6,122,354.
While no claim of precision is made for either figure, their range of
error is not large, and both provide good approximations. During
the intervening period, therefore, Mexico's population grew at the
healthy average annual rate of 2.2 percent.

Tremendous economic expansion, especially in the areas of mining and foreign trade, accompanied this demographic increase.
Table 8 shows the total value of silver and gold produced in New
Spain decade by decade in the eighteenth century. The large per
decade increase began in the 1770s and continued until 1810.

The prevalence of contraband interlopers and the use of the free

Table 8.   Peso Value of Silver and Gold Produced in New Spain, per
Decade of the Eighteenth Century

Decade	Value Expressed in Pesos
1700–1709	51,731,034
1710–1719	65,747,027
1720–1729	84,153,223
1730–1739	90,526,730
1740–1749	111,855,040
1750–1759	125,750,094
1760–1769	112,828,860
1770–1779	165,181,729
1780–1789	193,504,554
1790–1799	231,080,214

Source: Humboldt, *Ensayo político*, p. 388.

port system in the late eighteenth century exclude any comprehensive analysis of long-term trends in the volume of trade between Europe and New Spain. Nonetheless, there are some indicators that provide at least a partial picture of foreign trade in that century. The first, presented in Table 9, is a record of ships embarked from Spanish ports which docked in Veracruz (the only Gulf coast port of any consequence in the colonial period) in the periods 1728–1739 and 1784–1795. We have already seen that after the Seven Years War a good part of Mexican overseas commerce was conducted through extralegal channels and that Bourbon Spain responded by opening up imperial commerce to an unprecedented extent. The efforts of the home country were rewarded with some degree of success. While few nonfleet ships sailed to Veracruz from Spain in the 1728–1739 period, in the latter part of the century, even though Cádiz expanded its shipping to New Spain, it was quickly surpassed by the combined efforts of other Spanish ports, notably Barcelona, Santander, and Málaga.

During the years 1794–1820, New Spain officially imported an annual average of 7,445,004 pesos of goods from Spain, but of this amount an average of 3,133,812 consisted of foreign goods being transshipped.[3] Thus, even though foreign merchants increasingly bypassed the Spanish ports and shipped directly to the colonies,

Table 9.   Spanish Ships Docking in Veracruz 1728–1739 and
           1784–1795

Year	Number from Cádiz	Number from Other Spanish Ports	Total
1728	0	0	0
1729	20 (fleet)	0	20
1730	3	0	3
1731	0	0	0
1732	20 (fleet)	0	0
1733	0	0	0
1734	1	0	1
1735	1	0	1
1736	18 (fleet)	0	18
1737	1	0	1
1738	2	0	2
1739	1	0	1
	67	0	67
1784	18	7	25
1785	19	16	35
1786	11	18	29
1787	11	23	34
1788	12	15	27
1789	16	28	44
1790	16	28	44
1791	21	30	51
1792	25	47	72
1793	22	32	54
1794	26	41	67
1795	21	25	46
	218	303	521

Source: Miguel Lerdo de Tejada, *El comercio esterior de México desde la conquista hasta hoy*, (México: Rafael, 1853), Appendices 12 and 14.

Spain itself was still unable to escape the role of middleman for other countries or compete successfully against them. In an era of greatly expanding international trade, Spain did enlarge the scope of its colonial commerce, but at a rate slowed by the fact that ever more trade was occurring outside of its auspices. Even this heightened trade volume included a sizeable amount of transshipped merchandise. Both the interlopers and Spanish shipping carried greater amounts of foreign goods. As Spain could not compete with the manufacturers, it sought to increase its volume of trade and concomitantly its revenue through the established solution of transshipment, but even this approach was damaged by the naval blockades which the nation commonly experienced during the frequent European wars of this time.

New Spain, on the other hand, officially shipped goods of an average annual value of 7,914,143 pesos to Spain over the same period. Of these exports, about 75 percent by value consisted of bullion, 12.5 percent of cochineal, 3 percent of sugar, and the remainder of miscellaneous raw and agricultural products.

The colony's increases in domestic production and foreign trade are reflected in the revenue collected by both church and state. Annual government revenue averaged 10,087,329 pesos in the period 1765–1777 and rose to 17,946,350 in that of 1778–1790.[4] Church tithes averaged 1,669,644 pesos annually from 1771–1778, then ascended to an average of 1,835,382 annually over the decade 1779–1788.[5] All six bishoprics of New Spain reported an increase in their tithe income between the decades of the 1770s and the 1780s, several by well over 50 percent.

The Urban Setting

At this time in Mexico City, literally hundreds of people were actively engaged in commerce, though at a number of different economic levels. A summary of the 1790 census of the city lists 1,502 "comerciantes." The most successful of them refused to specialize in any one aspect of trade and hence cannot be described in any strict or exclusive sense as wholesalers or retailers, or as international or domestic traders. Perhaps the most striking features of the city's commercial life were the great number of participants and the wide variety of undertakings which they pursued for profit.

The colonists, and certainly the creoles, have been stigmatized in much of the older historical literature as anticommercial and nonentrepreneurial. Though scholars have charged that colonists sought to avoid identification with commerce because of the attendant threat to their social status, in fact, every citizen of late colonial Mexico City who had even the most tangential claim to merchant status asserted it vigorously given the chance. Whenever possible, whether in a notarized document or in court testimony, declarants identified themselves as commercially active citizens of the capital (*vecino y del comercio de esta capital, corte,* or *ciudad* was the typical form).

Though every international merchant of the city aspired to fashion through marriage a familial mercantile web which could dominate wholesale trade, such ambitions were inevitably stymied by the vastness and complexity of the city's commercial sphere and by the cutthroat rivalry which characterized it. The most powerful and wealthy merchants of the colony were those international traders who were members of the merchants' guild of Mexico City, the Consulado. Though Consulado members habitually formed themselves into consortiums and interest groups on grounds of consanguinity, affinity, and compatible economic interest, they composed too large a group of basically antagonistic competitors for any one subgroup to attain functional control over a major component of the city's trade.

The Consulado

By its own regulations, the Consulado was composed of men over twenty-five (the age of majority in colonial Mexico) who were not employees of another merchant and who wholesaled goods, though they were also permitted to operate retail outlets and did so to a man. Even these restrictions—and they appear to have been effectively enforced—regularly afforded membership to some two hundred merchants, all of whom acted independently in overseas wholesale trade, either alone or, at times, in partnerships and companies. Table 10 lists the number of Consulado members eligible to vote for officers at two-year intervals from 1809 until 1826 (the final interval is for three years).[6] For each year, figures are provided for total membership, the number of members who had held or were then holding one of the three major offices in the Consulado, and the number of new members admitted that year. In each case, when possible, the figures are further broken down to show membership in the Montañés and Basque parties which divided Consulado politics between them. Annual membership averaged about 185 over these seventeen years. As was the intent, the two political factions split membership, office holding, and new membership quite evenly.

Despite the relatively stable size of the Consulado, personnel turnover was large and continual among the heads of the great commercial houses (casas de comercio) of the capital, as becomes apparent when the names of Consulado members are studied over time. Much of the personnel movement, nonetheless, was only a management change within established commercial houses; that is, though new directors appeared, the firms retained their existing structures, spheres of economic activity, and webs of commercial affiliations in the city, in the provinces, and overseas. Yet some new trading houses were always emerging, frequently splitting off from established firms, while still others went into decline and even bankruptcy.

The division of the Consulado into Basque and Montañés parties dates from at least 1742, when the viceroy imposed a biennial alternation of major offices between the two factions in order to halt the internecine conflict that had long racked the organization. Every new member was required to affiliate himself officially with one party or the other. The titles of the parties are somewhat misleading. While all merchants of Basque and Montañés origin certainly belonged to their own parties, they were joined there by members from Mexico, other colonies of Spanish America, and other provinces of Spain. It should be noted that party affiliation did not prevent individuals from entering into commercial agreements, including formal partnerships, with members of the opposing faction. However, given the ethnocentricity of all Mexicans at this time, regardless of their origin, merchants did tend to favor associates with whom they had a regional affinity. This was, after all, the best guarantee of loyalty and trustworthiness available in the world of trade until later development of more structured banking and credit facilities and improvement in lines of communication.

Consulado elections were held under the supervision of an Audiencia judge appointed by the viceroy, who retained the post for the length of his judicial tenure. Every two years the Consulado elected a prior, as well as a consul who in his first year was desig-

Table 10. Voting Membership in the Consulado of New Spain, 1809–1826

Year	Total Member-ship	M	B	Former and Present Officers	M	B	New Members	M	B
1809	190	95	95	21	5	16	21	12	9
1811	183	91	92	13	5	8	9	5	4
1813	192	96	96	13	6	7	21	10	11
1815	209	107	102	13	7	6	72	36	36
1817	189	92	97	13	8	5	11	5	6
1819	170	84	86	13	8	5	2	1	1
1821	181	90	91	13	8	5	27	16	11
1823	171			10			31		
1826	177			11			40		

M stands for the number belonging to the Montañés faction.
B stands for the number belonging to the Basque faction.
Sources: AGN, Consulado, leg. 76, exp. 2, leg. 199, exp. 6, leg. 102, exp. 10, leg. 102, exp. 8, leg. 76, exp. 7, leg. 199, exp. 4, leg. 102, exp. 3, 5, and 6.

nated the junior (moderno) and the next year became the senior (antiguo). In the alternate year only a new junior consul would be elected. These three individuals served as the executive and judicial officers of the guild; they were joined by five deputies of much less authority. If all went according to schedule, the two parties alternated priors and each had a consul, alternating the junior and senior posts yearly. Before the election each party picked fifteen electors who in turn selected their party's candidates for that year. Each candidate was then formally elected by the thirty electors, usually with only a few dissenting votes. Each party was headed by a dean (decano), a prominent merchant who normally served for life and was very conspicuous in the planning of the carefully orchestrated electoral charade. The documentation makes it abundantly clear that an inner circle within each party chose its candidate well before the electoral meetings. However, the criteria by which a candidate was picked remain hidden.

Appendix A lists the prior and two consuls of the Consulado for every year from 1770 through 1826 (with the exception of 1823). Party affiliation of each officer is indicated when known. Rarely did any individual hold both of the main posts in his lifetime. All Consulado officers had similar characteristics, even those who took office when the alternating pattern was disrupted or when some disgruntled faction staged a rebellion. By the time of his election, an officer was typically established as the head of one of the major wholesale houses of the capital. (Its previous head might also have been an officer.) Many were titled, members of a military or honorary order, high officers in the colonial militia, or any combination of the three. They were equally likely to hold functional or honorary posts in the municipal and colonial governments.

With Independence, the Regency of the Mexican Empire (in accordance with the Plan of Iguala) ordered the end of the system of alternation in Consulado elections.[7] Nonetheless, every election through the last one of 1826 proceeded with protocol and structure identical to those of the colonial period. Both parties still functioned in this final year, and each was led by an officially recognized dean.[8]

The Consulado of Mexico City, founded in 1592 and the oldest in the Americas, was abolished in January 1827 by official order of the

Congress of the State of Mexico. It had already been stripped of its jurisdiction within the Federal District in May of the previous year.[9] Though the institution had adapted itself ably to many changes during the Wars of Independence, it was ultimately doomed in the early Republic by an onslaught of hostile forces, such as the entrance of a foreign merchant community, the thirsting of several governments for its financial resources, and the strong liberal campaign for the elimination of all special courts and fueros.

Credit and Capital Supplies

New Spain was chronically short of circulating medium, not only because of the efforts of Spanish kings, starting with Charles III, to impose a more perfect mercantilist system of trade on their colonies, but also because of the already great and growing export of bullion from Mexico to support the bureaucracy and to pay for defense and because of the payments to English merchants for products entering the colony outside of the sanctioned commercial network. Certainly the deficiency was nothing new, but the Bourbon Reforms exacerbated it through their efforts to stimulate the national and colonial economies as a means of producing yet more revenue for the royal government. At any rate, New Spain's economy, from local retail sales through major wholesale and real estate transactions, would continue to be based on credit. A major part of the total value of commercial establishments of every size and character in the city consisted of dependencias activas, the collective debts of the many customers compelled to buy on credit.

This reliance on credit dealings meant that the individual able to mobilize capital was in a position to reap substantial rates of return. Mexico City merchants were among those best able to assemble a cash surplus. They used these funds to expand their commerce, to invest in other fields of the economy, and, very importantly, to pay for their importations from Europe and the Far East. Their access to capital enabled them to strike favorable terms of trade vis-à-vis their Spanish suppliers at the annual Jalapa fair which endured until the free trade era and, after its demise, to deal directly with the individual English and Spanish merchants who brought their ships into colonial ports. A Mexican wholesale trader could not long survive without accumulating silver coin, since European suppliers sold to whoever could pay the most in cash, and to prosper within the Mexican economy one needed frequent sales of separate lots of goods and quick reinvestment in commerce.

By the late colonial period Mexico was shipping some agricultural products and raw materials to Europe, but silver remained the primary export, indispensable to the smooth operation of transatlantic commerce. It was equally indispensable to the Mexico City trading houses' maintenance of a web of correspondence accounts with local merchants in the provinces which enabled them to dominate interprovincial commerce at least down to the Wars of Independence.

Wholesale merchants involved themselves in silver mining in order to support the economy of the mining regions which served as prime markets for their merchandise, to diversify their investments as a hedge against failure in commerce, and to gain access to precious metal to pay for their imports. When a Mexico City merchant financed the operations of a miner or refiner, he was helping to sustain the economic life of an industry and a community which was consistently a major consumer of his goods. But he received an additional benefit, for the miner invariably agreed to ship all his bullion through the merchant in the capital, thereby assuring him a steady supply of the resource most vital to continued foreign trade. In this same era, merchants were quick to use companies to invest directly in mining. Here again, company agreements stipulated that all refined ore would be handled by the interested merchants, who would deliver it to the royal mint and receive back the coin.[10]

Merchants were not the only people who invested heavily in commerce. People from many sectors of the society—clerics, lawyers, bureaucrats, rural estate owners, women, and even some artisans—realized that supplying money to a merchant could prove a lucrative undertaking. Sometimes people provided the money in the form of direct loans, the depósitos irregulares that are scattered throughout the documentation on business transactions, but the return on these was technically limited to 5 percent simple annual interest in most cases and to ½ percent simple monthly for certain commercial loans. Therefore, many financiers chose to establish formal companies with merchants for one-half or two-thirds of the profits. Such arrangements riddled the colonial commercial world at every level, but were most common in retail trade. It was not uncommon for the retailer to move from company to company during his career, as investors sought to cash in on his business acumen. But a commercial company that proved successful, though originally founded for a span of three to seven years, could just as likely endure for decades.[11]

Capital was in such demand that it was rarely allowed to sit idle. Even merchants regularly loaned spare funds to each other, though commonly for short periods of time, as they needed its quick return in order to make the frequent wholesale purchases that typified their business.[12] Table 11 inventories the loans made to merchants by the mercantile house of Peredo y Cevallos which were outstanding as of January 1798. Such traders also utilized companies to mobilize their capital for the highest possible rates of return, but here, at this heady level of investment, most companies were between merchants to the exclusion of all others.

While it is well known that the diverse and autonomous branches of the church acquired and loaned out money, the manner in which they accumulated it and the variety of ways in which they distributed it are often less well understood. In the eighteenth century many individuals still left sizable bequests to church agencies, but the greatest part of these went to charitable establishments in the capital. Occasionally, some amounts were left to support convents or aging clerics. The other significant forms of church endowment were financing the admission of a daughter into a convent or founding one or more capellanías (chaplaincies) usually with the restriction that the income gained should support offspring of the benefactor or of his close friends. These latter methods enabled families to provide stable and honorable careers for some of their children.

None of the bequests mentioned alienated property from the family to the church. Rather, a church agency or an ecclesiastic was given a lien on a certain amount of income which the family derived from its holdings and business activities. In cases when the

Table 11.   Loans Made to Merchants by the Commercial Firm of
Peredo y Cevallos, outstanding as of January 1798

Name of Borrower	Value of the Loan[a]
José Antonio Cevallos (brother of the firm's partner and administrator, Francisco Antonio Cevallos), citizen of Veracruz	10,911 (pesos)
Francisco Antonio de la Sierra (future partner of Francisco Antonio Cevallos), citizen of Veracruz	38,983
Manuel Manso Cevallos (relative?)	1,409
José Franco Meca	631
José Vicente de Lara	20,720
Julián de Icedo	4,448
Diego Fernández de Cevallos (cousin of Francisco Antonio Cevallos)	20,171
Manuel de la Sierra	600
Francisco Emeterio de Elorriaga	2,000
José Sagarraga	10,496
Francisco Casasola	2,000
	112,369

[a] Here and elsewhere in this work, values have been rounded off to the nearest peso except when greater exactitude is required.
Source: AGN, Consulado, leg. 198, exp. 17.

family could no longer pay this money, the beneficiary had a legal claim to proceeds derived from debt or bankruptcy hearings, but not to the property itself.

The church was no monolith, certainly not in any economic sense, but a loose structure containing a panoply of agencies, including convents and monasteries, cofradías, obras pías, capellanías, the Inquisition, and such charitable organizations as hospitals, orphan asylums, and houses for the demented, each of which collected and managed its own revenue with little interference from higher ecclesiastical authorities. These bodies preferred to lend out their funds for a steady return of 5 percent annually rather than to invest directly in enterprises or to establish their own businesses. Consequently, they amounted to so many banking institutions available to the businessmen of the colony. While their frequent loans to agriculturalists, stock raisers, and urban real estate investors are a matter of common knowledge, the great number of loans they made to commercial firms is less well known. Table 12 relates a scattering of loans from cofradías, church-sponsored lay brotherhoods, to major commercial houses. The large amounts involved are evident. An advantage for the recipient was that these confraternities were normally quite content to receive just the annual interest and rarely called in the principal so long as it continued to be paid.

It was to be expected that cofradías would be notably active in the field of commercial loans, for merchants composed the leadership of some of them, especially those organized around the saint of their native province in Spain. It appears that some cofradías specialized in loans to their commercially active countrymen in New Spain. Most notable was the confraternity of Nuestra Señora de Aránzazu, which made frequent loans to merchants born in the Basque provinces.

An economy based on credit meant an economy based on trust, or at least on enforceable guarantees, and this proved both a boon and a threat to merchants. While some commercial loans were secured by real property, most were guaranteed by bondsmen. The guarantors were relatives, friends, or business acquaintances of the

Table 12. Some Commercial Loans of Cofradías

Year	Name of Cofradía	Amount of Loan	Length of Term[a]
1800	Tercer Orden de San Francisco (Lay Branch of Franciscans)	2,000 (pesos)	5 (years)
1800	Ecce Homo	8,000	5
1802	Ecce Homo	6,000	5
1786	N. S. de Aránzazu	20,000	5
1787	N. S. de Aránzazu	12,000	3
1789	N. S. de Aránzazu	12,000	2

[a] Always at 5% simple annual interest.
Sources: AN, Pozo, March 14, 1786, Feb. 28, 1787, and March 2, 1789; Joaquín Barrientos, Oct. 22, 1800 and April 28, 1802; AGN, Consulado, leg. 200, exp. 3, ff. 1–6, May 22, 1800.

borrower who attested to his trustworthiness and pledged themselves collectively to the repayment of the principal and interest if
he should default. This common practice, while placing a pre-
mium on a merchant's reputation for dependability, enabled him
to secure capital even when he lacked tangible collateral. Actual
default by a borrower, however, was no rarity and could bring his
bondsmen down in his wake. Occasionally, a businessman with no
financial troubles of his own was forced into debt or even bankruptcy when obliged to repay a loan on which he had posted
bond.[13]

Because of the prevalence of credit transactions and the inability
of merchants to control the activities of their associates once they
were beyond their immediate purview, colonial commerce was
characterized by chains of personal contacts. Through the years,
each merchant developed a range of contacts with other merchants
of various ranks in different locations and he came to rely on their
dependability for the long-term stability and growth of his business. As we shall see, when a merchant of the capital groomed a
successor, he not only taught him accounting and marketing skills,
but also had him travel to meet with provincial merchants so that
vital personal contacts might also be transferred.

Pursuing the goal of penetration into as many markets as possible, the successful Mexico City wholesale merchant counted on
overseas trade to provide him with the bulk of his merchandise,
which he then distributed by means of various outlets and mechanisms throughout the provinces and the capital. Naturally, the
mining regions of the North and the commercial agricultural and
small industrial areas scattered throughout the Center attracted
considerable attention, being integral parts of the national market
and wage-based economy.

Wholesale merchants rarely if ever specialized; it did not make
good business sense. Some emphasized certain products—silk, for
example, among those active in the China trade—but not to the
exclusion of other items. The internal market of Mexico lacked
the size, the amount of circulating coin or currency, and the rapid
transportation system necessary to support mercantile specialization. Though merchants sought payment in coin, extensive trade
and rapid inventory turnover demanded a willingness to accept

payment in a variety of products. To convert these new commodities from liabilities into assets required the merchants to seek out new markets and to elevate the volume of their trade. Thus, success at the higher levels of colonial commerce was predicated on continual innovation, expansion, and diversification. Bernard Bailyn has noted that the merchants of seventeenth-century New England, who also operated with a shortage of coin, responded in identical fashion.[14]

Patterns of Atlantic Commerce

The first part of the eighteenth century (up to the Seven Years War) was a flourishing period for the annual Jalapa trade fair, where the wholesalers of the capital met with Atlantic traders to acquire European goods. The Mexico City merchants enjoyed a good bargaining position at these fairs because of their supply of coin and their ability to wait out the Europeans, who were forced to sell to avoid taking a loss or returning with unsold goods.[15] Furthermore, after about 1765, British merchants began to bypass Spanish commercial firms and sent their own ships individually to Veracruz, where their counterparts from Mexico City would pay cash for their wares. In fact, it was the ability of colonial merchants to pay with silver that enabled the British commercial houses to abandon those of Spain, at least in part. This doomed the fleet system and impelled Spain to initiate its mercantilist free trade policy.

The economy of New Spain was growing, and the volume of foreign trade rose dramatically in the forty years before the Hidalgo Revolt. It would have been most surprising if, given this healthy economic climate, the merchants of Mexico City had withdrawn from commerce, and in fact they did not. But this is not to say that colonial overseas trade simply shifted into one or two new channels. The process was more complex. This was a time of transition, and as is typical in such eras, there was a combination of the old and the new. Some wholesalers of Mexico City continued to rely on long-established suppliers; many others utilized connections just emerging or even created them themselves.

It is clear that not all the leading merchant houses of Mexico City were independent of those in Spain. Some of the most prominent wholesale traders of the capital recorded their affiliation with counterparts in Cádiz, who were invariably their relatives. In his 1788 will, the Conde de Rábago acknowledged that he maintained regular accounts with a relative in that port. Three years later, in similar fashion, Diego de Agreda, the future Conde de la Casa de Agreda, affirmed business connections with kin located in the same still-thriving mercantile center.[16] When Isidro Bartomeu, a merchant of Mexico City, wished to pay off a debt of 5,000 pesos to Ramón Valiente of Cádiz, he merely turned over that amount in royal bonds to Roque Valiente, a brother of the latter and a successful merchant of the capital, for transfer to the Spanish merchant house.[17]

While such evidence establishes the existence of an ongoing commercial relationship between relatives at both ends of the major trade conduit between Spain and Mexico, its precise nature—especially the locus of power—remains hidden. Two cases from the early nineteenth century do, however, show that Spanish mercantile firms still dominated some Mexican trading houses on the eve of Independence. In 1808 Mateo Julián Gómez de Leís, a citizen of Mexico City, sold cacao from Guayaquil valued at more than 30,000 pesos to another merchant of the city. The transaction came under dispute, and testimony revealed that Mateo Julián was the Mexico City agent of a Cádiz merchant house operated by his father and brother.[18] In fact, the father traveled to Mexico with his son's power of attorney in order to straighten out the misunderstanding.

In 1819 Mateo Sánchez de la Concha, also of the capital, confirmed in judicial proceedings that he worked as an agent of a merchant of Cádiz. Acting in company with a peddler stationed in Veracruz, he traveled to that port and even to Spain acquiring merchandise for sale to provincial traders.[19]

Yet the merchants of Mexico City were so firmly in control of commercial operations in the colony that they were normally able to resist successfully the intrusion of commercial agents sent by Spanish factories and industrial consortiums. Two such attempts are preserved in the documentation, and both failed miserably. The best-known case was the stationing by the Cinco Gremios Mayores de Madrid of well-financed agents of their own in Mexico City and Veracruz. Pedro Basabe, the representative in the cap-

ital, withdrew within ten years after his 1784 arrival, having in-
debted the firm for around 200,000 pesos in that short time. The
Veracruz envoy, though in even slightly worse shape, was then
placed in charge of a consolidated operation. The best that can be
said of this reorganized branch is that it persevered; it certainly
never made money.[20]

Vico, Conti and Company, which opened a silk-stocking factory under royal protection in the Spanish port of Santa María,
dispatched an agent to Mexico City in 1785. He managed to make
profits for himself and the company until 1789, when he contracted debts from which he could not extricate himself or his firm.
Finally, he abandoned the company and secured employment in
the colonial bureaucracy. However, in this endeavor he accumulated even more debts and had to turn to his Mexican father-in-law
to bail him out. In 1799 he still owed over 50,000 pesos to the original investors in Spain.[21]

Mexico City wholesale dealers did not retreat into other forms
of enterprise in the free trade era; rather, they innovated and, overall, continued to thrive in the new commercial setting. There is no
question that at this time independent merchants were emerging in
Veracruz with the ability to purchase foreign goods and wholesale
them in the interior. But they did not wrest the main flow of goods
away from the merchants of the capital or supersede them as the
major suppliers to the provinces. Why did they fail?

It might be useful first to clarify why they came into being. The
reason, quite simply stated, was that the quantity of goods now
flowing to the colony through different channels from Europe was
too vast to ever again be completely controlled by the merchants
of any one city or region. But this is not to say that a group of
wholesale traders, those of Mexico City in this case, could not still
secure an overwhelming share of commerce, if they were able to
mobilize their resources and advantages. Veracruz did not enjoy
control over a sizable local market as did Mexico City. The port
had a population of around 4,000 in 1795, and many who made
their fortunes there chose to live far away because of its notorious
climate. Mexico City, on the other hand, had a population of perhaps 125,000 in the same year, and its merchants were unchallenged
there or anywhere in the surrounding Central Valley, which was, in

turn, densely populated and heavily involved in production for markets. Lacking control over a large local market, the Veracruz merchants could supplant those of the capital only if they were able either to assume control over large-scale acquisition of European finished goods or to take over distribution of them to the provinces. They succeeded in doing neither.

Merchants of the capital utilized two devises to prevent those of Veracruz from securing control over access to European goods. They stationed subordinates and business partners in the port itself to purchase directly from the incoming ships (their access to silver coin made them desirable customers), and they dispatched agents, again commonly as business partners, to Spain itself to acquire merchandise for shipment to Mexico City.

At least by 1800 Mexico City merchants were placing trusted associates as purchasing agents in Veracruz. These individuals typically started with tens of thousands of pesos in silver coin (and promises of more to come if business was good) and were given considerable discretion as to what they could purchase and from whom. They could buy on credit, though often with an imposed ceiling; they were also restricted from engaging in any enterprise outside of the company. Not salaried, the agents were entitled to a share—usually a third to a half—of the company's profits at the end of its term. Until then, they could maintain themselves by withdrawing funds which would eventually be subtracted from their share.[22]

The fact that the import trade was now conducted during the entire year and that the merchant was able to purchase relatively small shipments, often on credit, rather than entire shiploads, enabled capital merchants of middling rank to participate in foreign trade at an unprecedented level. While their large-scale operations, chains of distributing outlets, and unrivaled access to specie gave the mighty traders of the Consulado numerous advantages, they certainly did not monopolize this avenue of commerce.

As the head of a far-reaching and heavily capitalized commercial house, the Mexico City wholesale trader was definitely not a lone-wolf businessman. These commercial houses were typically family enterprises, often just one part in a complex of family investments. The merchant, whether creole or peninsular, was characteristically surrounded by blood relatives and in-laws. This is made manifest in the companies created to purchase goods in Spain. Needing trustworthy individuals in distant ports where agents were beyond immediate control, merchants normally dispatched relatives whom they made formal partners in the enterprise, thereby giving these persons a stake in the successful outcome of the undertaking. In 1783 the brothers Juan Francisco and José López del Diestro formed such a company with the capital of 16,000 pesos (8,500 pesos of it borrowed), which José was to use to purchase goods in Spain.[23] José, who would do the traveling and be in charge of overall operations, was entitled to two-thirds of the profits. In 1801 two other brothers, Manuel and Francisco Llano Velasco y Chavarrí, agreed to a simple understanding wherein Francisco was to travel to Spain with his brother's power of attorney and there acquire goods for shipment back to New Spain when the war with Great Britain ended.[24]

Showing his adaptability, in 1800 Antonio de Bassoco, perhaps the wealthiest merchant of the colony at this time and one of the main beneficiaries of the former fleet system, entered into one of the largest and most elaborate international trading partnerships recorded. He and his nephew, Bernardino de Arangoiti, one of five peninsular brothers active in the commerce of the capital under the tutelage of their uncle, formed a company for the duration of one ship voyage to Spain, with half the profits for each.[25] Arangoiti was to travel first to Havana, there to purchase a ship of some 300 tons, to take it to La Guaira, the port of Caracas, and to load it with 2,000 fanegas of cacao he was to purchase. He was then to proceed to whatever port in Spain offered the best profits from its sale, and with this money to acquire iron, steel, paper, or whatever product promised the best return when transported back to Mexico in the ship. The partners agreed to split all expenses evenly, and since Arangoiti would be amassing heavy personal expenses during his travels, he was to pay for only the first eighth by himself; the remainder would be divided equally. The contract even stipulated that if the company ship was waylaid by pirates, Arangoiti was empowered to negotiate with them for a ransom which the partners would pay to an agent of the raiders in either Cádiz or Veracruz.

Here again, the enormous expansion of foreign commerce enabled middling-level traders to participate. In one case, a partner in a haberdashery (mercería) traveled to Spain on business for his single store.[26] In 1802 Manuel García Herreros, a relative and former business associate of the prominent wholesaler Francisco Martínez Cabezón, now on his own, dispatched 502 tercios of sugar to Spain with another relative who would retain all profits from the sale, provided he used the original capital to buy goods in Spain for García Herreros.[27]

Dispatching partners and associates to Spain was not the only device utilized by Mexico City merchants; they also circumvented established Spanish merchant houses and contracted directly with independent traders of the peninsula. Once more, the company, that most versatile form of economic organization, played a prominent role. The Mexico City partner, either alone or with his Spanish associate, acted as the investor. The Spaniard typically installed himself in a seaport (Bilbao and Santander figure heavily in the documentation), and either received goods there or traveled about the country making purchases. The clauses of the contracts stipulated the rights and responsibilities of the two parties and provided each with grounds for legal redress if provisions were violated. Ideally, the fact that both partners stood to gain from the successful completion of the company would keep affairs in order.[28]

The Manila Galleon

Another extremely lucrative field of international commerce—the China trade, or as it has been more commonly termed, the Manila Galleon—was dominated by wealthy members of the Mexico City Consulado to the exclusion of all other merchants, whether from the capital or the provinces, through the final voyage in 1815. The galleon annually brought about 2,000,000 pesos worth of fine Chinese silks, ivory, jade, wood, and the like to Acapulco, where those products not already consigned to specific merchants were auctioned off.[29] Unlike trade with Europe, which now arrived in numerous small lots over the course of an entire year, the China trade still consisted of a single ship once a year, thereby enabling the most powerful wholesale dealers to maintain a monopoly. In 1810 six merchants of the capital formed a company that purchased the entire shipment of that year's galleon for the cash sum of 1,800,000 pesos.[30] One invested 550,000 pesos, another 350,000, and the remaining four 225,000 each. All profits were divided in proportion to each party's original investment. Even when the shipment was brought into the capital, it was not distributed to the partners, but sold off lot by lot at prices set by majority vote within the company, thus preventing the six investors from competing against each other. Only when all the goods had been sold did the partners split up the profits. No individual or group was able to curtail the activities of this company, and the only complaint registered came from another prominent Mexico City merchant who claimed that he had been excluded from the cartel after first being promised entrance.

But merchants of the capital were not content to purchase from the Manila Galleon only after it had docked at Acapulco. Often, brothers, sons, and other relatives were stationed as agents in Manila.[31] In addition, loans were made to other Manila merchants, who were required to repay with products on upcoming voyages. One major Mexico City trader and his business associate in 1805 loaned over 28,000 pesos to finance the return voyage of a Manila merchant then in the city. In payment, he committed himself to send goods worth 14,000 pesos on each of the next two Manila Galleons, plus the 25 percent markup common to overseas commercial loans and an additional 5 percent interest charge for the time that he held the money in Manila.[32]

General stores throughout the provinces and the capital regularly featured Chinese goods (silks and tapestries seem to have been greatly in demand) along with European imports and domestically produced items, and the dealers of the capital were their sole sources of supply. Beyond this, at least Mexico City supported a number of retail stores that specialized in silks (sederías). Individual wholesale transactions to either type of store could easily surpass 100,000 pesos.[33] The markups charged by the wholesalers varied incredibly and seemingly without pattern.[34] In 1803 José Bernardo Baz made two virtually simultaneous sales of Chinese goods to the same retail store; the first sale totalled 72,019 pesos, a price which included a 69½ percent increase over their value in Manila, but the second sale of 46,422 pesos carried an increase of only 21 percent.[35]

The Cacao Trade

The scope of the Mexico City merchants' trade in the Americas regularly transcended the political confines of New Spain and extended southward at least to Venezuela and Peru. In 1782 a group of three wholesalers purchased some Ceylon cinnamon from the Manila Galleon and shipped it to a consortium of Guatemala City traders.[36] Such activity was typical of the commerce carried on with Spanish South America. Based primarily on the cacao trade that had been dominated by Spanish traders of Mexico City since the late sixteenth century,[37] it was supplemented by a smaller importation of cotton, tin, copper, and even vicuña skins from Peru.[38]

Most of the colony's cacao came from three areas: Tabasco, Guayaquil, and Venezuela (Venezuelan cacao was divided into two types: Maracaibo and Caracas). Havana occasionally contributed an insignificant amount. The enormous volume of the trade is revealed in Table 13, which shows the total amount of cacao brought into New Spain as recorded by the customs service for the years 1758 and 1759. By a very rough estimate, the 1758 shipment

Table 13.   The Quantity of Cacao Received on Consignment in Mexico in 1758 and 1759 According to the Records of the Customs Service

Type	1758 Arrobas	1758 Pounds	1759 Arrobas
Cacao Caracas	55,243	2¼	27,840
Cacao Maracaibo	18,993	12½	8,112
Cacao Tabasco	28,602	14	2,584
Cacao de la Habana	656		
Cacao Guayaquil			38,592
Total	103,495	3¾	77,128

Source: AGN, Industria y Comercio, leg. 8, exp. 3.

Table 14.   Retail Prices in Mexico City of Some Types of Cacao[a]

Cacao Tabasco		Cacao Maracaibo		
1806	6½–7 (reales)	1805	5–6½ (reales)	
1807	7	1806	4½–5	
1812	12	1807	5–5½	
Cacao Guayaquil		1810	3½–4	
1805	1½–2 (reales)	1812	12	
1806	1½	Cacao Caracas		
1807	1½	1805	7	(reales)
1812	6	1810	3½	
		1812	12	

[a] All prices per pound.
Source: Weekly Retail Price Advertisements in the *Diario de México*.

would have retailed in Mexico City for approximately 1,800,000 pesos and that of 1759 for around 800,000. Table 14 lists some retail prices for different types of cacao in the city late in the colonial period. Overall, these prices were quite stable until the coming of the Wars of Independence, when they skyrocketed.

Broad participation by Mexico City merchant houses, a characteristic of commerce with Europe, was repeated in the cacao trade. Sixty-three firms were active in 1758 or 1759.[39] As shown in Table 15, twenty-one of them can be considered major dealers, importing more than 1,000 arrobas in a single year. For example, Esteban Buenvecino received more than 15,000 arrobas from Caracas, Maracaibo, and Tabasco in 1758, while Juan José de Fagoaga, a relative of the Marqués de Apartado, received more than 11,000. The following year, Francisco Martínez Cabezón imported over 19,000 arrobas of the same types, and Francisco Llano y Urresti over 35,000 from Guayaquil (over 90 percent of that year's shipment from that port).[40]

Some merchants had brothers or other relatives located in Guayaquil; others had long-term agreements with trading houses in Peruvian ports to receive periodic consignments.[41] Many persons in the China trade were also active in the trade to Peru. Some even employed their own ships in Pacific coastal shipping. In the early 1800s, Juan Lorenzo de Antepara regularly dispatched his corvette

Table 15.   List of Merchants Who Received More Than 1,000 Arrobas
of Cacao on Consignment in Either 1758 or 1759

Ventura Pablo Dies
Manuel de Leguinzabal
Juan García Trujillo
Miguel Alonso de Hortigosa
Antonio de Zavala
José de Matos y Rivera
José Joaquín de Ariscorreta
Diego García Bravo
Francisco Javier de Llano y Urresti
José de los Rios Mantilla
María Teresa Sáenz Rico
Pedro Therán
Esteban Buenvecino
Juan José de Fagoaga
Fernando González de Collantes
Francisco Martínez Cabezón
Juan Antonio Llanos Vergara
Agustín de Icaza
Manuel de Llantada Ibarra
Juan Tomás Meoqui

Source: AGN, Industria y Comercio, leg. 8, exp. 3.

to the ports of the South Sea (as the Pacific was still termed).[42] One
year Francisco Martínez Cabezón, heavily involved in both the
China and the cacao trade, borrowed 70,000 pesos to finance the
voyage of his ship from Acapulco.[43] His daughter married a
cousin, Diego de Agreda, who took over the merchant house and
continued trading along these established routes.[44]

Cacao from Guayaquil was normally shipped to Acapulco,
where agents—each of whom apparently represented several Mexico City traders—would prepare it for shipment to the capital for a
commission of 1 percent per pound, with each pound valued at
one real. Cacao was shipped in cargas weighing 78 pounds each.
The major expense upon docking was the seafreight charge, paid
at the rate of eighteen reales per carga to the master of the ship.
The costs of unloading were minimal, but those for storehouse

rental could quickly mount. These expenses and those for mule-teers to ship the cacao to the capital were customarily paid in cash, and the merchant might have to make a preliminary sale just to raise the necessary funds.

The Export Trade

To pay for the foreign goods it imported, Mexico had to export items of its own. The greatest external market, of course, was for silver coin. Over much of the colonial period, however, cochineal also constituted an appreciable part of the exports, and towards the end, several other commodities, especially sugar, began to figure in the trade.

The history of the cochineal trade between Mexico and Europe has already been well outlined, with a description of how the merchants of the capital utilized their ability to extend banking services to officials and local traders in Oaxaca to dominate this industry.[45] Still murky are the terms of trade between the merchants of Mexico and those of Europe who received the dye. It is unclear if the colonists were independent agents in this commerce or acted as factors of Spanish firms. From the evidence now available, the best that can be done is make the ambiguous statement that it was a combination of the two. The presence of the English seems to deny total control by Spanish firms; yet the occasional ability of these same trading houses to channel major shipments of the dye to themselves bespeaks a more than languid participation.[46]

It became increasingly apparent in this period that Mexico City merchants had the capacity to export colonial products to the peninsula at their own risk. I have already recounted the voyage, sponsored by Antonio de Bassoco, which dispatched a shipment of cacao from Venezuela to Spain, and the actions of Manuel García Herreros, who sent Mexican sugar to the peninsula. These are not isolated cases. After silver and cochineal, sugar was New Spain's leading export to the home country. Table 16 provides figures on the amount and value of cochineal and sugar shipped to Spain from Veracruz during the years 1796–1810. By weight, nine times as much sugar as cochineal was transported, but because of the much higher specific value of the latter product, its total worth exceeded that of sugar by a factor of 2.4. Still, the amount of

Table 16.   Export of Cochineal and Sugar from Veracruz to Spain in
the Years 1796–1810

	Cochineal		Sugar	
Year	Arrobas	Value[a]	Arrobas	Value
1796	6,122	439,609	346,361	1,347,231
1797	838	54,471	60,835	159,834
1798	12,220	804,903	79,568	212,691
1799	40,602	2,703,471	150,881	479,062
1800	5,150	379,256	87,570	287,277
1801	3,848	298,258	9,148	25,157
1802	43,277	3,303,470	431,867	1,454,240
1803	27,251	2,191,399	483,944	1,495,056
1804	11,737	1,220,193	381,509	1,097,505
1805	—	—	—	—
1806	4,254	425,400	25,857	64,642
1807	2,823	282,800	5,288	18,220
1808	7,374	737,400	19,917	39,834
1809	21,560	2,587,200	241,146	482,492
1810	20,415	2,449,800	119,726	269,383
Total	267,233	17,877,630	2,443,717	7,432,624

[a] All values in pesos.
Source: Lerdo de Tejada, *Comercio esterior*, Appendix 14.

sugar exported and its monetary importance (especially in those years when foreign wars did not impede Spanish commerce) were significant.

The merchants of the capital acquired the sugar in a manner not dissimilar to that which they used to obtain cochineal; they loaned the producers money against future harvests. Estate owners who needed funds or who sought a guaranteed return in advance of harvest pledged repayment in stipulated amounts of sugar over a certain number of years at a price that could not be altered by changing market conditions. While the producer customarily paid the shipping costs, the merchant assumed all additional expenses and government charges, as well as the risk involved in later shipping the commodity to Spain (a not inconsiderable factor given the disruption cause by Spain's then frequent foreign wars).[47] Table

16 reveals the curtailment in New Spain's overseas trade caused by conflicts in the years 1797–1801 and 1805–1808. Overall, however, despite growing demand overseas, Mexico City remained far and away the primary market for the colony's sugar industry.

The Spanish navy was ineffectual in challenging British control of the seas, and when the two powers were at war, few ships were able to break through British blockades. In 1796 a merchant of the capital attempted to send 36,000 pesos worth of sugar and nearly 23,000 pesos of Guatemalan indigo to the peninsula, but the ships were attacked and the entire value of the indigo was lost.[48] The traders of Mexico City learned from such occurrences. In 1804 Sebastián de Heras Soto, the future Conde de Heras Soto, ordered indigo and sugar loaded on a frigate docked in Veracruz harbor for shipment to the port of Santander (his hometown) where his creole son, located there to learn the ways of international commerce, was to receive the shipment.[49] But by the time the ship arrived at Havana in January of the following year, war had broken out between Spain and England, and Heras Soto, fearing to send the ship into the British-controlled Atlantic, sent a letter empowering an agent in Havana to disembark his goods and sell them anywhere (presumably in the Americas) he could obtain a favorable price.

The Silver Transporters

Silver shipment throughout the colony, and especially to the ports of Acapulco and Veracruz, was handled by a small number of commercial silver firms (conductores de plata) centered in the capital which emphasized this service, but again not to the exclusion of trade in other products. It appears that at any one time only two such businesses (and a total of three in all) transported bullion in the years after 1770. The merchant house of Pedro de Vértiz engaged in this aspect of commerce for at least three generations, achieving continuity through the familiar pattern of marrying daughters to peninsular nephews. But in 1802, now termed the house of Oteiza y Vértiz in honor of the latest nephew, the firm collapsed, falling into bankruptcy and taking down with it a number of smaller traders who had entrusted funds to it.[50]

Perhaps partly to fill the vacuum left by this collapse, Martín Angel de Micháus y Aspiros, already active in the commerce of commodities such as sugar and leather, founded a company with Captain Antonio de Uscola to ship bullion to the port cities.[51] To relieve the anxiety of potential customers, the firm guaranteed safe delivery of shipments through a fund of 200,000 pesos, composed of commitments of 25,000 pesos from each of eight prominent merchants of the capital.[52] The success of the company was immediate and enduring; Micháus y Aspiros was still shipping silver to Veracruz in 1823.[53]

The good fortune enjoyed by this new competitor inspired an immediate response from the long-established firm of Fernández de Peredo. Instituted by 1774 at the latest, this house in 1788 was operated as a company with equal division of profits between the partners Juan Antonio Vázquez and Juan Domingo Fernández, who had married María Guadalupe Vázquez, a daughter of his partner. Over the next decade and a half, though this business was restructured several times, it always operated as a company in which the partners were family members, usually nephews and cousins.[54]

In a two-page announcement in the February 18, 1804 *Gazeta de México*, Diego Fernández de Peredo, the latest director of the family firm, announced a new reorganization, the establishment of a partnership with yet another cousin. He noted the successful tactic taken by Micháus and Uscola of pledging a monetary bond to guarantee prompt delivery, and responded that his own company now offered security up to 300,000 pesos, made up of 12 bonds of 25,000 pesos each from leading Mexico City merchants. He proceeded to name them and to outline the basic provisions of his new company. These stipulated that the company was organized for the term of six years, that it would transport any amount of money to Veracruz and Acapulco for private individuals at the standard charge of 28 reales per 1,000 of silver and 12 reales per 1,000 of gold, that the shipments would go forth with the notorious promptness of never a month's interval between them, and that every person, within or outside the capital, might submit any amount and be assured of on-time delivery and payment of any bills of credit against the security of the 300,000 peso guarantee. The announcement concluded with a reminder to the public that this mercantile house had been in existence for twenty-eight years and that it had mule teams stationed at every appropriate staging point.

In sum then, if the wholesale merchants of Mexico City were threatened by the coming of the free trade era and the establishment of strong merchant communities in Veracruz and Guadalajara, they responded not by withdrawal from trade, but by innovating with methods and routes that successfully circumvented any takeover. Merchants of the capital remained in international commerce and prospered. They were gradually replaced and supplemented by a constant stream of new faces who assured the continued vitality of this entrepreneurial sector.

Significantly, if Veracruz traders were able to challenge those of the capital in trade with Europe, this was the only field of commerce in which they were able to do so. The lucrative China trade remained a monopoly of the Mexico City Consulado, as did the cacao trade with Spanish South America. Silver shipping was controlled by a small group of Mexico City merchants. If the port merchants were active in the export of colonial products to Europe, they were, at best, obtaining only a fragment of the trade.

The late colonial period as characterized by the rapid expansion of commercial activity as the population boom in both Mexico and Europe enlarged markets and as the nascent Industrial Revolution created a demand for more types of colonial products and for new markets in which to sell the finished products. The commercial world was expanding beyond the capacity of any one city or even region to dominate completely. In this new climate, Mexico City did not lose any of its established trade but rather shared the expansion with emerging regional centers. The merchants of the capital did not retreat to domination of the Valley of Mexico (still by far the largest market in the country) but continued their traditional hold over much of the interregional commerce of the wealthiest provinces of the colony. In the following chapter we will examine the mechanisms that enabled them to do so.

4 Provincial Trade

The merchants of Mexico City did not limit their activity to the capital and its immediate environs, but rather maintained a commercial domination over most of the country, especially over those parts of it engaged in the production of goods for interregional and international markets. As long as the wholesalers of the capital continued to dominate provincial trade, they would not be supplanted in their position of primacy in international commerce. For this and other reasons, the capital's merchants paid a great deal of attention to provincial trade, using a variety of methods to sell their merchandise not only in regional centers but throughout the countryside as well.

Provincial Companies

Merchants of the capital, including many without the stature to belong to the Consulado, owned great numbers of retail stores scattered throughout the provinces. Below the stratum of international traders flourished another of large-scale retailers who owned chains of specialty and general stores in both the capital and the countryside. These were the individuals who made many of the larger purchases—50,000 to 150,000 pesos—from wholesalers in order to stock their various outlets. In addition, some storekeepers of the capital were able to open single branches in nearby regional centers such as Toluca or Cuautla Amilpas.

While some merchants chose to operate these outlets through salaried employees, the great majority formed companies with the

77

managers of their stores, whether in Mexico City or the provinces. Their purpose in doing so was to instill greater loyalty and exact greater efforts from their associates by giving them a stake in the prosperity of the enterprise. A large retailer could thus maintain company contracts with the administrators of each of his outlets. Such arrangements relieved the owner of most operational duties; he remained in charge of purchasing while generally allowing his partners to run their stores with little interference. The contracts usually stipulated that there would be an annual inventory, that the manager could not extend credit beyond a certain stated limit, and that he would not involve himself in any business outside of the company. The manager's share of the profits varied between one fourth and one half (more often the latter), depending on his reputation and his ability to strike a favorable bargain.[1]

One Mexico City retailer whom we can use to exemplify some of the processes was Joaquín de Aldana, a native of San Juan Teotihuacán, who began his business career by marrying into a family active in the pulque trade. He soon assumed management of the family's operations and eventually came into ownership of a good part of them. Not content with this, he diversified into ownership of large bread-bakeries (panaderías) and retail stores. By the beginning of the nineteenth century, he owned several dry-goods stores in the capital and surrounding regions, including one in his home town.

An account of the management of the store in Teotihuacán over the period 1798–1804 shows how Aldana progressively elevated the status of an employee, José Basurto, as the latter proved his ability. In 1798 José Basurto was working as a salaried employee (cajero) in the Teotihuacán store under the supervision of its manager, the cajero mayor. The following year the manager left, and Basurto was given the post at an unstipulated annual salary. (The highest salary I have encountered for a store manager was 500 pesos; this was exceptional, and most earned from 300 to 400 pesos per year.) Basurto was so successful that by the beginning of 1800 Aldana owed him 1,150 pesos in salary and profits and thereupon installed him as a partner, though at a share of the profits left to the owner's discretion. But again Basurto displayed his business acumen, and at the end of that year Aldana rewarded him with a one-third share of the profits—a total of 2,794 pesos—and assured him a full half share in the future. They dissolved the company for unstated reasons at the beginning of 1805. In the period 1798–1804, Basurto had earned a total of 17,365 pesos in salary and profits, which minus his personal expenses of 3,723 pesos, left him an income of 13,362 pesos for his seven years of labor.[2]

Aldana used similar methods in the management of his Mexico City stores. In the 1780s, he took an orphan boy, Juan Reyes, into his charge and set about training him in the ways of commerce. He placed him under the supervision of the cajero mayor of his general store, the Alcantarilla, in one of the many small plazas in the capital. Reyes did so well that in 1788 Aldana gave him 2,000 pesos in salary and gratification. Then, when the cajero mayor of the Zorrilla, Aldana's other general store in the city, left his position, the owner installed Reyes as its manager, making him a partner. Table 17 relates Reyes' income as managing partner of this store in the years 1789–1799. His yearly income averaged slightly over 2,383 pesos during the eleven-year period. This successful company was dissolved in early 1800 only because management of Aldana's bigger store—the Alcantarilla, valued at 28,255 pesos— fell open, and the two associates decided that they would both benefit if Reyes became its managing partner.[3]

Most Mexico City merchants concentrated their provincial trade, in a general way, in a single broadly defined region. It was the rare merchant who had the resources and the organization to extend himself into several at the same time. The company contracts used to run these distant operations were usually for a period of anywhere from three to seven years; however, a successful provincial company could endure for twenty, thirty, or more years with the same supplier or his designated successor in Mexico City, while the body of personnel in the provinces might change or remain the same. Some retail companies involved only moderate investments (5,000 to 20,000 pesos), but these were typically located in towns relatively near the capital—Toluca or Cuautla Amilpas for example. Those in lucrative mining towns such as Rosario, Arizpe, and Zacatecas could easily elicit initial investments of over 70,000 pesos, all or by far the greatest part of which was put up by the Mexico City supplier; if the company prospered, even greater

Table 17.   Annual Profits Earned by Juan Reyes 1789–1799 While
Acting as Managing Partner of the General Store (Tienda
Mestiza) the Zorrilla, in Mexico City, owned by Joaquín de
Aldana

Year	Profit
1789	1,477 (pesos)
1790	2,124
1791	2,413
1792	2,543
1793	3,225
1794	2,350
1795	2,337
1796	3,788
1797	3,520
1798	4,290
1799	1,869
Gross Total	29,886
Personal Expenses	3,665
Net Income	26,221

Source: AN, Pozo, Feb. 15, 1800.

investment followed. Commonly, the partnership agreement provided that all merchandise in the store was to be purchased from
the Mexico City member, sometimes, it appears, at inflated prices.
Occasionally, however, the provincial partner was given the right
to purchase from whoever offered the best terms. The Mexico
City merchant received either one-half or two-thirds of the profits. The other party's freedom to sell on credit was often restricted
to a specific amount, and he was often enjoined from investing in
any local enterprise, such as a mine, at least without the consent of
the home partner. Almost universally, he was expressly forbidden
to act as a bondsman, since that might involve the company in litigation or even make it liable for the debts of a third party.

In provincial trade, as in international, merchants preferred to
place relatives in managing positions. When this was not possible,
the next best alternative was to station trusted associates from the
Mexico City trading house in the branch outlets. Thus there was a

constant flow of employees and partners from the capital to the provinces and back again; the persons returning were those who had proven their business aptitude and were now being promoted to the central office of the merchant house.

A company in a provincial store, especially one located in an economically promising setting, could attract a heavy initial investment, endure over decades, and maintain distinct articulation between investment, central management, and branch management. In 1777 José Luis de Fagoaga, a merchant of the capital and a cousin of the Marqués de Apartado, invested 80,000 pesos in a company in a general store in the mining town of Arizpe, Sonora for a period of six years. His partners were Manuel Jiménez del Arenal, who invested 20,000 pesos of his own, and Esteban Gach, who would administer the store. All three individuals were merchants of the capital, though clearly each was of different rank. Fagoaga, the major investor, removed himself from all active involvement in the company's affairs, except to exercise his right to one half of the profits. The other two partners were each entitled to one fourth. Jiménez del Arenal was placed in charge of overall administration and purchasing from his position in the capital. Gach, as the provincial manager, was instructed not to invest in any other enterprise on his own nor act as bondsman for any person not a merchant. Accounts of all store expenses had to be forwarded periodically to the capital for approval by the other two partners. However, Gach was permitted to select his own employees and was encouraged to establish branch stores in yet other mining communities.[4] In point of fact, the company survived the death of Gach in 1796 and endured twenty-two years until the demise of Fagoaga in 1799. Upon Gach's death, the two surviving partners reorganized the company, managing the Arizpe store through salaried employees and agreeing to divide future profits in the ratio of one third for Jiménez del Arenal and two thirds for Fagoaga. Between 1777 and 1796, Fagoaga increased his investment by an additional 37,868 pesos.[5]

Correspondence Accounts

Local retailers throughout New Spain depended upon Mexico City merchants for much of their merchandise. These storekeepers simply could not generate the volume of trade nor the liquid capital needed to purchase directly from overseas. Even when dealing with their suppliers in the capital, they were rarely able to pay cash for their orders. In fact, it was this dependence upon credit which bound provincial storekeepers to major Mexico City commercial houses.

The small merchant located in a regional trade center, mining town, or large village found himself forced by his limited resources and market into a retail trade depended upon extension of credit to customers and often the acceptance of goods in lieu of cash payment. This endemic reliance on credit and barter transactions, when combined with his relatively small scale of operation, placed the storekeeper in an inherently unstable situation. His survival was threatened by the continual ebb and flow of the local economy. When bad times occurred, the local storeowner's volume of trade decreased even further, and his clientele was even less able to pay off its accounts. He was a prime candidate for bankruptcy unless his own supplier could extend him credit over a long period and, perhaps, make him loans and provide other banking services. The economic vulnerability of the local retailers made them welcome the establishment of long-term correspondence accounts with major trading firms of the capital and the greater security that they provided.

Only Mexico City merchant houses had the capacity to operate on these terms. The scale of their business was so large that, except at times of acute economic depression, they could extend credit to all their clients, because at any one time they were receiving sufficient income from varied business interests (mercantile and otherwise) to avoid overextension.

Literally scores of wholesalers distributed goods throughout the countryside by use of correspondence accounts, sometimes with a number of retailers scattered across a wide area, but quite understandably with only one in each town. The retailer, on the other hand, dealt with only a single supplier, even to the point of issuing him bills of credit to purchase goods from other merchants.[6]

Table 18 shows some of the sales made to provincial storekeepers over a five-year period by a commercial company headed by José Gómez Campos. During the same five-year period, this

Table 18.   Partial Listing of the Sales Made to Provincial Clients by the
Company of José Gómez Campos in the Period 1785–1789

Year	Value	Occupation and Residence of Client
1785	6,876 (pesos)	Merchant of Real del Catorce
1785	27,874	Merchant of Durango
1786	4,674	Merchant of Zapotlán el Grande
1787	5,314	Same
1787	4,442	Mercader Viandante
1787	14,062	Merchant of León
1789	12,339	Miner of Real de Zacualpan
1789	17,867	Citizen of Pátzcuaro
1789	2,579	Merchant of Valladolid
1789	4,941	Two Citizens of Irapuato

Source: AN, Torija, Feb. 18, 1785, Dec. 3, 1785, Feb. 21, 1787, June 19, 1787, Sept. 10, 1787, March 12, 1789, April 23, 1787, July 11, 1789, Oct. 23, 1789; AGN, Civil, leg. 701, exp. 25, f. 1, March 23, 1786.

partnership also sold merchandise to retail distributors in the capital, as well as jewels and unworked silver to a local silversmith.[7] Few of these customers paid cash on the barrelhead, but rather delayed payment (con plazo).

These deferrals can be grouped into several different types. In one, the purchaser paid a certain amount upon receipt of the merchandise and committed himself to payment of the balance at the end of a set period of time, which might be anywhere from a couple of months to over a year. Just as frequently, the client paid no money down and pledged to settle the account on a fixed day in the future. In another variant, the customer obligated himself to make partial payments at several specified dates. In any of the arrangements, the buyer might be required to pledge real property or to secure a bondsman to assure prompt payment, but this seems to have been demanded mostly from new or infrequent clientele. In the same way, the supplier did not normally charge interest on the unpaid balance, but he might insist on it from those who were unfamiliar or known for their delinquency.[8]

Provincial storekeepers almost always came to the capital to select the goods they wanted and thus incurred all duties and freight
costs. They apparently did not trust their suppliers to provide the
items and the quality that they desired. However, payments for
these goods could often be made to business associates of the Mexico City merchants located in various regional centers. Wholesalers also made use of these agents to collect from delinquent
debtors.[9]

The Dependency of the Provincial Storekeeper

The commercial and banking services provided by the great trading houses of the capital were indispensable to the solvency of provincial storekeepers. The large firms typically handled whatever
business affairs the storekeepers had in the city, thereby buttress-
ing the latter's dealings with the power and reputation of major
financial institutions. This seems to have been an important consideration, for whenever the provincials encountered legal or economic difficulties, they were quick to appeal to their Mexico City
suppliers for succor. By honoring bills of credit issued against
them by their affiliates, these firms provided a bank's protection
against loss in the shipment of coin across country. They also acted
as banks by accepting bills of credit, even when there were insufficient funds in the storekeeper's account. Knowing the cyclical
nature of most regional economies and needing to maintain a presence in as many provinces as possible, the central merchant house
was willing to extend credit in this way. Not to do so would probably mean the demise of an associate's business and the creation of
an uncollectable debt. Credit extension offered a likelihood of at
least partial payment in the future and the preservation of another
market outlet for the present. No wholesaler prospered for long
unless he was able to support a chain of these regional affiliates.
Besides extending credit, the large trading houses had the resources to make their clients loans which were readily renewable
at the standard rate of 5 percent simple annual interest. Without
the availability of such services, the provincial storekeeper would
have been a most isolated and fragile economic being. And in
reference to him, perhaps the most appropriate question is not
whether he could pick and choose from among different merchant

houses but rather how he managed to survive without becoming formally appended to one of them.

Examples of dependence are seen in the dealings of Ramón de Goycoechea, who directed a commercial firm in the capital in the late eighteenth century and maintained a commercial agreement with a merchant in the mining town of Sierra de Pinos for a number of years. Goycoechea supplied the provincial trader with all his goods, received all the silver that he collected, paid all the libranzas he issued, and guaranteed all payments that he made. When the storeowner died, Goycoechea served as his executor along with the widow and dispatched two of his own cajeros there to run the business. One of them married the widow, the other one her daughter, and together they continued the association with Goycoechea.[10] Several years later, he made a major investment in two stores in another mining town, Real de Catorce, and to manage the business contracted a company with a merchant of the town who willingly divorced himself from all other commercial activities in order to work in partnership with Goycoechea.[11]

Securing Silver Supplies

Accumulation of sufficient silver coin to acquire goods from abroad and still to make occasional loans to affiliated retailers was a requisite for the long-term operation of a wholesale trading firm. Commercial houses, therefore, took every possible step to increase the amount of precious metal flowing into their coffers. They certainly could not expect a sufficient supply from payment from their provincial customers. The inability of the provincial merchants to make transactions in specie was at once the major factor binding them to specific wholesale dealers and the cause of the dealer's greatest worry: insolvency from overextension of credit.

Thus, quite frequently, at least in the late colonial period, major mercantile concerns of the capital used any of three methods to acquire silver: special arrangements with storeowners in mining towns, similar arrangements with the miners themselves, and direct investment in mines, usually in companies. In this era then, wealthy merchants invested in mining not as an alternative to international commerce, but as an essential part of it.

Shopkeepers in mining regions did in some cases receive a regular and sizable supply of silver through their dealings with mineowners. But these same provincial traders were typically associated with Mexico City commercial houses, either directly as their business partners in commercial companies, or indirectly (but still strongly) as regular customers dependent on the maintenance of long-term correspondence accounts. Though these local traders might accumulate considerable specie individually, they still could not generate sufficient trade volume, given their limited markets, to compete against the great firms of the capital in the wholesale purchase of foreign merchandise. Thus, they found it to their advantage to ship silver to one of the international firms, to purchase goods from it, and to receive credit, loans, and banking services when needed.[12]

Mexico City merchants frequently bypassed these nominally independent provincial traders and dealt directly with miners, usually through their own retail outlets in mining centers. Though these men of commerce might start off as nothing more than exclusive suppliers to a mine, once involved in the industry, they found themselves drawn ever more deeply into actual investment, and ultimately into partial ownership of these enterprises. And, it should be noted, most took these steps without the slightest hesitation. Mining investment through partnerships and joint-stock companies was a desirable form of economic diversification for the mercantile community of this period. Invariably, whether acting as supplier, financier, or owner, the merchant took steps to insure himself a regular supply of silver.

In 1789 José Gómez Campos was providing goods and interest-free loans to a miner in the Real de Zacualpan. Two days after purchasing a large shipment from this prominent wholesaler, the miner entered into an agreement with him, providing that in return for past favors, he would deliver all his silver to his benefactor's Mexico City trading house; as repayment, Gómez Campos was authorized to subtract 1½ reales from each mark (a mark in this period being equal to 8½ pesos or 68 reales) plus 20 reales from each bar worth more than 100 marks and turn over the metal to the royal mint. The arrangement was to be in force for three years with shipments made every two months.[13]

Manuel García Herreros, another merchant of the capital, went beyond this type of agreement and in 1801 entered into a formal contract with a miner to finance all necessary operations. The mine in the Real de Huautla was owned equally by Juan José de Apecechea and Juan Bautista de Fagoaga. According to the document, García Herreros, in return for 7 pesos out of each mark produced, would pay for the extraction of silver, the rental of the refining plant, and the cost of refining. He would receive Apecechea's share of the silver upon its arrival in Mexico City, turn it over to the royal mint, and receive back the coin. Other clauses stipulated that the first payment of nearly 6,500 pesos should go to the administrator of the mine (a relative of Apecechea), that Apecechea would be paid 300 pesos monthly for personal maintenance, and that the agreement could be abrogated by either party at any time.[14]

Steps taken by Manuel Bolado Regato exemplify the merchant's final step into actual ownership of a mine. In 1791, by means of a formal company contract, he agreed to become the financing partner of a miner in Pachuca. Bolado Regato pledged to provide all the money and supplies necessary to make the mine profitable; in return, he was made owner of half the mine. All silver produced was to be delivered to his firm in Mexico City, where he would keep the accounts and be free to use the specie in his commerce.[15] As was typical in mining companies, the mine administrator—the technical expert whose skills and initiative were of preeminent importance—was given a share; each of the two major partners gave him a sixth of his profits. However, he could not sell his shares without their permission.

A number of prominent merchants in the capital (along with some who were not so prominent) enthusiastically entered into part or complete ownership of silver mines. Some were content merely to finance operations, but others became directly involved with management, supervising the refining process and other operations.[16] In no known instance did a merchant abandon commerce for mining; the two fields of endeavor were perceived as complementary. Much provincial commerce was dependent on the health of the mining industry; maintenance of a successful wholesale trade, as we have seen, required regular access to specie.

Further inducements included the hope that the mine might turn out to be a bonanza and form the basis for a great family fortune, or at least serve as a hedge against possible bankruptcy in the always precarious field of international commerce.

In most cases, merchants entered the ranks of mine ownership through their increasing investments and loans to miners, but some did speculate in mining enterprises in which they had no previous involvement.[17] Prominent traders who became part-owners of mines typically did so by contracting formal companies with miners, but there is at least one case of a major wholesaler (José Gómez Campos again) dispatching a nephew as his agent to explore for mines in the province of Colima. Apparently, this nephew enjoyed some success, since the uncle filed for full rights and privileges pertaining to discovery of a mine.[18]

Eventually, by the 1780s at least, numbers of wholesale traders were investing together in mines through joint-stock companies. Several instances were found in which the merchant-owners or their deputies listed themselves in a document which gave their power of attorney to representatives who would oversee operation of the mine or mines. Table 19 records the members of a joint-stock company interested in mines in the Real de Bolaños. All seventeen individuals were almaceneros of Mexico City. They had joined together in 1788 to finance the drainage and development of eight Bolaños mines owned by Juan de Sierra Uruñuela, one of their number. He purchased five shares at 10,000 pesos each, and all the others invested 10,000 pesos apiece for a single share. They collectively turned over the 200,000 pesos to Francisco Martínez Cabezón, another almacenero of the capital long interested in mining. (Martínez Cabezón was the uncle and sponsor of Manuel García Herreros, a shareholder whose other mining activities were related previously.) He was entrusted with the acquisition and delivery of equipment to the mines, which were under the supervision of an experienced administrator.[19]

To sum up, Mexico City merchants regularly received shipments of silver during the late colonial period through a variety of mechanisms which centered around their commercial activities in mining regions and often came to include actual ownership of mining properties, usually through partnerships with the original

Table 19. Wholesale Merchants of Mexico City Who Were
Shareholders in the Mining Company in the Real de
Bolaños in 1788

Juan de Sierra Uruñuela
Antonio de Vivanco
Juan Casimiro de Ozta, Marqués de Rivas Cacho
Antonio de Bassoco
Manuel Ramón de Goya
Lorenzo de Angulo Guardamino
Gabriel Pérez de Elizalde
Juan José de Elías
José Adalid
Vicente Francisco Vidal
Sebastián de Heras Soto
Santiago García
Juan Fernández de Peredo
Juan Fernando Meoqui
Manuel García Herreros

Source: AN, Pozo, Feb. 28, 1789.

owners or joint-stock companies. This access to silver coin was vital to their ability to maintain dominance over interprovincial
trade, especially in areas producing for the international or colonial
markets. These commercial magnates viewed involvement in silver mining as a necessary aspect of large-scale mercantile operation and utilized the comparative advantage given them by access
to specie to expand their activities in trade rather than to retreat
from it.

Commodity Trading

Not all provincial trade involved local retailers. Merchant houses
also established long-term commercial agreements with large estate owners. (We have already seen that they did so with miners.)
This procedure was common with sugar estate owners of the Valley of Cuernavaca and equally with the great stock ranchers of the
desert North.[20] In almost every case the Mexico City dealer provided the estate with all needed supplies and was paid annually either in cash after the sale of the harvest or with the commodity

itself. The greatest concerns were the possibilities of a poor harvest and its reverse, a too abundant one, when a great supply would drive prices down.[21]

The merchant was as willing to be paid in goods as in cash because of the great demand for comestibles and raw materials in the heavily populated capital, a demand which supported numerous small processing and manufacturing plants in the environs. In addition, as already pointed out, given the shortage of specie and the lack of a stable circulating currency, wholesalers were forced to accept payment in a variety of products and to seek out new markets for them if they wished to thrive.

While Mexico City had to be supplied with all the basic foodstuffs, wholesale merchants found only meat and sugar sufficiently lucrative to merit their attention. This is quite understandable: prices for basic foods were low; transportation costs for these low-valued, high-bulk commodities were high; and there were many producers willing to market their own goods in the city. If prices did rise, there was no practical way to corner the market or drive prices up to a yet higher level.

But when a commodity had a high unit value and could bear transportation costs and still yield a substantial profit, wholesale merchants involved themselves heavily in its distribution in the urban market, and sometimes even overseas. Whenever possible, the merchant sought to obtain an exclusive contract with an estate owner rather than to purchase the harvest on the open market. Some merchants financed agriculturalists in return for delivery of the harvest at a guaranteed price, using their unrivalled access to coin to obtain produce at less than the going market rate. This approach was the same whether the producer was a stock raiser in the far North or a sugar harvester in the Valley of Cuernavaca, and bears a close resemblance to the company agreements which merchants struck with miners. The trader typically supplied all necessary goods to the producer, who in return gave him the right to a designated amount of sugar (the quality of which was specified in very exact terms) from the next harvest or perhaps several harvests, usually at a fixed price that could not be changed regardless of changing market conditions.[22]

Some of the major sugar producers of the Valley were Mexico

City merchants who chose this avenue of economic diversification. Martín Angel de Micháus y Aspiros, the previously mentioned silver shipper, and Lorenzo García Noriega, consul of the Mexico City Consulado in 1811–1812, are just two of those who acquired extensive sugar estates while continuing their careers in commerce.[23] But they did not seek to integrate their sugar production into their commerce; both men chose to sell their harvests through exclusive contracts with other merchants of the capital. In this they were typical of sugar producers generally.

Certain Mexico City merchants known as azucareros did specialize in the sugar trade. The 1753 census notes their presence, though it is possible that they concentrated on distributing the commodity within Mexico itself. Wholesalers in European and Chinese merchandise were also active in this field. In fact, it was these international traders who conducted every known overseas sale of sugar.

The value of sugar sent annually to Mexico City in the early 1790s approached one million pesos.[24] Ward Barrett reasonably estimates that this figure totals only one percent of the annual value of agricultural production in New Spain. But what is crucial here is not the percentage share of total annual production but rather the percentage share of those commodities sold in the marketplace. It must be remembered that at this time a significant part of agricultural production was destined for consumption by the family that raised it and was not intended for sale. Even more was traded in local markets and never entered the arena of the interregional economy in which the merchants operated. Furthermore, most agricultural commodities were not attractive to merchants, who only concerned themselves with commodities of high specific value which were in demand among urban residents with disposable income and which, at least periodically, could be sold for a substantial profit, not being price regulated or sold by so many agents that the profit margin was minimal.

Comestibles and alcoholic beverages were not the only commodities brought into the city for sale. Surrounded by numerous processing and manufacturing plants, Mexico City received a continual stream of raw materials for their supply. The most common items received were cotton and wool intended for the cloth obrajes.

Once again, merchants attempted to secure exclusive contracts to provision specific firms. Such agreements assured the manufacturer a steady supply of materials and offered the merchant possible high profits if, through negotiating with different producers, he could lower the initial purchase price, having already been guaranteed a constant selling price by the plant owner.[25]

Merchants of lower standing involved in provincial commerce were in a far poorer position to require payment in cash than were international wholesalers. Thus, they too regularly accepted payment in kind, relying on their ability to find new markets among the large population in the Valley of Mexico. Again, high transportation costs weighed against sale of low-value goods anywhere too distant from Mexico City. The greatest risk assumed by these small traders was apparently the quality of products received in payment. Merchants of this type turned to the Consulado for judicial relief against clients who had paid them with inferior or deteriorating commodities.[26]

Occasionally a merchant attempted to exploit price differences for a product between two regions and shipped comestibles from one place to another. However, it is obvious that these were irregular transactions, and no merchant attempted to build his career around them. By and large, the sale of comestibles and low-cost, domestically produced items was left to itinerant traders, who sought to market them in rural villages, sometimes with a notable lack of success.[27]

Some storekeepers of the capital did attempt to specialize in the sale of one commodity or another, but, with the exception of the sugar trade, such small-scale operations all drifted toward the same lamentable fate: bankruptcy. Whether concentrating on the commerce of a comestible such as wheat or a raw material such as cotton, no local specialist could control the pricing and demand patterns of the capital, and with a grim inevitability, economic collapse struck when the price level, for whatever reason (and they were numerous), fell below that which the merchant had anticipated.[28]

Yet other merchants participated in a field of commerce which did not directly involve the city. They regularly sent out agents— often relatives—supplied with cash, bills of exchange, and lines of credit to trade livestock in the provinces. The great wholealers stayed out of this trade; instead, the middle-level retailers with a good-sized store in the capital and perhaps one or two in the provinces regularly contributed participants.[29] The animals were never brought to the city, and their numbers were far too great to have been acquired just for a merchant's estate. (The prevalence of estate ownership within the merchant community will be discussed further on.) From all appearances, merchants dealt in this trade because of its financial appeal. Seemingly, considerable profits could be earned merely by transporting animals from an area with a surplus to another with a shortage, and these men of commerce occupied the best vantage point from which to ascertain which was which.

Government Officials

Certain officials of the royal government, especially those who were administrators in Indian districts or who supervised or held other high positions in royal monopolies, had much to offer the merchants of the capital: among their powers was the authority to restrict mercantile operations in their districts and to grant exclusive marketing rights of certain products. The merchants, on the other hand, had capabilities equally important to officials. They had the spare capital to post the bonds required of many government employees and the commercial apparatus capable of generating wealth if allowed to operate within an official's jurisdiction. Therefore, it is not surprising that government officials, both before and after the Bourbon Reforms, persistently entered into formal and informal business agreements with the great traders of the capital.

The best-known case of cooperation between merchants and government officials concerns the province of Oaxaca in the last half of the eighteenth century. In these arrangements, almaceneros of Mexico City posted the initial bond and then acted as bankers for the alcaldes mayores (and later the subdelegados) who were appointed to administer Indian districts and to deliver tribute from these areas to the royal treasury in the capital. Each merchant affiliated with the administrator of a given district and typically took care of all of his financial responsibilities, including delivery of the amount the alcalde mayor owed to the central treasury, in return for the exclusive right to trade in the district and to receive all the cochineal produced by its Indians. The government official was given a share of the proceeds in return for using his judicial authority to support the claims of his commercial associate against any recalcitrant local subjects or trespassing merchants.[30]

It has been argued that the free trade laws of the 1770s opened up the Oaxacan cochineal trade to the emerging merchants of Veracruz and that the reforms which replaced the alcalde mayor system of governance with the intendancy system in the 1780s irrevocably shifted control over this commerce from the merchants of the capital to those of the port city.[31] However, it appears to me that the detrimental impact of the free trade laws on the merchants of Mexico City has been overstated. It seems, rather, that the scale of cochineal production was rising so rapidly that it had grown beyond the capacity of any city to monopolize it, and in this situation Mexico City was reluctantly forced to share part of the cochineal trade with Veracruz.[32]

Furthermore, though the ordinances of the intendancy system outlawed the practice of merchants acting as business partners of the administrators of Indian districts, the new provisions did not eliminate the reason for the practice—the low salaries of these officials—nor develop a system to guarantee the punishment of offenders. This being the case, the new officials in charge of Indian districts, the subdelegados, looked to the merchants of Mexico City as had their predecessors.

A list from the early eighteenth century stating which districts in Oaxaca provided the greatest income to government agents placed the jurisdiction of Jicayán at the top.[33] In 1799, well over a decade after the intendancy reforms, Ignacio García Sáenz, a high-ranking member of the Mexico City commercial community, pledged himself as a bondsman for the sum of 2,000 pesos on behalf of the new subdelegado of that very district.[34] That same year, Pedro Alonso de Alles, the Marqués de Santa Cruz de Inguanzo, formerly a major backer of alcaldes mayores in the Oaxaca region, and four of his relatives and business associates served as bondsmen to the tune of 10,000 pesos (2,000 pesos each) for the sub-delegado of Teposcolula, another prosperous district of Oaxaca.[35]

Mexico City merchants served as bondsmen not just for officials in Indian districts but for all whose posts held some promise of profits. Tomás Pasarín acted as bondsman for his brother when he assumed the post of administrator of the royal tobacco monopoly in the district of Sierra de Pinos.[36] Diego Gómez de Barreda looked outside of the government bureaucracy and loaned 3,500 pesos for 6 months to the new tithe collector for the bishopric of Valladolid (Michoacán).[37] The eighteenth century was a time of enormous economic growth in Mexico, with much of it occurring in provinces that had previously been peripheral contributors to the colonial economy. In this changing business climate, it is understandable that some provincial centers began to rival Mexico City's traditional dominance over the most lucrative aspects of the economy, at least in some limited way.

Nor was acting as bondsmen the only approach used by merchants to affiliate themselves with officials at every level. More direct avenues, including loans, formal companies, and intermarriage, linked the bureaucracy to the mercantile community. When the peddler Silvestre Llampallas loaned 3,000 pesos interest-free to a subdelegado, he certainly did not do so without expecting something in return, and what greater reward could a subdelegado give an itinerant trader than access to the Indians of his region? Other merchants were even more blatant in their business arrangements with this new class of officials. In 1807 José Aniceto Ortega of Mexico City reported that he first loaned 600 pesos to the sub-delegado of Tixtla and then entered into a formal commercial company with him. He was now suing his former partner over his share of the proceeds. Ortega had become ill, and the subdelegado had managed the entire company, profited, and then refused to pay him.[38]

The merchant Juan José de Elías had regularly contracted with alcaldes mayores, supplying the royal treasury with funds which the officials owed but had diverted to personal use. In 1787 he turned to yet another branch of the bureaucracy and in a formal public contract loaned 4,000 pesos to the new administrator of the royal tobacco monopoly in the villages of Apan and Otumba in the northern part of the Valley of Mexico. In return, the administrator designated Elías' stores in the two villages as the exclusive dealers in tobacco products. Elías further agreed to pay the administrator a salary of 50 pesos per year as an employee.[39]

Government officials throughout the colony were active in local commerce. Some were regular purchasers of merchandise from Mexico City wholesale houses. Because regional officials occupied positions of power and status in their communities, merchants found them useful business associates. When Fernando Hermosa y Miranda purchased an outlet in Cuautla Amilpas for his Mexico City warehouse, he installed the local administrator of the mails as his managing partner.[40]

The most prominent merchants and businessmen of the capital bound their families to those of high-ranking royal functionaries—intendants, oidores, and viceroys—by marrying their daughters to these men or to their sons, as will be seen later in detail.

Viandantes

Among the mechanisms used by merchants of the capital to distribute goods throughout the provinces, though one of the least important, was the employment of viandantes, those marginal, itinerant, and petty regional traders who were present in Latin America from the earliest days of the colonial period.[41] A viandante usually approached the individual merchant and entered into a one-term contract to take his goods into the hinterland, usually either "tierra adentro," the mining regions of the North, or "tierra caliente," the heavily Indian regions of the South. There the merchandise would be sold from muleback in small villages which could not support a full-time merchant. The viandante's greatest fear was that the regional market would already be satiated and that he would have to sell at a loss or move on to another territory, assuming rapidly escalating transportation costs.

Suppliers used two different methods of financing viandantes, both of which were about equally common. As these itinerant traders were incapable of assembling a large amount of capital, they invariably bought on credit. In direct credit purchases, portions of the total purchase came due on specified days in the future.

As was common in credit sales at every level of commerce, bonds-men normally guaranteed faithful payment.[42]

The other option which suppliers regularly exercised was to enter into a one-time partnership with the viandante for the term of his expedition. As a rule, profits were divided equally between the partners; when one of them received a greater share, it was the supplier who got two thirds. Rarely did the two parties renew the agreement, and when they did, it was always a new one-time agreement, never a long-term understanding. This makes sense, for viandantes only filled in the commercial interstices, usually receiving small odd lots of merchandise for sale in areas outside the perimeters of established provincial trade.

Yet the viandantes' operations can be considered small only in light of the magnitude of the commerce carried on between the capital and the hinterland. Viandantes regularly handled goods from Europe, China, and New Spain itself, along with agricultural produce, in amounts exceeding 10,000 pesos per trip. Neither the mightiest nor the more modest traders of the capital hesitated to use these agents to enlarge their markets. In particular, dealers of agricultural and locally manufactured products turned to itinerants for distribution outside of the capital, presumably because the scope and profitability of this trade were too small to warrant establishment of permanent branches outside of the greater Mexico City area.

The viandantes themselves, creole or peninsular, composed a uniformly marginal sector of urban society. They maintained residences in roominghouses or in the houses of better-off relatives and spent most of their lives traveling from village to village selling their wares. Their possibilities for upward mobility were sharply limited. About the best they could hope for was to become the managing partner of a company in a small retail store and perhaps to buy it at a later date. But even this slight elevation in status was not common; aspirations to own a rural estate or even a house in the city were out of the question. Viandantes, despite their dependence on established merchants, were unaffiliated with, or perhaps better said, unprotected by any larger commercial firm. They were not invited to become permanent employees or to take over part of the business. When misfortune struck, there was no powerful institution to intervene on their behalf and possibly soften the impact. Antonio Zayas, illiterate and with no wealth besides his good name (so he declared), who relied upon his occupation as a viandante to maintain his family, can provide us with an example. Zayas regularly bought goods on credit from merchants of the capital and transported them for sale in Oaxaca. His limited freedom was revealed when he had to return to the same dealer who he complained was selling him goods at inflated prices and forcing him into debt. This supplier even required him to take along one of his own assistants at salary to watch over the supplier's interests. In 1812 these afflictions, coupled with the damage to regional commerce brought about by the Insurrection, forced Zayas into bankruptcy proceedings before the Consulado.[43]

Silvestre Llampallas, another viandante, was born in Barcelona and died in Mexico in 1810 at the age of thirty. He had come to the colony as a youth and spent his short adult life as an itinerant trader under the sponsorship of an uncle, who always served as his bondsman. In 1807 Llampallas entered into a company to manage a general store for its owner; however, this arrangement quickly broke down and he once again assumed his life as a viandante. At the time of his death, his material possessions consisted of 900 pesos in silver, 4 gold watches, clothing, and 21 mules with equipment then under the care of a dependent. His financial picture was more complicated. Two men in Acapulco owed him a total of 5,700 pesos for goods he had sold them on credit; another in Teposcolula owed him 2,100 pesos for the same reason. Llampallas also had loaned 3,000 pesos without interest to one of the subdelegados of the Teposcolula region and another 900 pesos to a cotton grower, who was to repay him in one year with cotton from his harvest at the rate of 8 reales per arroba. However, Llampallas himself had not yet managed to pay off merchants of Mexico City for the goods he had bought from them on credit. He owed one 3,200 pesos and another 4,000 pesos. All in all, Llampalla's assets and debits indicate the scale of operation attainable even by an itinerant with no real property.[44]

Viandantes were useful in economically peripheral areas of the country, and agreements with government officials also facilitated trade in regions generally outside of the mainstream of interprovincial commerce, but for most of their business in provincial centers and along thriving trade routes (places where a high percentage of the population had disposable income), Mexico City wholesalers relied primarily on other methods of distribution: the establishment of companies in their own branch stores and the maintenace of long-term correspondence accounts with provincial storekeepers.

5   Retail Trade in the Capital

Commerce in some aspect or another provided the economic livelihood for a large segment of the population of Mexico City in the late colonial period. There were different tiers of individuals who identified themselves as merchants ("comerciante" or "del comercio"),[1] starting at the top with the wholesale traders, and moving down through the owners of chains of stores, large establishments that emphasized imported merchandise, specialty shops, neighborhood grocery stores, liquor stores, small stands, and finally to those who traveled to homes and factories selling inexpensive goods to the individual. In the 1790 census, 1,502 inhabitants labelled themselves as "comerciantes." The 1816 survey of local stores specified roughly 700 retail establishments within the city proper. As we shall see, a significant number of women were active in retail trade at every level but the highest. And beyond the persons who specified commerce as their occupation were many others gainfully employed in other fields who nevertheless engaged periodically in retail trade or invested directly in local stores and depended upon partners or dependents to run the business. Most of the individuals in this latter category will be discussed in the chapters that treat their primary occupations.

Ownership and Rental of Buildings
Overall, there was a distinct division between ownership of a building containing a store or stores and ownership of the store itself in late colonial Mexico City. Only those wholesalers who

maintained distribution centers in their own homes, plus a few retailers, chose to possess the actual structures. All other local merchants, whatever their status, rented their facilities. Store inventories prepared prior to sale of the business never included the physical plant. Many retailers noted the rent they paid as a business expense in their financial statements. The 1816 survey of commercial establishments in the city makes this pattern abundantly clear; it lists the owner of each building, the proprietor of each business in it, and the rent he paid. (All indications are that renting was also the norm in the Parián and other governmental structures.) Liquidity was a vital economic consideration to these businesspeople; success demanded, among other things, the ability to lay one's hands on capital when needed, whether to diversify into other fields, to enlarge an existing business, or to pay off a threatening creditor and thereby stave off bankruptcy. Only the most successful retailers were able to accumulate the surplus capital required to purchase or construct a house, and of these, not all chose to devote this scarce resource to a domicile which might provide greater comfort and perhaps prestige, but which consumed money without rendering direct profits.

Not all wholesale traders operated out of their residences. Among the many stores in and around the central plaza were some large distributing centers belonging to the merchants who operated out of them. They were easily distinguishable from neighboring retail stores by their size and value. Instead of just one store, the wholealer often had two, three, or even four adjacent, all containing similar merchandise and under the same mangement.[2] Their combined worth regularly exceeded 100,000 pesos and might reach up to 200,000.[3] It was from these outlets that wholesalers supplied both provincial and local merchants, besides themselves retailing the products they imported from abroad. Here cloth, ironware, porcelain, and finery could be found in great variety. Notably absent were domestically manufactured items, perishables, and the petty daily necessities of life. These were available in other types of stores.

The wholesale merchants of the capital did not limit themselves to ownership of large stores. Instead, they often acquired small shops that were, at best, only marginally integrated into the normal wholesale trade of their owners. Thus the head of a major trading house could readily own, besides his international and provincial operations and his warehouse and distributing center in the city, one or more cajones and one or more stores of other types that, though smaller, could still render profits.

Though the records of scores of sales of retail stores of every size and type were examined, in not a single case did a buyer pay cash for his new business. Liquid capital was too scarce and too dear to be available in such a lump sum. Invariably, the purchaser made a down payment, and then he and the seller arranged a schedule of payments, which usually extended over a couple of years, though the installments could stretch up to seven years. Sometimes 5 percent simple annual interest was charged on the outstanding balance and sometimes not.

Store Management

The head of a trading house usually attended to purchasing and to overall supervision of his commercial holdings. To manage his different city retail operations, including his primary distributing center, he most commonly entered into company agreements with each of his store administrators. In 1780 José Gómez Campos, as proprietor of four contiguous stores on the ground floor of the Mexico City cabildo, decided to hand over their management to Pedro Marín. To this end the two contracted an equal partnership for the term of three years.[4] Gómez Campos invested the value of the stores, 150,000 pesos, and Marín put up 25,000 of his own, plus 20,000 that he borrowed. Marín enjoyed total control over the operation of the company and was specifically permitted to sell on credit to whatever extent he thought necessary. He was, as usual, forbidden to have any business dealings independent of the company or to act as bondsman for any person during its term. He could withdraw money from the general fund for his personal maintenance, salaries, store upkeep, and the interest on his 20,000 peso loan.

Gómez Campos chose not to renew this partnership when it expired, but rather formulated a new company arrangement, elevating two of his cajeros to managing partners for the next four years.[5] The four stores were now valued at 180,000 pesos, and only one of the two managers put in any money, a mere 1,195 pesos. As in the earlier contract, they could not pursue any business independent of the company nor act as bondsmen. Perhaps dissatisfied with the performance of his previous partner, Gómez Campos stipulated that he would now have the right to approve all business deals. Nonetheless, he remained content with a half share of the profits; his two partners were to divide the other half equally. Very satisfied with the success of this company, in 1788 the three men renewed their contract with the same terms for an additional two years.[6]

Kinship ties between partners in business were often important in the organization of companies. Yet at times the economic health of a retail company was so solidly based that it could survive the death of one or even both of the original partners. For years Pedro Alonso de Alles, the Marqués de Santa Cruz de Inguanzo, had managed his store in the Parián through a company with a nephew, Simón de Somoano Alonso, who received one third of the profits.[7] When this nephew died in February 1802, Alles turned over the store to Mateo Rubio y Benito, one of its employees, for a salary of 500 pesos for the remainder of that year and a third share of the profits in subsequent years. That same year the marqués himself died, and his successor, Antonio González Alonso, another nephew who had acted as business agent for his uncle, renewed the agreement with Rubio y Benito.

Company contracts in retail stores could become very complicated as different parties became involved at different levels. In 1803 Sebastián de Heras Soto, a knight in the order of Carlos III and that year consul of the Mexico City Consulado, decided to acquire a retail outlet in the Parián and agreed to pay some 93,000 pesos for two adjacent stores, putting 40,000 pesos down and promising to pay the remainder in one year. But at this point Juan Antonio Cobián, another prominent wholesaler, sought to invest in the business, and Heras Soto allowed him to assume overall supervision of its operations. The stores had been managed by two cajeros who wished to remain, and as they impressed Heras Soto with their abilities, he consented to a company contract with Cobián and the two young men. The enterprise was valued at slightly over 103,000 pesos;[8] Heras Soto and Cobián each invested 41,000, one cajero nearly 15,000, and the other over 6,000. These latter two men would jointly manage the stores, but could not go in debt for over 8,000 pesos without permission from the two major investors. Heras Soto, typical of the capitalist who invested in retail companies, removed himself from actual operations and left Cobián to assume overall responsibility for the undertaking. The company employed two other men in the stores, each of whom was entitled to 500 pesos a year plus 4 percent of the profits and the other to 400 pesos a year plus 2 percent. The partners would divide all profits or losses into equal fourths.

From Manager to Proprietor

Cajeros employed by trading houses were in a position to become managing partners of some branch of the enterprise and perhaps even to acquire it for themselves. As we shall see, in allowing commercial employees and partners to purchase all or part of their operations, wholesalers were acting like merchants at every other level of local trade. In 1796 Lorenzo Angulo de Guardamino, a prominent wholesaler, agreed to sell his two adjacent cajones in the Portal de Mercaderes to their two cajeros—who had joined together in a company—for their appraised value of nearly 116,000 pesos payable in installments over the next seven years and with an interest charge of 5 percent annually on the outstanding balance (a sum that would ultimately total nearly 139,000 pesos).[9] The company between the two new owners was for the same seven years, with equal division of profits and losses. As it turned out, they dissolved the company in 1801, selling off one of the stores. One partner exited, receiving 13,000 pesos in profits from the other, who gained sole ownership and a debt of almost 17,000 pesos at interest still owed to Angulo de Guardamino.[10] But this remaining partner was unable to make it on his own. He accumulated more debts over the next decade and by 1814 was in bankruptcy proceedings before the Consulado. This body authorized the sale of the store and its merchandise toward the payment of his creditors, Angulo de Guardamino included.[11]

An alternative to this approach was for the former managing partner to become established in a new business of his own, using as capital profits earned from the company and any further amount his former employer might be willing to loan him.[12] The commercial world of Mexico City burgeoned with individuals who proved their business aptitude by managing stores through company agreements and who hoped that good fortune and the sponsorship of a prominent wholesaler, plus the profits earned in these companies, would enable them to set themselves up independently as major retailers and perhaps someday even to ascend to the status of wholesaler. Some, in fact, did make it all the way up the ladder.

Ignacio García Sáenz prospered in the 1780s as a managing partner of the enormously successful commercial company of José Gómez Campos. By the 1790s, he had attained his independence and borrowed large sums of money from wealthy relatives and businessmen to finance his operations, which included the provisioning of viandantes bound for the mining North and the underwriting of subdelegados in the cochineal-producing districts of Oaxaca. By 1797 he owned both a warehouse and store in the capital and was empowering merchants of the highest rank to care for his affairs while he was absent from the city.[13]

In the late 1780s, José Sánchez de Espinosa, a wholesaler and rural estate owner who had entered the priesthood after the death of his wife, wished to secure skillful management of the cajón which now belonged to his two minor sons. He therefore arranged for them to enter into a company with Pablo Vicente de Sola, who would manage the store for a period of seven and one-half years; Sola was to receive a third of the profits the first four and one-half years and a full half the remaining three.[14] By the mid-1790s, Sola had become the independent owner of a warehouse and store in the central business district and was borrowing 50,000 pesos to expand his commerce. He now organized his own operations into a company and turned over their management to two partners who were to divide half the profits equally between themselves.[15] Just a few years later, one of these two partners attained commercial independence in turn, purchasing a cajón for nearly 68,000 pesos (25,000 in cash with the remainder due in installments).[16]

Ownership of Small Stores by Wholesalers

Never reluctant to broaden their economic interests, Mexico City wholesalers frequently purchased one or more of the different types of smaller neighborhood stores that filled the daily needs of the populace for food, drink, and a variety of household items.[17] Depending on the volume of sales and the spectrum of goods carried, such stores were termed tiendas mestizas, pulperías, and cacahuaterías.

The great merchants usually entered into company agreements to manage these smaller stores. Not uncommonly, they had separate contracts, each with distinct terms, with each of their managers.[18] It does not appear, however, that these managing partners were in line for promotion into the trading house proper. The wholesalers perceived both these stores and their operators as peripheral members of their economic empires. There was a quite well-defined social boundary in the commercial world of the city between, on the one hand, those who worked in the trading houses, their main retail ranches, and other independently owned, large-scale general merchandise stores and, on the other hand, those employed in the lower levels of local commerce, the retail sale of liquors, groceries, basic household items, and domestically produced goods.

The Large Shopkeepers

Despite the strong presence of international traders, the retail sale of imported items in Mexico City was unquestionably dominated by other merchants who owned one or two cajones apiece. The central business district was replete with these stores. In 1816 the Parián alone, with few shops that were not cajones, contained at least 180 such stores owned by over 150 different merchants, few of whom were almaceneros. Each establishment was usually valued at somewhere between 30,000 and 70,000 pesos, though some were worth considerably less, especially those farther away from the central plaza. Their owners, like storekeepers of provincial towns, relied on merchandise supplied them by the wholesale merchants and on the lines of credit which these great traders allowed them to maintain. But unlike their counterparts in the hinterland, Mexico City retailers could purchase from different suppliers. Thus their accounts normally included outstanding debts totalling thousands of pesos owed to local trading houses (5 to 8 in most cases) which were being paid off in installments. Some proprietors had several cajones located in the capital and provincial centers. They and other prosperous cajoneros were candidates to marry into landed families or acquire estates on their own. They might even entertain the possibility of making the most difficult jump in commerce: advancement into the realm of wholesale trade.[19]

Most cajoneros, however, never ascended to such lofty heights in Mexico City society. Prosperous by comparison with other storekeepers of the city, they remained nonetheless subservient to the wholesalers. Though generally able to enjoy a comfortable existence, few could assemble the capital or property necessary to develop a large family fortune. Many, in fact, did not even own their own homes. No evidence was found that these enterprises were passed down from generation to generation; rather, competition at this level of commerce seems to have been particularly fierce, with numerous bankruptcies and sales of stores. Cajones were frequently acquired, often with borrowed money, by their managing partners or by unaffiliated individuals rising from the ranks of commercial employees.

A cajón could represent the entire estate of a family. Antonio Martínez de Soto invested his inheritance and that of his two sisters in one such store.[20] Such a store was equally inviting as an investment to the migrant from the provinces who wished to settle into a comfortable existence while making no claims to elite status. Francisco Ramón Espinosa de los Monteros, a peninsular, first resided in the Real de Rosario in the far northern province of Arizpe, where he married a local woman and worked as a notary in the registry of mines for the royal treasury. However, by his own statement he was enamored of the better social and educational life that Mexico City could offer his two daughters. He therefore sold his position in the government and moved to the capital, where he purchased a cajón and lived a prosperous and respected existence, basking to some extent in the social glow cast by his brother-in-law, a prebend of the metropolitan cathedral.[21]

Most cajones were acquired and run by individuals with much the same career goals as the cajeros of the wholesale merchants, but being economically one step further down the ladder, they sought to gain control over one substantial store rather than a diversified commercial enterprise. Though it was not unknown for an individual to rent a cajón from its owner,[22] it was far more common for several persons to organize themselves into a company. In 1788 Juan Kelly, a native of Cádiz, entered into an equal partnership with José de Villar and José González.[23] Kelly invested 20,000 pesos in merchandise from Spain, Villar put up 18,000 pesos borrowed at interest from a cofradía, and González agreed to manage the store. Kelly had come to New Spain with these goods and had originally sold them on credit to González, then the owner of his own store.[24] However, the latter was unable to make a go of it and soon descended to the level of store manager with no other capital than his personal industry. Kelly removed himself from all store operations, Villar assumed overall responsibility, while González served as manager. The partners could sell on credit up to 30,000 pesos beyond the original investment, but could not act as bondsmen. González was allowed 1,000 pesos yearly from the company's general fund for personal subsistence, and Villar 600.

In 1794 Kelly and González, this time without Villar, formed a new company to operate the same cajón, but the capital invested now totalled nearly 62,000 pesos, composed of 42,000 in profits made by Kelly from the earlier company, nearly 20,000 that he had made after its dissolution, and over 9,000 that González had been able to muster.[25] In this and in any other joint ventures they agreed to divide profits equally. Again, González was to manage the store. He could give credit up to 3,000 pesos, but was expected to favor Kelly in any purchases made. He was entitled to an annual subsistence allowance of 1,500 pesos, but was once again forbidden to act as a bondsman.

Specialty Shops

Specialty shops throve in Mexico City. Their number and variety distinguished the Mexico City market from those of provincial centers. Counting just the retail outlets of wholesale traders and cajones, the city contained easily 200 distributors of imported goods (most of them, it is good to remember, of substantial size). Nonetheless, shops that carried just one type of merchandise—such as glass, ceramics, silk, or tapestries—also prospered. The larger nonspecialty stores also sold these wares, which can be found in surviving inventory lists. But demand for certain luxury or especially well-crafted items was so large that these other ventures, themselves usually valued in the thousands or even the tens of thousands of pesos, found their niche.

Such stores were typically owned and operated by the same sort of people who owned and operated cajones. Proprietors tended to be fairly well off and willing to increase their investments or expand their businesses into nearby provincial centers.[26] Some used their profits to acquire rural estates. Whenever possible, they utilized the company form of business organization. Once again, there was a distinct bifurcation between ownership and management.[27] Proprietors frequently looked to family members—brothers and sons—to manage these stores on salary or for a share of the profits, thereby receiving training for eventual takeover of the business.[28]

Neighborhood Grocery Stores

So far in this section we have discussed only that part of retail trade which emphasized imported merchandise. As we have seen, this branch was both large and complex, but another aspect of local commerce was even more so: the supply of food, drink, and basic necessities to the greater urban population. The general stores of the capital fall into two categories, tiendas mestizas and pulperías. (There seems to be no substantial difference between a pulpería and a cacahuatería; they were apparently synonymous.) Both regularly carried some small amounts of imported goods, especially cloth and ironware, besides an incredible variety of hardware, locally produced cloths, mats, food staples, and beverages.

The factors separating tiendas mestizas from pulperías were matters more of scale and emphasis than of character. As defined by the regulations for the direction of such establishments, a pulpería was a store inside a building (to differentiate it from the open-air stands and tents which sold comestibles and inexpensive items throughout the city), containing a counter and facing onto the street, which sold petty lots of comestibles and diverse products—including candles, charcoal, lard, chile, and beans—to its customers. It made change and accepted payment both in tokens that it devised and registered and in items pawned by its clientele.

It was distinguished from a tienda mestiza, which sold the same merchandise in larger amounts (pounds rather than ounces). When a tienda mestiza accepted payment in tokens or in pawned items, it had to register itself with the Cuerpo de Comerciantes Pulperos.[29] For all intents and purposes, tiendas mestizas were simply larger pulperías (though some of the former could be quite small and some of the latter could attain considerable size). Table 20 lists the values of some different types of stores as stated in annual inventories or at the time of their sale.

Tiendas mestizas often resembled cajones and specialty shops in many of their basic characteristics. Their owners were frequently people from the same social and economic levels who later chose to expand their operations or to diversify into other fields of the economy. Able to acquire small landed estates, they might marry into solid, respectable creole families.[30] They sought to manage their stores through companies, and those with chains of several stores would customarily maintain a separate company with each of their managers. The managing partner was in good position to purchase the store if the proprietor decided to sell.[31]

Pulperías were far more numerous. A 1795 survey taken to determine which stores should sell bread from which bakeries identified 154 separate establishments owned by a total of 131 individuals. Unlike the case of larger retail businesses, few proprietors of pulperías owned more than one outlet, and no case was encountered where a pulpero owned a store outside of the city. Of the 131 owners, 2 had three stores, 17 had two, and the remaining 114 just a single store each.[32] Also, while only a few women were scattered among the proprietors of larger retail stores, they became somewhat more common at this level of local commerce.[33] The 1795 report included nine women owners of pulperías.

The division between ownership and management was as characteristic of pulperías as of larger commercial establishments; the vast majority of these stores were operated by cajeros or administrators. Male relatives of retail proprietors often served these functions, and it was not unknown for pulperías to be managed by wives of proprietors, and in the cases of female ownership, by daughters.[34] The upward mobility of these retailers was sharply limited. None advanced to the higher levels of mercantile enter-

Table 20. Listed Total Values of Different Categories of Stores at the Time of Their Sale or Inventory

Type of Store	Value	Year	Sale or Inventory
Cajón	67,975 (pesos)	1798	Sale
Cajón	10,413	1799	Sale
Cajón	5,900	1812	Sale
Mercería	11,690	1797	Sale
Semillería	2,526	1809	Sale
Botica	4,847	1797	Sale
Tienda Mestiza	7,823	1785	Sale
Tienda Mestiza	884	1787	Sale
Tienda Mestiza	10,000	1800	Inv.
Tienda Mestiza	28,000	1800	Sale
Pulpería	4,623	1786	Sale
Pulpería	1,894	1787	Sale
Pulpería	1,286	1789	Inv.
Pulpería	929	1789	Inv.
Pulpería	235	1790	Sale
Pulpería	4,258	1791	Sale
Pulpería	2,376	1795	Sale
Pulpería	1,360	1795	Sale
Pulpería	8,500	1802	Sale
Pulpería	1,657	1804	Sale
Pulpería	1,015	1808	Sale
Pulpería	3,900	1813	Inv.
Pulpería	1,265	1817	Inv.
Pulpería	594	1825	Inv.
Vinatería	1,895	1787	Sale
Vinatería	10,653	1794	Inv.
Vinatería	850	1804	Sale
Vinatería	603	1804	Inv.
Vinatería	1,239	1813	Inv.

Source: GM, Nov. 12, 1795; AGN, Consulado, leg. 127, exp. 1, Sept. 12, 1786, leg. 48, exp. 6, f. 1, Sept. 25, 1788, leg. 221, exp. 5, f. 1, Feb. 3, 1789, leg. 127, exp. 16, f. 1, March 15, 1790, leg. 160, exp. 11, f. 5, Nov. 26, 1802, leg. 25, exp. 12, f. 1, Oct. 26, 1804, leg. 14, exp. 2, f. 1, Sept. 19, 1804, leg. 75, exp. 23, f. 1, Dec. 14, 1808, leg. 130, exp. 1, f. 1, Dec. 30, 1809, leg. 67, exp. 13, f. 2, Dec. 28, 1810, leg. 88, exp. 9, f. 1, Jan. 26, 1813, leg. 94, exp. 15, f. 3, Dec. 13, 1813, leg. 47, exp. 5, f. 1, Dec. 22, 1817, leg. 11, exp. 36, f. 1, Oct. 26, 1825; AN, Pozo, Oct. 14, 1785, March 6, 1787, July 17, 1787, March 21, 1797, May 2, 1798, June 6, 1800, and Nov. 9, 1812; Burillo, Feb. 7, 1794, June 26, 1797, Dec. 9, 1799, July 24, 1800 and Aug. 25, 1804; Torija, Sept. 1, 1787 and Oct. 10, 1789; Ignacio de San Martín, March 21, 1791.

prise; marriage into well-off families was not a possibility; sons were not likely to receive advanced education or to enter the professions or the bureaucracies. The ownership of rural estates, investment in mining, and movement into manufacturing or processing were very rare. One pulpero did have two plants which manufactured noodles, and another sold his store to acquire a mill.[35] Save for these minor exceptions, those pulperos who were able to accumulate the necessary funds preferred to purchase a house for use as a personal residence or to rent out as a rooming-house.[36]

Pulpería ownership was a goal of those who occupied the lower levels of commerce: viandantes and owners of small stands.[37] To make the jump to actual possession of a store, no matter how small its operations, demanded a concerted effort and considerable risk-taking by these people. Sometimes a purchase claimed the savings of an entire family.

While a few pulperos prospered, led comfortable lives, and left a significant inheritance to their children, far more commonly the fortune of an owner comprised only a few thousand pesos, much of it composed of debts that might never be collected. These persons rarely enjoyed any economic breathing space and were fully aware that their financial collapse could be brought about by factors not under their control. Even some of the more established members of their trade sank into bankruptcy.

Pulperos were organized into a guild-like body governed by a detailed list of regulations. One of these required that they select one of their most respected members to serve as their legal representative (apoderado). Early in the nineteenth century, two of these representatives were forced into bankruptcy proceedings before the Consulado in order to request esperas.[38] A wife of one of the men demanded to be listed among her husband's creditors for the value of her dowry; the other man instructed the executors of his will to sell off all of his possessions to pay his debts and give anything that remained to his widow and children.

Pulperías were customarily run by administrators, who might be either salaried employees or partners with the proprietor. Like their counterparts in other forms of retail trade, these individuals were closely affiliated with their stores and could well remain with the business even when it was sold. A transfer of ownership could even bring about a promotion.[39] Tomás Castro managed the pulpería of Vincente Bustillo at salary, but when Bustillo sold the store to Joaquín Palacios, the latter retained Castro as administrator and advanced him to full partnership.[40] Three years later, their company a success, they renewed it under new terms. Palacios now invested 4,800 pesos (an amount greater than his original purchase price), and Castro put in 1,289 pesos of his own money.[41]

We have already seen how a store manager could advance from salaried work to full partnership and then to actual ownership; the process could also work in reverse. In 1802 Matías de Alcedo bought a pulpería for 8,500 pesos, but was unable to make a go of it. Three years later he sold the store for slightly less than 6,500 pesos, but in the sale agreement consented to stay on as managing partner for half of the profits.[42]

Grocery Store Regulations

Table 21 summarizes the variety of goods found in the 1786 inventory of a pulpería. The predominant quantity of food items and condiments was supplemented by kitchenware, clothing and sewing items, some furniture, and even riding equipment, plus a few items which defy easy categorization. These neighborhood groceries provided the populace, especially the lower sectors, with many of their basics, and the municipal government regulated the terms of trade, even setting the prices every four months.[43]

At some earlier time pulperías had only been allowed on street corners, but by the late colonial period they were permitted anywhere along a street. Nonetheless, previous practice and the better location dictated that nearly half of these stores were still located on corners in 1796.[44] Women and the poor could sell from accesorías, small niches on the sides of buildings, but they could not deal in goods normally carried by pulperías. Regulations decreed that every new pulpero initially had to invest at least 1,000 pesos in his business and post a bond of 1,500 pesos with the government to guarantee tokens issued and goods received in pawn. No pulpero was to interfere with the persons bringing in goods from the countryside for sale in the plazas or, through membership in a militia unit or as a familiar in the Inquisition, claim a separate juris-

Table 21.   A Summary of the Variety of Merchandise on Sale in a
Mexico City Pulpería as Extracted from an Inventory of
1786[a]

Lard	Saffron Oil	Wine Sacks
Rice	Chocolate	Chairs
Chile	Cinnamon	Tables
Peppers	Wine	Bedframes
Starch	Aguardiente	Skins
Cooking Oil	Thread	Wax
Cacao	Buttons	Iron
Lentils	Silks	Wooden Shovels
Honey	Ribbons	Lanterns
Olives	Cloths	Paper
Beans	Chinese Vermillion	Crystal
Cheese	Kitchen Containers	Ink
Shellfish	Pitchers	Quills
Eggs	Bottles	Machetes
Almonds	Cascara	Copper
Bread	Candy	Rosaries
Sesame	Copal	Vinegar
Salt	Incense	Halters
Anise	Cord and Rope	Petates
Sugar	Cinches	

[a] In the original inventory many of these items are subdivided into a variety of types.
Source: AGN, Consulado, leg. 127, exp. 1, Sept. 12 and 13, 1786.

diction in any litigation bearing on his business. The stores could
be open from 5:30 in the morning until 10:00 at night.

Retail Credit Sales

Of all retail establishments, pulperías catered most directly to the
needs of the masses of the city. As most people were poor and
often without access to coin and as many of the items they purchased were valued at less than a real, the smallest coin of the
realm, these outlets were authorized to issue tokens and to accept
goods in pawn, but only under rather detailed regulations from the
municipal government. All pulperías were required to accept
pawned items as payment for goods purchased; as noted by the
government, the poor had no other means of acquiring the neces-

sities of life. Clothes, both new and used, and inexpensive jewelry were to be accepted, but no one was to accept valuable jewelry, any religious icons or utensils, dishes, books, keys, saddles, harness, instruments, or artisan equipment; in short, nothing which might be stolen or which might be necessary to the labor of an artisan. The storekeeper could advance up to two-thirds of the value of the pawned items (a list of which was to be posted at the front entrance to every store), and after six months, if the person did not redeem the pawned item, the tradesman could sell it with the permission of local officials. (Judging from some oblique references, special auction houses existed that concentrated on the sale of pawned merchandise.) When a pulpería was sold, the new owner was required to honor all pawned transactions made by his predecessor. He likewise had to honor all tokens previously issued. Each storekeeper was permitted to use registered tokens that were distinctive to his store. Of course, he had to accept them in all future payments; it is unclear if other merchants also accepted them.

Though only pulperías were required by law to accept pawned items in payment, in actuality, every retail outlet at whatever level did so. Whenever a store was inventoried, whether for an annual inspection or in preparation for its sale, a significant portion of its value always consisted of prendas (pawned items) and dependencias activas (debts owed the store). As related earlier, retail shops bought their merchandise on credit from wholesalers. Typically then, at any given moment, these businesses owed great amounts of money, were in turn owed other amounts (often a considerable share of the total value of the store), and held in pawn a certain amount of goods belonging to their clientele.

Table 22 summarizes five pulpería inventories from the late colonial period. In the first, about 42 percent of the total worth of the store consists of pawned items and of debts owed by the clientele. Twenty-three individuals owed nearly 1,520 pesos; the largest single debt was for 200 pesos, the smallest for only 3 reales. Nineteen of the 23 debtors owed at least 25 pesos, roughly a month's salary of a commercial employee. The second pulpería was clearly bordering on collapse, being owed four times as much as the value of the stock on hand. Most often, bankruptcy threatened these stores

Table 22.   Financial Summaries of Five General Stores in Mexico City

A Breakdown of the Inventory of the Pulpería Sold by Vicente
Bustillo to Joaquín Palacios in 1786

Géneros (Sale Goods)	1,890 (pesos)
Aperos (Store Equipment)	500
Prendas (Pawned Items)	431
Dependencias Activas (Money owed the Store)	1,520
Uniforme (Uniform)	19
Reales (Cash on Hand)	1,081
Dependencias Pasivas (Debts owed by Store)	818
Líquido (Total Value of Store)	4,623

Source: AGN, Consulado, leg. 127, exp. 1, Sept. 12, 1786.

A Breakdown of the Inventory of the Pulpería Sold by Antonio
José Esquivel y Vargas to Francisco García in 1790

Géneros	118 (pesos)
Aperos	400
Prendas	180
Dependencias Pasivas	468
Líquido	235

Source: AGN, Consulado, leg. 127, exp. 16, March 15, 1790.

A Breakdown of the Inventory of the Pulpería Sold by José Pérez
Chacón to José Rafael Márquez in 1817

Géneros	460 (pesos)
Aperos	700
Prendas	128
General	1,288
Líquido	1,265

Source: AGN, Consulado, leg. 45, exp. 5, f. 1, Dec. 22, 1817.

Table 22.   (continued)

A Breakdown of the Inventory of the Pulpería Sold by José Vicente
Berruecos to José Antonio Beristáin in 1808

Génros	448 (pesos)
Aperos	400
Prendas	190
Líquido	1,015

Source: AGN, Consulado, leg. 75, exp. 23, ff. 1–6, Dec. 14, 1808.

A Breakdown of the Inventory of the Pulpería Sold by Ramón
Rosales to Francisco López de León in 1788

Géneros	281 (pesos)
Aperos	290
Prendas	166
Líquido	462

Source: AGN, Consulado, leg. 48, exp. 6, ff. 1–7, Sept. 25, 1788.

after they overextended credit to their customers and were then
unable to pay off their suppliers when bills came due. The third
and fourth listed stores enjoyed sound financial health. In both
cases prendas made up less than 20 percent of the net value, and
debts were small. The fifth, though, carried a considerable outstanding debt of its own, while prendas composed over a third of
its worth.

Liquor Stores

It is more difficult to generalize about vinaterías, the retail outlets
for European and domestic wines and liquors. They served both
men and women; the customers could drink on the premises (the
shops were popular gathering spots in the evenings) or take their
purchases with them. Overall, despite great variation, vinaterías
were valued on a par with tiendas mestizas, worth less than cajones and more than pulperías. More so than owners of pulperías,
vinatería proprietors might own several stores in the city plus

Table 23.   Financial Summaries of Four Vinaterías in Mexico City

A Breakdown of the Inventory of the Vinatería Sold by José
Hernández to Rafael Pineda in 1804

Géneros	292 (pesos)
Aperos	200
Prendas	111
Líquido	603

Source: AGN, Consulado, leg. 25, exp. 12, Oct. 26, 1804.

A Breakdown of the Inventory of the Vinatería Sold by María
Manuela Segura to Pedro Troytinas in 1799

Géneros	3,339 (pesos)
Aperos	400
Prendas	74
Dependencias Activas	1,751
Gastos (Reimbursement to the Owner)	263
Entregado (A Sum Repaid to the Owner)	27
Reales	53
Dependencias Pasivas	3,446
Líquido	2,440

Source: AGN, Consulado, leg. 36, exp. 11, Oct. 29, 1799.

A Breakdown of the Inventory of the Vinatería Owned by José
Pérez de Tagle in 1808

Géneros	1,352 (pesos)
Aperos	2,500
Dependencias Activas	6,998
Dependencias Pasivas	10,866
Líquido (In Debt)	16

Source: AGN, Consulado, leg. 68, exp. 4, June 25, 1808.

Table 23.   (continued)

A Breakdown of the Inventory of the Vinatería Sold by Juan
Danz y Freire to Justo Gutiérrez de la Iguera in 1805

Géneros	2,683 (pesos)
Aperos	2,000
Prendas	101
Uniforme	25
Reales	16
Dependencias Pasivas	5,044
Líquido (In Debt)	220

Source: AGN, Consulado, leg. 38, exp. 3, Oct. 8, 1805.

other forms of enterprise as well. Often, they operated their own aguardiente distilleries and purchased rural estates or stores of other types.[45] On the other hand, a considerable number of these enterprises ran into financial difficulties and ended up in bankruptcy proceedings before the Consulado court.[46]

Table 23 offers summaries of four vinatería inventories. Here again, as with cajones and pulperías, a significant part of a store's worth could consist of pawned items and debts owed. The merchandise itself typically included a great variety of European wines and liquors and several types of domestic aguardiente. Pulque was never sold in these stores, but rather in special outlets, pulquerías, which we will discuss below. Nonalcoholic goods such as glassware, containers, and such food items as sugar and dried fish were also generally available.

Most vinatería owners chose to operate their stores through companies with their managers.[47] Pedro de Caso, perhaps the most successful vinatería owner of the capital in the late colonial period, had companies with the managers of each of his three stores. In one case the manager was entitled to one half of the profits, in another case only one third, and in the third only one fourth. Caso himself prospered to the extent that when he drew up his will in 1810, he had expanded his property to include an aguardiente distillery outside the city, a tienda mestiza, two houses in the city (including that in which his family resided), and two haciendas in the Valley of Mexico.[48]

Again, as with pulperías, women were well represented among the owners; like their male counterparts, they too made heavy use of companies to run their businesses, but some also used marriage as a device to secure managers—not always with the happiest of outcomes.[49]

As was so commonly the case, managing partners were in a good position to acquire a business if the owners chose to sell.[50] Or if the enterprise was transferred to a new proprietor, the administrator could well remain in the same post.[51]

The Pulque Trade

The organization of the pulque trade in Mexico City was unlike that of any of the other fields of retail commerce. One reason for this difference was the structure of pulque production. Some of the wealthiest families of the colony were predominant producers, and not satisfied just to cultivate the maguey cactus and distill the sap into the valued intoxicant, they generally sought to control the distributing outlets in the city, the pulquerías.

In 1784 the Audiencia legally sanctioned forty-five pulquerías in greater Mexico City. Of these, eighteen were in the city proper, defined by the Audiencia as the territory inside the bridges spanning the canals around the city center, and twenty-seven were outside the city, that is, beyond the canals but in close proximity and under the city's jurisdiction. Table 24 provides a list of these pulquerías according to their location and also the names of their owners when known. I have found the proprietors of thirty (67 percent) of these establishments at some point during the time span 1783–1807. Of the thirty whose owners are known, twenty-four belonged to the proprietors of pulque ranchos or their direct descendents. It does not seem that pulquerías were often sold. Those transfers that appear in the documentation examined are clear cases of inheritance.

Eleven pulquerías belonged to the descendants or business associates of the original Conde de Jala. Six were owned by the two daughters of the original Conde de Regla, and two by the Marqués de Vivanco. These distinguished personages and their relatives

Table 24.   Pulquerías of Mexico City in 1784[a]

Within the City Proper:

Name	Owner (Year of Ownership)
Pelos	Ignacio Adalid (1805)
Calderas	Conde de Tepa (1800)
Puesto Nuevo	Conde de Tepa (1800)
Arbolillo	María Ignacia Romero de Terreros (1787)
Risco Nuevo	María Ignacia Romero de Terreros (1787)
Retama	Antonia Gómez Rodríguez de Pedroso, Marquesa Viuda de Selvanevada (1794)
Puente Quebrada	Juan del Valle (1796)
Tumbaburros	Parcialidad de San Juan Tenochtitlán (1794)
Celaya	Bachiller José Sánchez de Espinosa (1787)
Mixcalco	Doctor José Ignacio García Jove (1796)
Maravilla	Marqués de Vivanco (1796)
Romero	María Dolores Romero de Terreros (1802)
Florida	María Dolores Romero de Terreros (1802)
Recogidas	No Owner Listed for This and Those Below
San Felipe	
Rodríguez	
Solano	
Buenavista	

Outside the City

Orilla	María Isabel López de Ortuño (1807)
Madrid	María Isabel López de Ortuño (1807)
Papas	María Isabel López de Ortuño (1807)
Montiel	José Adalid (1799)
Lagunilla	José Adalid (1799)
Cuajomulco	Ignacio Adalid (1805)
Nana	María Josefa Rodríguez Pinellos y Gomez (1797)
Granadas	María Josefa Rodríguez Pinellos y Gomez (1797)
Soledad	Ana María Rodríguez (1783)
San Martín	José Montero (1785)
Cantaros	Antonio Gómez Rodríguez de Pedroso, Marquesa Viuda de Selvanevada (1794)
Navarra	Conde de Tepa (1800)
Tepozán	María Ignacia Romero de Terreros (1787)
Biznaga	María Ignacia Romero de Terreros (1787)
Jardín	Francisco Antonio Villaverde (1794)
Alamedita	Lugarda Maria Ana Fragoso (1786)

Table 24.   (continued)

Outside the City

Jolapa	José de la Torre Calderon (1785)
Bello	No Owner for This and Those Below
Hornillo	
Candelaria	
Camarones	
Carbonero	
Altima	
Organo	
Tenexpa	
Jamaica	

ᵃ Several other names of pulquerías in Mexico City were encountered in the documenta-tion and appear to have been nicknames for some of the same ones listed. As there was no way to determine which nickname corresponded to which establishment, they were ignored.
Sources: AGN, Padrones, 79 and 80, 1796, Civil, leg. 966, exp. 7, ff. 1–20, March 9, 1785; AN, Burillo, Dec. 4, 1783, Aug. 27, 1784, Feb. 1, 1786, Jan. 24, 1794, May 9, 1796, Dec. 29, 1797, Sept. 3, 1799, May 23, 1800, Dec. 30, 1802, Jan. 2, 1805, and Sept. 17, 1807; Torija, Nov. 8, 1783 and July 28, 1787; Pozo, Dec. 20, 1785 and June 4, 1787; "Informe sobre pulquerías y tabernas el año de 1784," *Boletín del Archivo General de la Nación*, primera serie, 18:2 (1947), p. 205.

were joined in pulquería proprietorship by members of less prom-inent but still respected Mexico City families whose wealth did not approximate that of the highest elite. Such families commonly participated in hacienda ownership, were active in commerce (oc-casionally overseas, though on a small scale), enjoyed academic ti-tles, occupied professional positions, and pursued and sometimes received formal recognition of their achievements or the quality of their bloodlines. One pulquería was owned by Doctor y Maestro José Ignacio García Jove, a native of San Luis Potosí, who was a catedrático of surgery and anatomy at the university and pro-tomédico for the entire colony.[52] His three sons all received ad-vanced degrees and enjoyed prominence as lawyers and clerics.[53]

Few owners of pulquerías chose to operate their businesses di-rectly. Those who did belonged to the group that had only a single outlet and no pulque ranchos. More commonly, owners rented out their enterprises to other individuals under long-term lease agreements. When the pulquería owner also had pulque ranchos, the rental agreement would commit the renter to the purchase of all or a fixed quantity of the pulque produced on these ranchos at a predetermined price. At times, a family rented out all of its pulquerías and all the pulque from its ranchos to a single contractor. It was not unusual for the owner of a pulquería to rent another outlet from someone else and then to rent out both to yet another party. On the other side of the coin, the renter might be content with the rental of one or more pulquerías from a single individual or family, or he might seek to rent simultaneously the businesses of two or more owners. Likewise, he might then decide to subrent any or all of them to a third party, unless this act was expressly forbidden in the contract.

Not surprisingly, certain pulquerías were worth considerably more than others, but all seemed to render a good income, and there is no evidence in the records examined that activity in the pulque trade ever proved unprofitable or ruinous. In 1783 José Adalid let out his three pulquerías for a total annual rent of 3,468 pesos; in 1796 he rented out two for an annual income of 2,509 pesos.[54] Also in 1796, Doctor José Ignacio García Jove gained 726 pesos for the rental of his single establishment.[55] Again that same year the Marqués de Vivanco, the owner of two outlets, derived an income of 1,095 pesos from one, but only 568 pesos from the other.[56] The highest annual income gained from the operation or rental of a single pulquería was 1,700 pesos by the parcialidad (Indian district) of San Juan Tenochtitlán from its sole establishment in 1784.[57] The lowest income was the slightly more than 205 pesos received by José Montero in 1785.[58] Virtually all rentals expressed the rate on a daily basis with actual payment made monthly. Most contracts specifically stipulated that the agreement was abrogated if the renter fell three months behind in his payments.

While the contracts for the mere rental of one or several were quite simple, those that combined rental with guaranteed purchase of pulque from certain ranchos could become very complex. In 1800 the Conde de Tepa, then in Spain serving on the Council of the Indies, owned (as widower of the Marquesa de Prado Alegre, a granddaughter of the original Conde de Tepa) five pulquerías and three pulque ranchos in Mexico. His nephew, Guillermo de Aguirre y Viana, was currently an oidor in Mexico and, therefore, in a good position to protect his uncle's interests. But for business matters the Conde relied on his apoderado, Rodrigo Sánchez, a fellow peninsular and a member of the Consulado of Mexico City. That year Sánchez, on behalf of the Conde, rented out all five outlets for a period of seven years to Raymundo Oqueli (O'Kelly) for a total of 10 pesos a day, with the stipulation that Oqueli had to accept all the pulque produced on the Conde's ranchos.[59] Oqueli was not inexperienced in such matters; he had regularly rented pulquerías and the product of pulque ranchos for at least several years from different owners, including the Conde de Tepa. Sometimes he operated the facilities directly and other times he chose to subrent them to other individuals.[60]

Doctor Luis Gonzaga González Maldonado, a lawyer, regidor of Mexico City, and owner of a pulque rancho, apparently used his official position as legal representative of the parcialidad of San Juan Tenochtitlán to secure rental of its pulquería for a five-year period through 1785 at the annual rate of 1,700 pesos. But he was seemingly not concerned with making a profit from the rental of the outlet, for when he proceeded to subrent it to different individuals for shorter periods of time, he charged them only the same rate that he himself was charged. In 1782 he sublet the pulquería to Juan Julio Cortés for 1,700 pesos annually, with the stipulation that the latter buy 45 cargas of pulque each week at the rate of 2 pesos per carga from the rancho owned by González Maldonado.[61] In 1784 González Maldonado sublet the establishment once again for the annual rental of 1,700 pesos, but this time to Juan Bolío, who agreed to purchase 25-30 cargas of pulque weekly from his ranchos at an unstipulated price.[62] González Maldonado was most desirous of renting a pulquería, even if he promptly sublet the business to another person, because only such a rental ensured him a market for the product of his own ranchos.

Pulque was not wholesaled on a free-market basis; even owners of a single pulquería who had no ranchos entered into exclusive contracts with producers. A pulque producer who did not assure himself an outlet could anticipate being squeezed out of the market. An examination of a number of these contracts leads to the conclusion that while pulquería ownership or rental would proba-bly prove profitable, the greatest profit accrued from the whole-saling of pulque to retailers. Therefore a person owning both pul-querías and ranchos always stipulated that the renter would buy a fixed quantity or the entire amount of pulque that he produced. Similarly, it was quite beneficial to the owner of a rancho to pos-sess at least one outlet in order to guarantee himself a market. The rental of one or more pulquerías to another party afforded the owner a secure and steady income, while the stipulation in the con-tract to buy a set amount or all the pulque produced on the owners' ranchos provided him an even greater secured income and elimi-nated his fear of losing his share of the market.

These rental agreements reveal the existence of individuals in late colonial Mexico City who systematically rented and operated such enterprises for prolonged periods as the mainstay of their livelihoods. Some of these people, Martín de Barandiarán for ex-ample, seem to have concentrated on renting these businesses from their elite proprietors without ever successfully branching out into any other form of enterprise.[63] Others, such as José Ber-nabé de Isita, did manage to diversity and even to become owners of local stores or processing plants. In 1801, Isita, though still rent-ing pulquerías from their owners, purchased a wheat hacienda for 35,000 pesos and a panadería in the capital for 22,000 pesos.[64] Isita is also typical in that he did not attempt to challenge the elite's domination of the large-scale production of raw materials and comestibles. The small-scale renters and owners of pulque enter-prises expanded horizontally into other forms of commerce and product-processing and did not seek to ascend to the heady level of production, where only those with the resources of the elite families could prosper or even survive. Of course, not everyone viewed pulquería rental as the first step toward independent own-ership. The trade was sufficiently lucrative to attract individuals looking for a profitable activity secondary to their careers. Juan Navarro, a peninsular, was the director general of internal customs collection on alcoholic beverages, including pulque, but he also, in contracts in 1783 and 1785, rented individual outlets from different owners.[65] He made public contracts for both activities and seemed not to fear, nor in fact to receive, any reprimand or punishment for dealing in the very commodity he was encharged to oversee.

As most Indians and many members of the various castes lived on the outskirts of the city, it is not surprising that the majority of pulquerías, 27, were found there. Ordinances, repeated and revised over many years, clearly stated how a pulquería was to be constructed. The jacal,[66] as the public area was termed, was not to exceed a space of 20 by 16 varas, and the bodega, the storage area, was to be 22 by 9 varas in size. As the authorities desired the customers to consume their pulque and move on quickly, seating facilities for the public were not allowed. The only article of furniture permitted was the bar itself, ideally placed before the storeroom to block entrance to the public. The public areas were to be open on all three sides not fronting the bodega in order to permit authorities to observe behavior inside the facility without actually entering.

Drawings of five pulquerías of Mexico City in the late colonial period are preserved in the ramo of the AGN entitled Policía.[67] The five—Celaya, Papitas, Teposán, Tenespa, and Granaditas by name—were located along alleyways and dead-end streets or tucked into corners. In all cases the roof over the public areas was nothing more than a peaked covering, apparently of canvas, held up by poles and ropes. There was no wall of any sort, though one side was blocked by the front of the bodega. The bodegas were all solidly built structures, larger and higher than the public areas. Two pulquerías had adjacent indoor latrines, while two others had corrals that served the same function.

But the reality of pulquería construction differed greatly from what was prescribed. Of the forty-five pulquerías, no more than seven were open on the required three sides, while eleven were open on only one side, and eighteen were totally enclosed. Some, especially the newer ones, were larger than the regulations permitted, and, in addition, permitted the public into the storage areas.[68] These drinking establishments had become incredibly large operations; it was calculated that most could hold 500 to 600 persons. These burgeoning businesses were hard pressed to serve their clientele adequately. To better accommodate the people, many facilities had added extensive seating areas, both along the walls and at large tables on the floor.

The seating arrangements were certainly a convenience for the large number of individuals who passed much of their day inside. Despite the hope of the authorities that people would buy and quickly consume their beverage, in actuality, many customers lingered for prolonged periods. While the exact daily schedules of these businesses remain hidden, pulquerías opened at a very early hour, for they were able to serve the Indians going to work on the 6 a.m. shift of the cigarette factory of the royal tobacco monopoly. Not surprisingly, some of the workers never made it to their place of employment. It was recommended at one point that pulquerías be open only from 8:00 in the morning to 5:00 in the afternoon on work days and stay closed until 1:00 in the afternoon on Sundays and holy days.

Because pulquerías attracted a steady clientele willing to pass time in the establishments, a variety of ancillary services and entertainments existed on the premises. Sellers of lunches and other comestibles frequented these spots to find ready customers. Musicians came to play before the preassembled (and hopefully paying) audience. Dancing was common, but it was the card playing and other forms of gambling which most disturbed the authorities.

By law all pulquería employees were supposed to be women; in fact, however, because of the type of labor required and the general environment in these establishments, few women worked in them. A pulquería typically employed about ten men and a boy: an administrador to manage the business, a probador to test the liquid, a tinero to serve the product, a sobreasaliente to break up quarrels in the establishment, six cajeteros to solicit customers in streets near the facility, and the boy to gather up any unbroken clay cajetes, the shallow bowls in which the pulque was served. The customers normally hurled the emptied bowls to the floor, and the jagged shards could be used as weapons in the quarrels so common in these places.

Pulque itself was classified into three descending grades: fino, ordinario, and otomite, the last being a form of the Nahuatl word

"Otomí," then and now meaning anything bad, small, or inferior.[69] Neither the procedure for determining the quality of the liquid nor the retail prices of the different grades could be determined from the materials studied. The pulque fermented in leather hides used to transport it from the countryside to the city. The fermentation process took from two to four days and was begun by any one of a variety of catalysts which each producer used and tried to keep secret from his competitors. Before the newly-tapped pulque reached the consumer, it was commonly treated with any of several contaminants designed to preserve or dilute it. To keep the pulque fresh for longer periods, the producers added active lime or chinchona, the by-products of which could do damage to the consumer. Arrieros who transported the pulque to the city on muleback, two cargas per mule, often took some for their own profit, replacing it with water. In the pulquería the intoxicant was adulterated once again by the operator and was then served in either of two types of containers. One, the cajete mentioned above, held three cuartillos (pints) and sold for half a real; the other, the cubero, was larger, held twelve cuartillos, cost two reales, and was purchased by groups drinking together. Although pulquerías were forbidden to sell their product on other than a retail basis, they also wholesaled it to nearby luncheon stands which sold the beverage along with the food.

There was one other grade of pulque, not sold in pulquerías. Tlachique[70] was pulque of distinctly inferior quality produced by individual Indians from wild, uncultivated maguey cacti. It was brought into the city and sold out of large pots by Indian women gathered around the fountain of the central plaza. Because of the poor quality of the product, these women sold three containers for half a real, a larger portion than what the same price could purchase in pulquerías.

Tobacco Stands

Far lower on the scale than any of the retail establishments already discussed were the exclusive outlets for tobacco in the city (estanquillos or cigarrerías). As a general rule, the more modest the store, the more common the presence of women as owners and operators. This was the case with pulperías and proves to have been even more so with estanquillos. In 1753, before the formation of the tobacco monopoly had turned these outlets into its adjuncts, 49 of 149 recorded owners of cigarrerías were women. Of these, 26 were widows, while 6 were married. Even at this low level of retail trade the overwhelming majority of women were Spanish, but other ethnicities were beginning to appear. Four mestizas and two mulatas were also proprietors.

The female presence in this line of commerce seems not to have diminished after formation of the royal tobacco monopoly. In 1793 María Josefa Betancurt recorded her ownership of an estanquillo de puros y cigarros, and typical of retail store owners, she turned over its management to another person. She had posted a 400-peso bond with the monopoly, the value of her monthly allotment of tobacco.[71] Even more striking is the success and entrepreneurial spirit displayed by Josefa Delgado y Sotomayor. In 1821 she stated that she was a spinster of over forty years of age, had always owned an estanquillo in the city, and had never been late in her payments to the monopoly. She enjoyed such success that she had also acquired a pulpería, administered by a man for a half of the profits. She likewise owned two houses which she had bought, reconstructed, and now rented out.[72]

In some cases, retailers in other lines diversified into ownership of tobacco stands. The evidence indicates, however, that only proprietors of small retail operations did so. José de Rojas, for instance, in 1796 owned a fonda worth a total of 1,200 pesos, six puestos de ropa y fierro (a stand selling clothes and metalware) in the Baratillo (a block in the city set aside for second-hand shops), and an estanquillo which he had financed with his own funds and 300 pesos which he had borrowed.[73]

A man such as Rojas, with a variety of shops besides his tobacco stand, would characteristically look to other persons to manage his businesses. Employment of professional administrators was standard behavior for retailers at every level; of course, these administrators occupied very different social positions and entertained widely divergent aspirations, and it should not be assumed that managers of grocery stores and tobacco stands could ever anticipate being employed in similar posts in the establishments of international traders and retailers of imported merchandise.

The Difficulties of Retail Companies

So far I have emphasized the advantages of the company form of business arrangement for managing a store and acquiring greater amounts of working capital. Retail companies were certainly common and frequently successful. Some, however, did result in economic catastrophe for one or both of the partners. Illness, death, misunderstanding, and dishonesty imperiled more than a few companies. Juan Manuel Guilez assembled 83,000 pesos, 60,000 of it borrowed at interest, to form a company in a city store to be administered for one-third of the profits by Domingo Busce. Unfortunately, Busce became too ill to work, and the company terminated with a loss of around 5,700 pesos; Busce pledged himself to pay off his third of the losses.[74] Santos Beato suffered an even worse fate; he invested 4,330 pesos in a company in a provincial store, but his partner ran off with all the money.[75]

Sometimes, one partner would extract too much of a company's funds during its operation and end up in debt to the other at the final accounting. Francisco Noriega managed a vinatería in a company with Manuel Joaquín de Hidalgo, the investor of 2,000 pesos; when they terminated the partnership, Noriega was unable to repay the capital and therefore assumed the entire amount as a loan for four years at 5 percent interest with a bondsman guaranteeing the payment.[76]

A misunderstanding or possible duplicity on the part of one partner could bring about the downfall of the other. The most usual difficulty was that the capitalist would commit himself to even greater investment, and the manager would expend money against the promise but find himself in trouble when the funds were not delivered. In one such case, a manager extracted money from a company to maintain his family when his partner was slow in delivering promised funds. Upon the manager's death, his wife was sued by the partner for repayment from her own money.[77] Another time, a man administering a store for the widow who owned it claimed that, acting with her promise to supply the necessary capital, he had purchased another store in order to set himself up as an independent shopkeeper but that the woman then reneged on her commitment, leaving him with substantial debts and without the house which he had sold to make the initial payment.[78]

Ambulatory Vendors

Of course, not all commerce in the city was conducted inside permanent buildings; many impoverished individuals went from door to door selling petty merchandise. One, María Galindo Gutiérrez, related how for eight years, because of her husband's ill health, she had bought goods on credit from stores and then sold them directly to the workers at the factory of the tobacco monopoly, who paid her back in weekly installments. (Note how lines of credit were necessary at every level of commerce. No one, not even the wealthiest of the city, regularly purchased goods and services on a cash basis.) The storekeepers who supplied María, themselves feeling a credit pinch, were forced to pressure her for more prompt payment. As her own customers could not pay more rapidly, she repaired to the Consulado court to request esperas, arguing that she would be able to repay everybody if given the time.[79] In a society so dependent on credit, when a large merchant shortened his credit lines the shock waves reverberated down to the lowest social stratum.

Commercial Agents

There remains one other group heavily involved in retail commerce, though its members owned no stores: the commercial agents (corredores de comercio). These men made their livings by arranging sales between wholesalers and retailers, both within Mexico City and in the provinces, and by conducting many of the inventories required by commercial establishments. (It was not possible to determine what percentage of each transaction or what salary corredores received.) Though these agents made a comfortable living, none ascended into the ranks of prominent merchants nor acquired large estates. They were organized into a guild under the auspices of the Consulado and maintained a corredor mayor, deputies, and inspectors of their own. While the Consulado authorized only sixty guild members, normally up to ten more than that figure were allowed to practice as long as they obeyed the regulations of the organization.

Retail commerce in the capital was a vast and diversified field. It supported over a thousand owners of businesses, even more managers, and thousands of sales personnel and commercial apprentices. The stores, both general and specialized, sold great varieties of imported and domestic merchandise intended for all sectors of society. Proprietors of these establishments fell along a social spectrum from the most wealthy international wholesalers to those whose single stand was the only barrier between themselves and impoverishment, and in every type of retail trade, managers at times advanced into ownership, while some proprietors descended into bankruptcy.

6 Patterns of Advancement in the Commercial World

The Separation Between Ownership and Management

As has been shown in the previous three chapters, a sharp distinction prevailed between ownership and management of commercial establishments at every level in late colonial Mexico City. Whether a business was humble or exalted, its proprietor, if possible, removed him or herself from daily operations and left them to either a salaried employee or, preferably, a managing partner who received between a fourth and a half of any profits or losses. The documentation makes it abundantly clear that both owner and employee sought to enter into a company agreement if at all possible. A supervisor with a financial stake in a business was more likely to stress its efficient operation and thus provide greater income to himself and the proprietor. Managing partners often earned several times the salary of employees in equivalent businesses. Overall, salaried employees were used only when owners lacked a person of proven competence who might be elevated to partnership status.

The Definition of "Cajero"

The term *cajero* was applied generally to all sales and management personnel of a commercial firm irrespective of their rank. Therefore, although usually referred to as *administrador*, the managing

135

partner was at times called *cajero mayor*. In turn, *cajero mayor* commonly indicated the salaried manager of an enterprise, but he might as easily be termed just *cajero*. Below him were one, two, or several employees, all of whom were labeled *cajeros*, though they might each have different responsibilities and earn different salaries. Thus the word *cajero* used out of context could signify any member of a commercial establishment other than the proprietor. He might be the managing partner and nephew of the owner or just a lowly clerk with limited prospects for advancement.

Complementing the business structure was another based on kinship and marital ties. Often, merchants employed brothers, nephews, cousins, and other relatives as managers and clerks. Though just one relative might be involved in a small firm, commercial houses and large stores frequently utilized several at the same or different ranks. They were not all destined to enter the ranks of the commercial elite or even to become independent proprietors of their own stores; only those who demonstrated their business acumen could entertain such expectations. There were thus two separate but closely intertwined bodies of personnel here: employees and relatives. Let us look at each in turn.

The Role and Status of Cajeros

Given the broad meaning of "cajero" at this time, it is no surprise that there were many individuals so described in the capital. Despite their large numbers, they had little property and even less prestige in this society. Totally dependent on their employers for their subsistence, they were never considered for any honor or position of responsibility. Those who were not related to a merchant found themselves in a very precarious situation as they set out on their careers. Without influence or connections, they had to wander about soliciting employment anywhere in the colony they might have a chance to display their supervisory abilities. Juan José García and Leonardo Trejo, among others, turned to advertising in the Mexico City newspapers in their attempts to secure positions. García stated that he desired a post as a cajero, concierge (portero), or mayordomo of a hacienda either in the capital or in the provinces; Trejo declared his ability to work as a cajero, horse-breaker, or administrator of a rural estate.[1] The immigrant from

Spain and the creole from the provinces found themselves in the same predicament.

But securing employment in the field of commerce by no means guaranteed success or even a comfortable living. Salaried commercial employees of whatever rank never acquired any personal property of great value. As stated in their wills, cajeros characteristically owned only their clothes, perhaps along with a bit of jewelry and a few sticks of furniture. They never owned their residences, let alone rural estates or other properties. Their only income was their salaries; they typically named their employers as executors and often as heirs. Though some of these people lived in the roominghouses so common in the city, many resided in the same building that housed the stores they worked in. Managing partners often retained the authority to hire and fire at will. Frequently, company contracts stipulated that a certain amount from the general fund should be used each week to house, feed, and maintain the managing partner and the other employees living in the building containing the store, if not in the store itself. Noncommercial employees commonly included a cook, a maid, a guard who might sleep nightly within the store, and one or two other custodial workers.

Those cajeros employed in the main distributing outlet of a large trader, usually situated in his house, normally lived there with him. An examination of the residential groupings recorded in the 1811 census of the city confirms this. The heads of international trading houses commonly reported anywhere from five to ten commercial employees residing with them. This census further reveals that several (if not a majority) of these cajeros were relatives or countrymen of the merchant and that a good number of them never advanced into independent ownership of a business. Some were already in their late thirties or even their forties, unwed, and still situated as a dependent and employee of the master of the house (and business).

Salaries of commercial employees were customarily low, barely providing enough for personal maintenance in the urban Spanish world. Examples of salary levels for administrators and cajeros in different types of commercial establishments are provided in Table 25. Generally, the former made about twice as much as the latter,

Table 25.   Salaries of Some Commercial Employees in Late Colonial
Mexico City

Administrators (including cajeros mayores) Store Type	Year	Salary
Cajón (Parián)	1802	500 pesos per annum
Tienda	1786	400
Vinatería	1794	400
Vinatería	1781	300
Semillería	1809	1 peso per day

Cajeros Store Type	Year	Salary
Cajón (Parián)	1792	200 pesos per annum
Tienda Mestiza	1803	200
Cerería	1799	200
Tienda	1789	150
Tienda	1785	150
Tienda	1778	100
Tienda de algodones	1800	100
Semillería	1809	12 pesos per month

Source: AGN, Consulado, leg. 47, exp. 2, leg. 216, exp. 3, leg. 130, exp. 1, leg. 142, exp. 7, leg. 225, exp. 5, leg. 166, exp. 8, leg. 226, exp. 2; Civil, leg. 703, exp. 4; AN, Burillo, Nov. 15, 1792, Feb. 7, 1794, and Nov. 12, 1799; Pozo, April 2, 1800; Puertas, April 30, 1786.

and neither earned enough to provide more than a subsistence living. The attainment of economic success in the commercial world required the individual to advance to the level of ownership, or at least to that of managing partner.[2]

Some employees were unable to continue long at this level of existence without tapping into the invested capital or profits of the proprietor. Scattered throughout the records of the Consulado are cases in which the owners of businesses sue their former workers to recover funds that the latter have taken not for investment but for subsistence. José Montenegro left the employ of the merchant Manuel de Frago in 1799 after nine years of service as both a salaried employee and a managing partner. The final balance found him in debt to Frago, even though he had already sold the employer some of his furniture. Six years later, Montenegro, by now pulling in an inconsequential salary as an employee in one of the royal monopolies, was still indigent and in debt to Frago, despite having given him a pair of mules to sell and a share of his salary.[3] His was not an isolated case. Many cajeros left their posts in debt and found themselves legally hounded to make repayment, even though they personally owned little property and earned only a meager income.

The Path of Advancement

The successful cajero in a large firm typically proved his aptitude over a rather lengthy apprenticeship before eventually rising to become the cajero mayor. From there the next big step was to become the managing partner of an enterprise and then possibly to acquire it or some other through use of personal savings plus funds loaned by the former employer, by relatives and friends, or by an independent agent or organization. (Of course, even these funds normally sufficed only for the down payment; the balance was paid off in installments.) Here it is necessary to remember the sharp distinction between commercial employees of stores selling imported merchandise and those of pulperías and other types of grocery and general stores. Only the former could aspire to acquisition of a cajón or eventually to head a trading house. The best the latter could achieve was to possess for themselves the type of store that they had formerly managed. Cajeros in provincial branches of trading houses were in no way excluded from advancement in the Mexico City home office. In fact, sometimes the most promising employees were dispatched to the provinces for a while to become better educated in the operation of a far-flung commercial empire.

Administrators and managing partners advanced into ownership in three ways: (1) by acquiring a new business that was nominally independent but in actuality maintained close affiliation with the sponsoring merchant; (2) by purchasing one of the stores of the sponsor and operating it as an appendage of his commercial network; and (3) by taking over the trading house directly, which often entailed marriage into the family of the sponsor. An individual head of a trading house could use all three approaches with different employees. But to make full sense of this pattern of sponsorship, it is first necessary to understand how these magnates surrounded themselves with relatives and countrymen, whom they both used and favored.

Kinship and Commerce

Uncommon was the Mexico City wholesaler who did not enjoy the companionship and business support of one or more blood relatives from his own generation and from those on either side of it. Francisco Alonso de Terán, for example, served as prior of the Mexico City Consulado and headed its Montañés party in the early nineteenth century. He could always depend on the support of another member of the party, his brother Antonio. Francisco himself was not the first member of his family to have held that exalted position. Earlier his uncle and benefactor Gabriel Gutiérrez de Terán had occupied the priorship. Gabriel too had a brother in the city, Damián, who worked in a commercial company with him. In fact, Francisco Alonso de Terán married María Ignacia, a daughter of Damián. In turn, Francisco and Antonio had with them their own nephew, Gregorio Mier de Terán, who they were training in the ways of commerce.[4]

This is not an isolated case. Some brothers established themselves independently in business, though often with the support of some senior relative; more frequently, one served as a managing partner or other type of commercial dependent of the other. Examples of both types can be found in a single family. The brothers José, Manuel, and Lucas Palacio y Romaña, natives of Santander, all took slightly divergent paths after initially involving themselves heavily in commerce. The first two prospered to the extent that each married into prominent, monied creole families. José continued to emphasize his wholesale business, while Manuel opted to involve himself deeply in the manufacture and distribution of the pulque on which his wife's family had based its fortune, and he employed his brother Lucas as a business associate.[5]

International trade in late colonial New Spain rested primarily in the hands of peninsular immigrants. This remained the case because wholesalers regularly brought over nephews from their home area in Spain to train in commerce. First outlined by Lucas

Alamán, this practice has been more fully described by D. A. Brading.[6] Normally, however, a nephew did not come over alone and was not preselected as the exclusive heir to his uncle's mercantile business. Rather, relatives came in groups, brothers and cousins, with the result that each head of a trading house had a retinue of nephews to whom he could turn for help and whom he was expected to train. But this also meant that there would be competition among them to determine who would take over the firm. Those who displayed considerable business abilities were eligible; those who did not remained as dependents and commercial employees. The situation had to be handled in a way that would avoid cajero rivalry from alienating some members and fragmenting the family business. The goal after all was to have the family members work together in harmony in an enterprise with each having different but complementary roles under the directorship of the family head. It was vital that every relative (whether through blood or marriage) who possessed business acumen should participate as an adjunct rather than establish himself as a competitor. The upshot was that several methods were used to establish these young men in business either jointly or, more commonly, apart, though still in affiliation with or dependent on the main trading house.

The intricate interconnections between business and blood ties is exemplified by Fernando de la Barcena and his family. Fernando was a wealthy merchant who maintained several stores in the capital. His two brothers, Patricio and Juan, worked with him. By the 1780s, he had been joined by four nephews from Burgos: the brothers Gaspar and Juan Antonio López Herrero, their cousin Antonio López Herrero, and Fernando Barcena e Izquierdo, whose relationship to the other three is unclear. In the 1790s, Fernando and his nephew Gaspar maintained a company in a couple of the uncle's stores. Earlier, the cousins Juan Antonio and Antonio López Herrero had worked together as partners in another store, apparently owned by the former.

In 1804 Antonio Mariano del Toro, seemingly unrelated to the family, was persuaded by Fernando to enter into a company to administer a store owned by Juan Antonio López Herrero. As owner, Juan Antonio was entitled to one-half the profits; as administrator, Toro earned one-fourth; the other fourth went to the third partner,

Patricio de la Barcena, uncle of Juan Antonio and brother of Fernando. The store employed two cajeros; one was an unnamed nephew of Juan Antonio and the other an unnamed nephew of Antonio Mariano. The store also employed a porter, a cook, and her assistant. All these people, with the exception of the owner, Juan Antonio, were to be maintained on 12 reales a day from the firm's general fund, but this proved impossible.

Inadequate funding for maintenance was only the first of the complaints which Toro, the apparent outsider, brought against the above arrangements. In a sworn statement he averred that Patricio did absolutely no work, nor did the cajero who was a nephew of the owner. Toro claimed that he himself had to wander through the streets daily to purchase goods to be sold in the store and that he had to leave the establishment in the hands of the other cajero, his own nephew. This situation prevailed until 1807 when the patriarch Fernando de la Barcena, having rented a hacienda, invited his brother Patricio to join him in its operation and to leave Toro alone in management of the store, now with a third share of the profits. For this reason the firm took an inventory and discovered, to everyone's delight, that in two and a third years it had earned profits of 3,700 pesos. Because of the surprisingly good return, Patricio decided to remain in the company and to forego the hacienda partnership with his brother. Unfortunately, Toro's reaction was not recorded. An interesting footnote to all this is that Fernando de la Barcena, who had never married, named none of these individuals as his executor or heir. Rather, he designated a well-established wholesaler of the capital, who was seemingly another distant relative of his.[7]

As related in Chapter 5, Pedro Alonso de Alles, the Marqués de Santa Cruz de Inguanzo, employed one nephew as a managing partner of a large store in the Parián and another, who would eventually marry his widow and succeed to his title, as his business agent, but there were at least three other nephews around. They all worked singly or in pairs in different branches of his business, mostly in commerce, though at least one relative was employed as the administrator of one of the family haciendas. Despite their specialization, they still cooperated economically for the good of the larger family. As seen in Chapter 4, the first Marqués and five of his nephew-employees each posted 2,000 pesos bond for the new subdelegado of Teposcolula. Money was readily shifted from one branch of the family to another; when one nephew needed 20,000 pesos for his commerce, he borrowed it at the standard rate of interest for five years from the widow of one of his cousins and was able to claim the first Marqués and yet another relative as guarantors of the loan.[8] And though they managed separate stores, several of the nephews joined together to buy a shipment of Chinese goods from a local wholesaler, pledging themselves jointly to payment on a specified date.[9]

Naturally, the presence of so many commercially aspiring relatives required the merchant head of a family to find suitable positions for all who proved themselves competent. Overall, perhaps because of the breadth and diversity of the holdings of the major traders, this does not seem to have been a very large problem. Francisco Martínez Cabezón, who was heavily involved in trade with Europe, Manila, and Spanish America, helped three of his nephews establish themselves in commerce. The first, Blas Martínez Cabezón, was apparently the least competent of the three. He worked in his uncle's commercial house for some years until 1777, when he was given 4,000 pesos, followed by an additional 5,777, so that he might run his own business. For many years he carried on a typical correspondence account with his uncle's trading firm; he bought goods on credit and periodically paid off outstanding debts. When he died in 1804, he had not expanded his business significantly and still maintained his relationship with the parent commercial house; in fact, he was in debt to it for a relatively small amount.[10]

The second nephew, Manuel García Herreros, had been a partner in his uncle's trading house until the company was finally dissolved by the senior member's death. García Herreros acted as executor and heir not only for his uncle but also for his aunt.[11] But this is not to say that he assumed sole control over the entire diversified commercial empire. By no means, for there was yet another nephew present who had also demonstrated his business skill and had been given a large share of the business. Diego de Agreda, the future prior of the Consulado and conde of that name, did not need to inherit from Martínez Cabezón or his wife, for he had already implemented another procedure for gaining control over all or a substantial part of a trading house: he had married his cousin, María Ignacia Martínez Cabezón y Sau, his uncle's only child.[12] By doing so, he had received a dowry of 60,000 pesos and, just as importantly, obtained official affiliation with her father's firm, with access to all of his business associates and contacts. Thus, we can see that the great merchants had no fear of dividing up their businesses, so long as the split did not substantially weaken either branch or set them in destructive competition against each other. In fact, such a division provided greater opportunity to more of the ambitious younger relatives and better enabled the family to expand itself economically and socially.

A wholesaler could help establish a flock of aspiring nephews in the commerce of the city without ever turning over part of his own holdings to them. In the last decade of the 1790s, Antonio de Bassoco watched over his own business affairs and some of those of his cousins, the mighty Castañiza family; in addition, he had under his wing five nephews, the Arangoiti brothers, who had come over from the Basque country. He never made any of them a managing partner nor gave them a share of his wealth (none of them are even mentioned in his will of 1798), but he was nonetheless instrumental in setting them up in business. In the early 1790s, Bernardino de Arangoiti had a company with a local merchant of Durango. By 1800, he and his brother Pedro were in Veracruz, apparently acting as commercial intermediaries between ship captains and the merchants of Mexico City. In that very year Bernardino entered into the previously recounted company agreement with his uncle which would take him on an extensive commercial voyage to Venezuela and Spain and finally back to Mexico for an equal share of the profits. Little other information is available on Pedro, but what does exist indicates that he never advanced in business and remained a commercial dependent of his more successful brothers. Again in 1800, another brother, Juan Miguel, who had already established himself as a merchant in the capital, served as Bernardino's legal representative (apoderado general). The following year he borrowed 20,000 pesos at 5 percent for five years from his uncle to expand his commerce. By 1809, he was a member of the Consulado.

Perhaps the most successful of the Arangoiti brothers was Francisco. In 1805 he purchased a cajón in the city and to supply it borrowed 40,000 pesos, at 5 percent for five years, from his uncle. Four years later he too was recorded as a member of the Consulado. By 1814, he owned a panadería and that year again borrowed from his uncle to expand his business, this time 10,000 pesos for five years. The following year he served as legal representative for the head of the other major branch of the family, the Marqués de Castañiza, then bishop elect of Durango. The remaining brother, Bernabé, is encountered in 1807 working as a viandante in Durango, having been supplied goods by his brother Francisco.[13]

All five brothers worked to set themselves up in commerce with the support of their influential uncle; they also manifested considerable internal cohesiveness, dealing with each other commercially and willing to help one another out when needed. Furthermore, they cultivated the full range of their family ties, interacting also with the Castañiza branch. Two of the five never advanced very far even with this formidable assistance; they remained business dependents of their more capable kin. None of the three successful brothers became the heir apparent to the estate of their uncle. Rather, before his death in 1814, Bassoco summoned yet another nephew from his home province and left him his wealth and title. By the following year, this young man, José María de Bassoco, was admitted into the Mexico City Consulado and maintained himself as a member of the capital's elite well into the Independence period.

The Route in From the Provinces

Not all peninsulars who became members of the Consulado inherited their trading houses from uncles or other relatives. In Chapter 5 we saw how young immigrants, though unaffiliated with any major mercantile family, could prove their abilities as commercial employees, rise to the status of managing partners, and ultimately use funds they saved and borrowed to make the quantum jump into wholesale commerce. Some other aspiring immigrants first demonstrated their business acumen out in the provinces, either on their own or as employees of branches of Mexico City merchant houses. Almost invariably, these young men married into a prominent provincial family which was anxious to join fortunes with a person who had proved his ability in their locality and seemed likely to ascend to the heady social and economic level of a merchant in Mexico City. These associations were mutually beneficial. The newcomer now had the considerable resources of the family to use in his business, and the family could ride his coattails out of the provinces and into the elite world of Mexico City.

The career of Bruno Pastor Morales well illustrates this pattern. Born in Catalonia, he came to New Spain as a youth. There he began his career as a cajero in a store in the city of Valladolid, marrying into a landed family of that province. He took over the business affairs of his new family and succeeded to the extent that he was able to move to the capital, where he again prospered in commerce, though without abandoning his strong interest in commodity trading. He became a captain in the militia regiment of the Mexico City merchants and then, upon the demise of his wife, resolved to enter the church. In no way did his new calling cause him to diminish his mercantile activities. He continued to operate rural estates and to deal in agricultural commodities. He managed his store in the capital in the name of his three children, whom he had made its owners, and he even continued as a captain in the militia. In fact, instead of relinquishing the position, he obtained the additional post of proprietary chaplain of the grenadiers.[14]

Other people entered the field of international commerce from other professions. Jorge Hourat, who legally adopted the name of Diego José García, was not even Spanish by birth. A native of French Navarre, at the age of eleven he went on his own to Andalusia, where he lived in Cádiz for a decade, much of the time as a dependent in the house of the Conde de Reparaz. When his master journeyed to Mexico, Jorge came along as his business agent. He decided to remain and enlisted as a soldier in a militia company of the capital. He then married a native of the city and quickly established himself in commerce and in agriculture, acquiring an estate near the capital for 20,000 pesos. He prospered to the extent that in the late 1790s, after twenty-one years of residence in the colony, he petitioned for membership in the Mexico City Consulado. Though he owned a certified almacén (commercial warehouse) and had been naturalized the year previous, no other non-Spaniard had ever been admitted to the merchants' guild and an extensive court case ensued. To Jorge's great delight, he won when both parties of the Consulado agreed to recognize his fitness.[15]

Antonio del Frago, a native of the Basque Provinces, did not start his career in New Spain as a merchant; rather, he served as director of the royal tobacco monopoly, a most prestigious and potentially profitable government post. Not enough information is available to ascertain if he used his lucrative position to further his commercial interests, but in 1785, retired as director of the monopoly, he remained active as a wholesale trader in the capital.[16]

The Limits of Peninsular Inheritance

There are several dangers in emphasizing the preponderance of immigrant nephews who took over their uncles' Mexico City commercial houses. First, it is often assumed that control over the trading firm entailed oversight of the entire estate of the late merchant, when in fact the deceased's diversified investments might well be in the hands of other family members. Second, such an emphasis leads one to downplay the very significant and powerful presence of native-born wholesalers, many of whom were themselves the sons of merchants. Third, one should not fall into the belief that there existed some sort of competition and resentment between the creole and peninsular members of most families, when typically the two parts were well integrated into a harmonious whole. Fourth, an entire trading house did not always pass down intact to a single heir; as shown above, occasionally the firm itself was divided among relatives, while yet others were given control over subsections or were established in their own nominally independent businesses, which usually maintained a working relationship with the family trading house even though they were installed as Consulado members.

As discussed earlier, in 1803 Sebastián de Heras Soto formed a complicated company in a store in the Parián. In it were two of his nephews who, though brothers, occupied unequal positions. Manuel de Heras was one of the two managing partners, entitled to a full fourth of the profits; his brother José was employed as a cajero with an annual salary of 400 pesos and a 2 percent share of the profits. At about the same time, Sebastián's own son, Manuel de Heras Soto, was stationed in Santander, his father's home town, where he was learning the ways of international commerce among his kinfolk. By 1813, he had returned to Mexico and in that year joined the capital's Consulado. He was certainly not without friends in the organization the year of his entrance or for the remainder of his tenure until the Consulado's dissolution in 1826. His father, by now the Conde de Heras Soto, was one of the leaders of the merchants' guild as a former consul. His cousin, Manuel de Heras, had also joined by 1809. The patriarch Sebastián died the following year and in 1815, for unknown reasons, the nephew Manuel also disappeared from the guild membership. But this is not to say that Sebastián's son Manuel, now the second Conde de Heras Soto, was without kin in the organization, for that same year two more cousins, Francisco Javier and Miguel de Heras, were admitted into the body. These were later joined by two other relatives: Javier de Heras in 1823 and Ignacio de Heras Soto in 1826. Thus, an extensive kin group operated within the Consulado under the overall supervision of a creole son who was carefully trained by his father and who functioned much like him.

Creoles and Wholesale Trade

Creole sons of merchants might choose from a variety of professions; one that they did not slight was their fathers' own. They were frequently trained in commercial practices under the watchful eyes of their fathers or other relatives both in Mexico and abroad, and assumed control over the family mercantile enterprises upon their fathers' deaths, even succeeding to the latter's seats in the Consulado. Manuel de Heras Soto was by no means unique when he followed in his father's footsteps and became the head of a diversified trading house. Of the three sons of José Melchor de Ibarrola, a leading wholesaler of peninsular birth, two made their careers in commerce. Francisco Javier de Ibarrola was clearly the most successful and was a member of the Consulado by 1809. But his brother Ignacio José also achieved a great deal in his own right. In 1805 he reported that he had maintained a correspondence account for many years with a Querétaro merchant, sending him goods and honoring his drafts. At that time his provincial associate owed him over 2,340 pesos.[17] The one brother who did not become a merchant, Luis Gonzaga, entered the legal profession and served many years as the chief notary (escribano mayor) of the Consulado, was twice elected rector of the lawyers' guild (Colegio de Abogados), and was appointed honorary secretary to the viceroy.

In 1786 Miguel Francisco Sánchez Hidalgo, another peninsular-born merchant, served as consul of the Consulado. That same year he made out a will listing his four children. His eldest, a daughter named Ignacia then still unmarried, would later marry José Palacio y Romaña, one of three immigrant brothers discussed earlier. Palacio y Romaña would remain active in the family's commerce, often working as a managing associate, and ultimately entered the Consulado. The second oldest child was Ignacio María. By 1787, he had his doctorate; by 1792, he was a practicing attorney; in 1793, though the only member of the family who was not formally a merchant or married to one, he, as patriarch of the family, supervised its financial affairs and introduced himself and his siblings into a company contract with a partner who was to manage one of the family stores in Zacatecas. All goods were to be purchased from the family's central outlet in Mexico City then under Ignacio María's directorship, with a 1½ percent markup. Ignacio María operated yet another commercial company with his two brothers-in-law until 1795, when he became a cleric and removed himself from it to become curate of one of the parishes of the capital. The other daughter, María de Guadalupe, married the peninsular-born merchant José Vicente de Olloqui, who in 1807 ascended to the priorship of the Mexico City Consulado. But he was still not sole head of the family's financial fortunes, even now that Ignacio María had removed himself from commerce. The youngest of the four children, José Miguel, had involved himself in wholesale trade while still in his twenties and was himself a member of the Consulado by 1809.[18] Once again, we can perceive both the extent and diversity that a family fortune could attain in this era. At one time or another all four male members of a generation were actively involved in the family's economic affairs, with no apparent divisive strains; ultimately, three of them functioned independently enough at a sufficiently large scale to merit simultaneous membership in the guild of wholesale traders.

Nor were all creole members of the Consulado sons of merchants. Both Francisco Maniau y Torquemada and José Sánchez de Espinosa were sons of government officials, and they achieved commercial success through their own efforts. The former was one of four sons of an accountant for the royal tobacco monopoly, all of who were born and raised in Jalapa. Francisco was the only one to become a wholesaler; however, his brother Ildefonso José was one of his most dependable associates.[19] The other two brothers made names for themselves in the service of the crown and the church.

José Sánchez de Espinosa was a native of the capital whose father was a treasury official (factor) for the crown in the port of Acapulco, but whose family on his mother's side enjoyed a long and prestigious history in the colony. His greatuncle had been archdean of the Mexico City cathedral chapter and had founded a massive obra pía from lands concentrated in San Luis Potosí. José's own uncle, a cleric and attorney, had been its first administrator; in his will he made his nephew his sole executor and heir and the new administrator.[20] José pursued his mercantile interests alongside his agrarian ones. He had already earned the appellation "almacenero" while still in his twenties and throughout his lifetime added additional estates to the family holdings, though he did not attach them to the obra pía.[21] He married a daughter of the first Conde de Nuestra Señora de Guadalupe del Peñasco, and his eldest son eventually became the third Conde.[22] After his wife's death, José entered the priesthood, but his clerical status did not curtail his business activity.

The Peninsulars and International Trade

Overall, the creoles maintained a healthy presence in the ranks of overseas traders, and their numerical domination of the lower levels of commerce in Mexico City is beyond question. Many creoles not formally merchants were also active in commerce on an occasional basis. But given these facts, we must nonetheless account for the heavy peninsular role in the colony's overseas trade. Certainly it cannot have been because of an entrepreneurial spirit native to the metropolis and foreign to the colony, for if any economy was stagnant, it was that of Spain, and if any economy was flourishing, it was that of Mexico. Furthermore, far from all of the aspiring immigrants became successful businessmen. As shown earlier, often a number of nephews and cousins came from Spain to work under a sponsoring merchant, and of these, only one or two might ever ascend to the rank of international trader. The majority never advanced from employee status, or at best rose to become a managing partner or proprietor of a modest retail establishment.

Some, in fact, were complete financial failures. Perhaps the most notable example was Francisco Antonio Adalid, the peninsular nephew of the mighty Mexico City almacenero José Adalid. (A son of Diego Adalid, who had been a kinsman and cajero of the original Conde de San Bartolomé de Jala and who had prospered in the pulque trade under his aegis, José himself married the eldest daughter of the fifth Marqués de San Miguel de Aguayo.) In 1784 Francisco Antonio borrowed nearly 6,000 pesos for his business from four capellanías; he also received nearly 4,500 pesos in 1790 as a dowry. Nonetheless, he was a complete failure in commerce and by 1792 had declared bankruptcy. Four years later, his uncle José agreed to assume all of the nephew's debts, including restoration of the dowry.[23] At this point Francisco Antonio disappears from the documentation. José himself died in 1799 hounded by creditors.[24] His family managed to reestablish its solvency by abandoning commerce and concentrating on agriculture. No Adalid was listed in the 1809 Consulado or in any of those subsequent.

What must be remembered is that even in the more open and flourishing world of international commerce characteristic of the late colonial period, the establishment and maintenance of a web of reliable overseas contacts remained the key to the survival of an international trading house. Though clearly not in a dominating position, Spanish merchant houses still played a significant role in colonial commerce. Even the Mexico City wholesalers who launched their own commercial ventures overseas in this time normally utilized contacts in other port cities or at least sent along a designated agent, often as a partner in the undertaking. Trading

houses of the capital regularly stationed agents in Manila, Guayaquil, Acapulco, Veracruz, Santander, Bilbao and other ports where
they had dealings.

This being the case, the best commercial apprentices were those
young men who were most dependent on the head of the trading
house for their livelihood and advancement (the better to insure
their loyalty), who already had contacts with relatives and other
business associates in Spain (the better to foster the personal contacts on which the commercial system rested), and who were not
averse to being stationed throughout the colony and across either
ocean (the better to learn the practicalities of international trade
and again to promote personal contacts). On every count immigrant relatives were superior to those who were Mexican born,
not because of any greater entrepreneurial spirit or frugality, but
because they had fewer viable economic alternatives available to
them and were therefore more willing to accept the rigors, travel,
and demands inherent in commercial apprenticeship. A youth
born to the creole elite had other fulfilling career options open to
him which did not demand such sacrifice with so little guarantee
of success. In similar fashion, the creoles, unlike their foreign relatives, did not have the same initial access to and familiarity with
that vital web of kin and commercial associates. And finally, as argued in the next chapter, these immigrant merchants were not desirable marriage partners for the wealthy creole elite until they had
proved their business acumen beyond a doubt and had acquired
status and honors in this society. Wholesale merchants did not occupy the pinnacle of Mexico City society. That position was held
by the great creole families with their diversified economic interests. Those international traders who married into these families
did not take them over, but rather were integrated into them along
with their business holdings.

The Role of the Company in Commerce

Because of the various functions that it could serve and its adaptability in changing circumstances, the company was the basic
form of commercial organization in late colonial Mexico City. It
channeled fresh capital into a business, bound management to
ownership by giving it a greater stake in the outcome, permitted

businessmen to expand within certain fields and to diversify into others, facilitated the extension of the city's commercial tentacles into provincial economies, and provided for the training and promotion of relatives and underlings in a controlled setting.

Company agreements were ubiquitous at every level of commerce. A single wholesaler could simultaneously maintain separate contracts with an associate overseas, with the head manager at his almacén, with the administrators of branches in provincial centers, and with his agents running neighborhood grocery stores. All of these companies were within the sphere of commerce. Since merchants commonly diversified into other fields of the economy, the same wholesaler could have yet other company agreements with the administrator of his hacienda complex, with the owner of a bakery or a slaughterhouse in which he had invested spare capital, and with an artisan with whom he had done the same.

The company, then, enabled the entrepreneur dissatisfied with the customary 5 percent return on loans to let out funds to specific enterprises for a stipulated share of the profits and to set certain terms to guarantee his investment. It was the device by which nonmerchants were able to tap into the profits available in the commercial world. It allowed the small businessman to expand by giving him access to capital reserves otherwise beyond his reach. It was, in short, perhaps the primary vehicle for business expansion and investment in the society.

By contracting a number of separate agreements, wealthy businessmen were able both to secure and to expand their fortunes through diversification. The company gave them the means by which to involve themselves in a variety of enterprises by turning to competent managers and undercapitalized proprietors in different fields, all the while maintaining the distinction between ownership and management. Lacking the company as an organizational device, powerful individuals and families would have found it much more difficult to expand beyond a certain point simply because they would not have been able to control their investments adequately. Contract provisions limiting the activities of managing partners, giving them a set share of any profits (and often losses) and setting up periodic inventories and inspections, heightened the investor's sense of security and his ability to direct broad policy. After all, the capitalist utilized the company exactly to exempt himself from responsibility over daily operations of his businesses. It was the existence of these managing partners that freed him to concentrate on wholesale transactions and broad questions of business administration.

The managers themselves stood to gain much from successful companies. Their share of the profits could earn them far more than straight salary, and success enabled them to negotiate for a yet higher percentage in the future, to move into more lucrative agreements with other investors, and even to advance into ownership itself. A few former managing partners actually made it to membership in the merchants' guild. More commonly, however, they were able to acquire one or two major stores in the capital or in outlying towns. This done, they characteristically entered into company agreements with their own managers.

The frequency of company contracts even at the lower levels of retail trade bespeaks the entrepreneurial activity which pervaded every sector of the economy. The small shopowners, by the limits on their wealth, were effectively prevented from investing in some fields of the economy, mining and agriculture most notably. Nonetheless, many of them were not satisfied with the income provided by the operation of just a single store and used the profits to purchase yet other stores or unrelated businesses or to back already-existing concerns for a share of future profits. Either way, the investor, though operating on a very modest scale, still maintained separation of ownership and management.

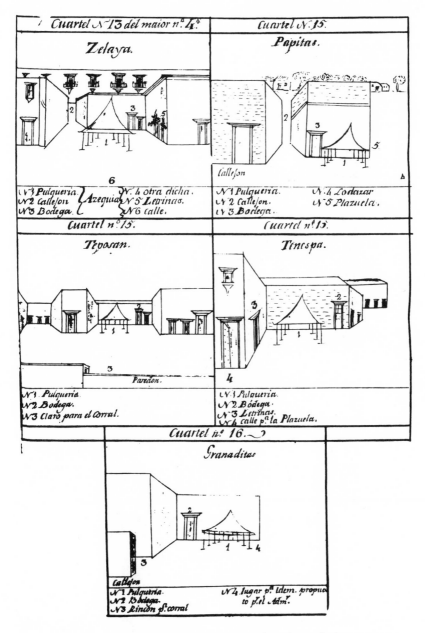

Drawings of five *pulquerías* in Mexico City that show their openness.

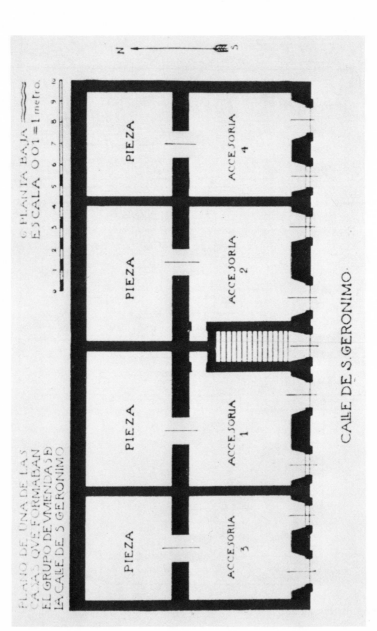

Plan of the main floor of an eighteenth-century apartment house.

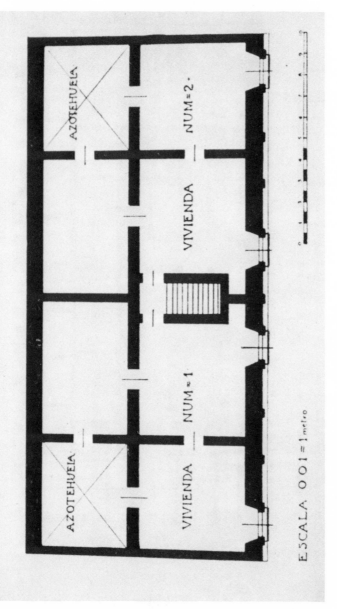

Plan of the second floor of the same apartment house.

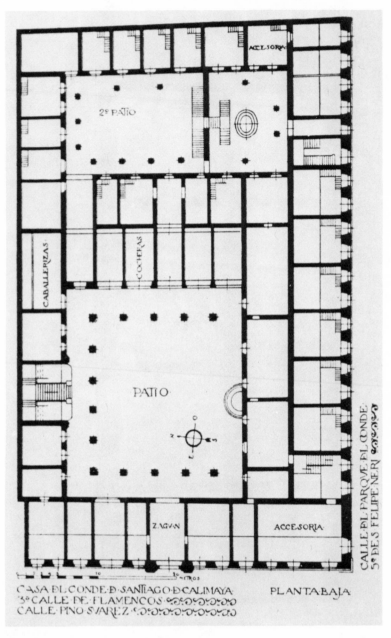

Plan of the main floor of the family mansion of the Conde de Santiago de Calimaya.

Above: The House of Tiles, the family mansion of the Conde del Valle de Orizaba. Below: family mansion of the Conde de Heras Soto.

Interior patio of the family mansion of the Marques de Jaral de
Berrio.

Above: The Parián and the Cabildo building in the main plaza of Mexico City. Left: the dress of a regidor in the late colonial period.

José de Cevallos, Prior of the Consulado.

José Mariano de la Cotera, Marqués de Rivas Cacho, Knight of
Santiago.

Servando Gómez de la Cortina, Conde de la Cortina, Consul of the Consulado.

Miguel González Caldéron, Consul of the Consulado.

Gabriel Gutiérrez de Terán, Prior of the Consulado, Alcalde Ordinario of Mexico City.

Francisca Javiera Tomasa Mier y Terán.

Domingo de Rábago, Conde de Rábago, prominent merchant.

Juana María Romero.

Francisco Antonio Sánchez de Tagle, Knight of Calatrava, Regidor of
Mexico City, Prior of the Consulado.

Manuel Antonio Valdés, printer, publisher of the *Gazeta de México*.

Mariano José de Zúñiga y Ontiveros, printer, publisher of the *Guías de forasteros* and the *Diario de México*.

7 Consolidation of Position
Marriage, Investments, and Honors Among Merchants

Elite Families and Consulado Membership

The number of creole sons and immigrant nephews of merchants entering into international commerce, together with the frequency of intermarriage among different merchant families, created powerful extended families of merchants within the Consulado. In any single year several members of the merchants' guild might be blood or marital relatives formed together into a formidable power bloc. In 1809 José María González Calderón, a creole member of the Consulado, was a direct descendent of two of the most powerful merchant families of the colony and related by marriage to another. On the paternal side, his grandfather was Francisco José González Calderón, a peninsular who had emerged as one of the great wholesaler traders of the mid-eighteenth century. One of Francisco José's four children was Miguel, the father of José María and himself a power in the guild, serving as consul in 1792–1793. Bárbara, a sister of Miguel, married the international trader José de Cevallos, who was a consul in 1772–1773 and prior in 1789–1790. Her son married the fifth Marquesa de Guardiola; their son in turn inherited the title and was present in the 1809 Consulado.

On the maternal side, José María's grandfather was yet another great wholesale merchant, Francisco González Guerra, who had maintained a commercial company with his equally prominent

155

Table 26. Select Genealogy of the González Calderón, González Guerra, and Gutiérrez de Terán Families.

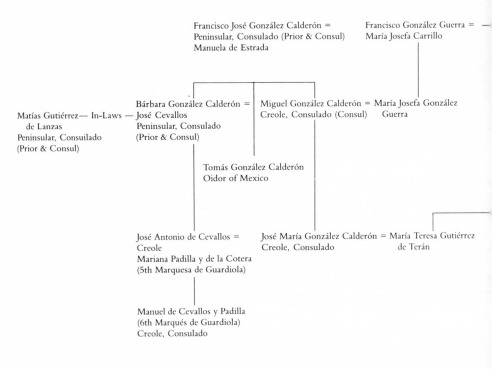

Table 27. Select Genealogy of the Icaza and Iraeta Families.

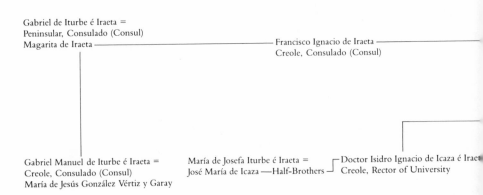

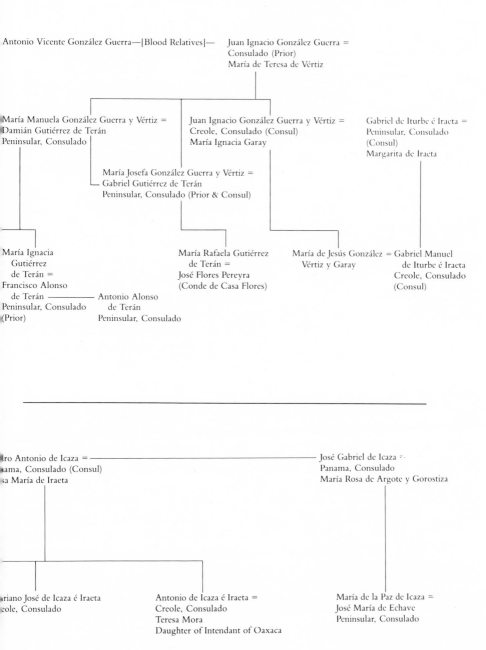

Antonio Vicente González Guerra—[Blood Relatives]—   Juan Ignacio González Guerra =
                                                       Consulado (Prior)
                                                       María de Teresa de Vértiz

María Manuela González Guerra y Vértiz =   Juan Ignacio González Guerra y Vértiz =   Gabriel de Iturbe é Iraeta =
Damián Gutiérrez de Terán   Creole, Consulado (Consul)   Peninsular, Consulado
Peninsular, Consulado   María Ignacia Garay   (Consul)
                                                                                       Margarita de Iraeta

                    María Josefa González Guerra y Vértiz =
                    Gabriel Gutiérrez de Terán
                    Peninsular, Consulado (Prior & Consul)

María Ignacia   María Rafaela Gutiérrez   María de Jesús González = Gabriel Manuel
Gutiérrez   de Terán =   Vértiz y Garay   de Iturbe é Iraeta
de Terán =   José Flores Pereyra   Creole, Consulado
Francisco Alonso   (Conde de Casa Flores)   (Consul)
de Terán ———— Antonio Alonso
Peninsular, Consulado   de Terán
(Prior)   Peninsular, Consulado

ro Antonio de Icaza = ——————————————————————————— José Gabriel de Icaza =
ama, Consulado (Consul)   Panama, Consulado
sa María de Iraeta   María Rosa de Argote y Gorostiza

riano José de Icaza é Iraeta   Antonio de Icaza é Iraeta =   María de la Paz de Icaza =
eole, Consulado   Creole, Consulado   José María de Echave
                                Teresa Mora   Peninsular, Consulado
                                Daughter of Intendant of Oaxaca

brother Antonio Vicente, the founder of a leading family with marriage ties to important creole families. There was yet another González Guerra, Juan Ignacio, whose exact blood relationship to the brothers I have not discovered, but who was prior in 1770 and whose creole son, Juan Ignacio González Vértiz, served as consul in both 1804 and 1807. In turn, Juan Ignacio's daughter married yet another creole member of the guild, Gabriel Manuel de Iturbe e Iraeta, who was the son of an 1805 consul, and who had joined in 1811, to be elected consul in 1826.

All these members of the Consulado were direct blood relatives of José María. To them we should add the relatives of his wife, María Teresa Gutiérrez de Terán. María Teresa's father, Damián Gutiérrez de Terán, had been an international trader along with his brother Gabriel, who himself had held the office of prior in 1785. Their successors in commerce were two nephews, the brothers Francisco and Antonio Alonso de Terán, both of whom were Consulado members. These family and marital connections are laid out graphically in Table 26. As stated earlier, Francisco was the dean of the Montañés party for many years and served as prior in 1809. Assuredly, his ties to all of the above gave him a solid bloc of votes on which to base his long-term guild leadership.

This was not the only network of interrelated families present in the Consulado at this time. When Mariano José and Antonio de Icaza entered the organization in 1811, they were able to count on the support of a couple of relatives already present and on the prestige of their family, which had given several leaders to the guild. This family's presence in the Consulado and its marriage patterns are illustrated in Table 27. The brothers Isidro Antonio and José Gabriel de Icaza had come to Mexico from their birthplace in Panama and had quickly established themselves as leading members of its mercantile community. Isidro Antonio married twice, the first time to a relative of Francisco Ignacio de Iraeta, a consul in 1789–1790, and of Gabriel de Iturbe e Iraeta, who occupied the same office in 1805–1806. Isidro Antonio himself held that post in 1801–1802. Of his three sons, two, with their father's encouragement, became international traders.

In 1804 Isidro Antonio reported that his son Mariano José had shown an inclination and aptitude for commerce and that he had employed him in the family almacén. Now, to promote his commercial career even further, they joined together in a commercial company. Each invested 10,000 pesos, and the son was to run the enterprise over the next five years for an even share of the profits.[1] His success is manifested by the fact that he was accepted into the merchants' guild as an independent and prosperous wholesaler just seven years later.

José María de Echave had worked as the cajero mayor of the Icaza merchant house in the 1790s. By 1809, he had married a daughter of José Gabriel (Isidro Antonio's brother) and was himself a member of the guild. Gabriel Manuel, the son of the Icaza in-law Gabriel de Iturbe e Iraeta, had married a daughter of the wholesaler Juan Ignacio González Vértiz, who was also related by blood and marriage to the just described González Calderón—González Guerra—Gutiérrez de Terán clan, and thereby linked, at least at this one point, these two very powerful families. (Interestingly, while the one family was solidly ensconced as a power in the Montañés faction of the Consulado, the other was nearly as powerful in the other, the Basque.) Finally, the bond between the Iturbe e Iraeta and the Icaza families was tightened when the daughter of Gabriel Manuel married a son from Isidro Antonio de Icaza's second marriage.

Of course, this pattern of intermarriage among prominent families was by no means restricted to the merchant elite of the colony. Doris Ladd has documented how the noble families of late colonial Mexico repeatedly married into each other over the course of generations.[2] D. A. Brading has also shown that wise marital alliances could bind together families influential in government, mining, and commerce.[3]

Intermarriage With Government Officials

Marital alliances with prominent government officials, especially those from Spain, always held attraction for the landed and mercantile elite of Mexico. Such marriages proved mutually beneficial; the official gained access to great wealth and affiliation with a powerful and respected Mexican family, while the local family gained not only heightened prestige but also an advocate in the governmental bureaucracy, potentially a most useful instrument in sustaining a family fortune over the long term.

Overall, titled creole families had the greatest success in snaring high-ranking grooms for their daughters. In 1771 María Josefa Rodríguez Pablo Fernández, the future Marquesa de Prado Alegre, exchanged vows with Francisco de Viana, an oidor of the Audiencia of New Spain and later member of the Council of the Indies who himself gained the title of Conde de Tepa. He would survive his wife and continue to enjoy the considerable income from her family's pulque estates, overseeing them from Spain through a Mexico City merchant who held his power of attorney. Around this same time, María Dolores Romero de Terreros, daughter of the first Conde de Santa María de Regla, became the spouse of Vicente Herrera y Rivero, an alcalde del crimen and later oidor of the Audiencia who later entered the Council of the Indies and became the Marqués de Herrera. In 1784 Juana María, daughter of the Conde de Santiago, married the oidor Cosmé de Mier y Trespalacios. This pattern of marriage between the creole elite and high-court judges was not at all unique to the late colonial period. Already in the 1720s, the daughter of an earlier Conde de Santiago had wed a peninsula oidor, Domingo Valcárcel.

By and large, while members of well-established creole elite families could marry with high-ranking colonial officials, persons from newly wealthy, commercially based families were able to wed only the daughters of government officeholders rather than officeholders themselves. Merchants tended to marry into the families of officials whose positions afforded access to capital or to trade in a province of the colony. José María de Echave, in his second marriage, wed the daughter of the accountant of the royal lottery, while Simón de Somoano Alonso wed the daughter of the chief accountant of the Audiencia of Quito.[4] As related earlier, Domingo de Rábago wed the daughter of the director of the royal mint of Mexico City.[5]

When the crown extended the intendancy system to Mexico, part of its intent was to prevent individual merchants from dominating the commerce of provincial districts. But at least a couple of intendants would have had to work against the interests of their sons-in-law if they did so. A daughter of the intendent of Guanajuato married Jaime Salvat, a major wholesaler with diverse economic pursuits, and, as cited in Chapter 2, Antonia Mora y Peysal, the daughter of an intendant of Oaxaca, wed Antonio Icaza e Iraeta, the merchant son of Isidro Antonio, who himself had maintained a strong presence in the commerce of that province for most of his career.[6]

Dowries

In general, merchants were able to command substantial dowries when they married. On the other hand, a certain number of merchants, even wholesalers, were unable to garner any dowry at all. In fact, one receives the impression after examining marriage patterns among all occupational groups in this society that the dowry was diminishing in importance as a mechanism for transferring wealth across generations. Only wealthy merchants plus the landed and mining elites were able to obtain dowries with any frequency, but again, far from universally. Even when given, the dowry might consist of clothes, jewelry, and furniture for the wife, items which were not translatable into liquid capital or usable real property. The dowry brought by José María de Echave's bride in 1815 was valued at 3,224 pesos, but was composed exclusively of clothes and jewelry.[7] Similarly, the dowry received by Mateo Julián Gómez de Leís totalled 11,685 pesos, but was largely made up of clothes, jewelry, and furniture.[8] Even the 29,170-peso dowry given to Francisco de Chavarrí contained only 20,000 pesos in liquid capital, the remainder once again being clothes and jewelry.[9]

Indications are that it was becoming more common to marry with prior assurance that a specific maternal or paternal inheritance would be passed on to the wife upon the death of a parent. This is difficult to trace and must be inferred mostly from the phrasing used in various legal documents. No husband among all the people studied ever complained about the lack or the small size of a dowry; frequently, the arrival of an inheritance for the wife was recorded in a document in a manner which suggests that the act fulfilled a prior understanding between the parties involved.

Arras

The husband was not without contractual obligations of his own. Many pledged arras—a sum of money representing usually either a tenth or a fifth of their wealth at the time of marriage—to their wives. The value of arras could approximate or even exceed that of the dowry in some cases. If widowed, the woman received not only her original dowry and the arras of her husband, but also a share of the profits earned by her late husband from his use of these sums.[10] In their wills, husbands commonly stated their wealth at the time of marriage so that their executors could better compute the amount earned during marriage and thereby determine how much should go to the widow. In bankruptcy cases, by Spanish law the wife's dowry had first claim to any property or income remaining to her spouse. Thus, in many bankruptcy proceedings, wives were prominent among the creditors, averring the preeminence of their claims on the remaining goods of their husbands. Of course, just as frequently wives used the dowry for their mate's benefit. Often, wives pledged dowries to assist their husbands out of financial difficulties, to secure loans, or otherwise to help them make their way in business.

Table 28 offers a compilation of dowries, inheritances, arras, and statements of the husband's worth upon marriage drawn from documentation left by wholesalers and their spouses. There is no noticeable disparity between the dowries given to merchants who married children of other merchants and those given to ones who married children of government officials. Marriage into the established creole elite, however, might convey a tremendous dowry, with the promise of even greater wealth through inheritance. When Angel Pedro de Puyade married into the wealthy Mero family, his enormous dowry exceeded that of any other merchant studied by a factor of three, and later, upon the death of her mother, his wife received an additional sum of almost equal value that passed into his control. Again, it bears repeating that this property was not alienated from the wife. The husband obtained the right to use it to increase his fortune, but upon his death the wife was entitled to both it and a share of the wealth obtained from its use. If she died first, it was passed on to her children as

Table 28. Wife's Dowry and Inheritance and Husband's Arras and Capital in Merchants' Marriages (expressed in pesos)

Name	Dowry	Inheritance	Arras	Capital
Diego de Agreda				
(first marriage)	60,000		8,000	
(second marriage)	40,355	49,746		
Baltasar de Casanueva	6,082			83,000
Domingo de Castañiza		9,361		25,000
Francisco de Chavarrí	29,170		5,000	
Félix Clemente Garrido	11,619		2,100	
Mateo Julián Gómez de Leís	11,685			
Ignacio García Sáenz				30,272
Fernando Hermosa y Miranda	27,500			
Manuel José de Horcasitas	2,000			11,000
Francisco Antonio de Horcasitas	40,268		800	
Jorge Hourat	10,800			20,500
Antonio Ibáñez de Rivero	6,360			10,500
Isidro Antonio de Icaza				
(first marriage)	20,500	14,988	8,000	
(second marriage)	15,185		8,000	184,479
José María de Echave	3,244		6,000	78,170
Francisco Martínez Cabezón	27,000			
Martín Angel de Micháus y Aspiros	6,082		3,000	
Roque Pérez Gómez		46,950		
Angel Pedro de Puyade	180,244	170,465		
Francisco Antonio del Río	4,800		4,000	
Simón de Somoano Alonso	29,265			
Jaime Salvat	1,300			
Francisco de Soberón y Corral	20,799			
José Sánchez de Espinosa	64,400			

Sources: AN, Torija, May 25, 1782 and May 24, 1784; Burillo, Jan. 27, 1789, Dec. 9, 1793, March 15, 1798, Aug. 17, 1799, June 26, 1800, and Nov. 29, 1800; Pozo, Sept. 5, 1794, June 14, 1797, July 8, 1797, Nov. 15, 1797, June 9, 1798, May 28, 1799, June 20, 1800, Oct. 25, 1800, Nov. 4, 1801, Feb. 22, 1802, Jan. 13, 1805, Jan. 3, 1806, July 10, 1811, Feb. 4, 1813, and Feb. 17, 1815; AGN, Tierras, leg. 1288, exp. 4, March 21, 1797.

part of their maternal inheritance. The wife retained the right to initiate judicial proceedings against her husband for misuse or squandering of the dowry.

The sums listed in the table under "Inheritance" should not be seen as final figures. They usually designate amounts given while some of the wife's near relatives were still alive and thus in a position to add to her wealth.

The groom often swore that the amount he proffered as arras represented a tenth part of his wealth or, infrequently, a fifth part. Sometimes, as revealed in the two cases where we have figures for both arras and capital at the time of marriage, it actually represented a smaller percentage, though it still totalled a substantial amount of money. (It should be further stated that neither groom in these two cases misrepresented either the arras or his capital at the time of his betrothal.)

Absorption of Peninsulars into the Creole Elite

To aspiring peninsular merchants, marriage constituted a primary mechanism for the acquisition of landed estates, without which no family fortune could endure over generations, and for entrance into the dominant creole elite. Though these immigrant traders might give their names to the families into which they wed, in actuality, they, their skills, and their wealth were assimilated into the spouses' families to be used on the latter's behalf. In no sense did the new couple consider itself an autonomous family unit, but rather as just another branch, of greater or lesser importance, of the long-established and typically quite extended creole kin group. In other words, the immigrant groom was an outsider who, however desired, was still seeking acceptance into a powerful native-born elite with stringent rules for acceptance. He might become the titular head of the family, or at least its economic manager, but he was still adding his holdings to immense others already in existence and managing them as a unit for the greater benefit of his wife's family. He himself was normally the only one of his immediate blood relatives who was joining this already large and imposing creole family. By no means was he socially superior to it. Rather, by having proved his business aptitude and thereby building up a considerable fortune of his own, he had made himself a candidate for inclusion in the colonial elite. In no way was it preordained that he would do so. Out of the multitude of immigrant commercial apprentices, only a handful ever attained truly towering positions in the world of trade. These few, by having done so, were eligible for marriage into the highest ranks of society. All others lacked the slightest chance.

Because immigrant merchants had to demonstrate their abilities and social respectability beyond the shadow of a doubt before becoming serious candidates for marriage into the Mexican elite, many of them wed late in life to women far younger than themselves. It had already taken them a good part of their lives to make their fortunes and assemble some honors. No daughter of an elite family would consider them as suitable marriage partners until they had done so. Therefore, for these merchants to marry young meant to marry a woman of lower social position. In fact, a significant portion of these men never wed, no matter how wealthy they became. On the other hand, young men from prominent creole families benefited from already high social rank and proven wealth. They therefore did not suffer from the same handicap as did their peninsular counterparts and commonly married earlier. Young Spanish immigrants received no assumption of high social standing from the Mexican elite. While many of them lived out a very comfortable existence, neither they nor the creole elite considered them to be among those at the summit of Mexico City society. They lacked the blood lines, wealth, honors, personal connections, and marriage partners required to ascend to these social heights. Few among them would ever garner the necessary attributes. Table 29 records the known age differences between some successful peninsular merchants and their first wives.

Investment Patterns of International Merchants

In a very real sense it is misleading to divide the elite of Mexico City into landed families and merchant families, for both occupied points along the same continuum. Though a family might pursue a specialized economic endeavor—mining, commerce, government service, or the different types of agriculture and livestock raising—to ascend into the ranks of the elite, once there, it quickly began to diversify and invest in a variety of enterprises. Given the cyclical nature of the colonial economy and Mexico's dependence on foreign economic currents, it only made good sense to invest in different fields as a hedge against the reverses that could be ex-

Table 29.   Age Differences Between Some Peninsular Wholesale Merchants and Their Creole Wives

Name of Merchant	Age Difference
Manuel Fernández Sáenz de Santa María	30 (years)
Simón María de la Torre y Albornoz	22
José Manuel Hurtado	21
Fernando Hermosa y Miranda	20
Francisco de Soberón y Corral	19
Roque Valiente	19
Sebastián de Heras Soto	18
Roque Pérez Gómez	17
José Nicolás Abad	16
Manuel del Valle	14
Martín Angel de Micháus y Aspiros	12
Esteban Vélez de Escalante	9
Nicolás Noriega y Escandón	8
Manuel de Urquiaga	8
Pedro Marcos Gutiérrez	7
José Martínez Barenque	3

Source: AGN, Padrones, vols. 53 and 54, 1811.

pected periodically in any one of them. No case has been found where a mercantile family had not acquired enterprises outside of commerce by its second generation. In fact, it is difficult to find any merchant, first generation or second, who did not invest in mining and agriculture—and sometimes in both—as soon as he had the capital, borrowed if necessary, to do so. Typically then, a successful young merchant acquired one or more estates as soon as possible and continued to employ himself in both commerce and agriculture for the remainder of his career. Marriage was certainly a convenient way to accumulate estates, but the merchant might also purchase some on his own before betrothal.

None of the merchants studied declined the opportunity to acquire estates on any grounds; certainly none ever described estate ownership as economically unattractive. In fact, men of trade thought agriculture potentially so profitable that they were quite willing to lease haciendas, calculating that they could obtain a return sufficiently over the rental fee to earn a profit. This willingness to lease rural estates indicates that at least some agricultural enterprises yielded profits higher than the 5 percent guaranteed annual return that money lending offered. Finally, it must be remembered that given the general scarcity of specie, the lack of any trustworthy paper currency or redeemable bonds, and the character of international commerce at this time, in which the multiple contacts developed by individual traders were vital to success, real estate constituted the only form of wealth which could be reliably transferred across generations and also be conveniently subdivided among a number of heirs.

Whatever other enterprises they might invest in, merchants almost invariably acquired at least one substantial landed estate. That these men perceived estate ownership as profitable emerges repeatedly in the documentation. Francisco Antonio del Río stated in his will that he had invested the profits from his two cajones in the purchase of estates and had thereby increased his wealth from 51,000 pesos to over 100,000 in only five years.[11] Yet others manifested their confidence in the possibilities of agriculture by leasing haciendas from their owners. Francisco Ignacio de Iraeta leased one the very year he served as consul of the merchants' guild.[12]

Sugar haciendas were popular items for both ownership and rental among merchants. Angel Pedro de Puyade obtained most of his agricultural holdings from his marriage with Josefa de Mero, who left a fortune composed mainly of sugar and sheep-raising estates valued at some 400,000 pesos. Besides overseeing his wife's vast holdings and running his own commercial affairs, Puyade found the time to lease yet another sugar estate for a period of five years.[13] Gerónimo de Mendoza was another merchant who moved quickly to diversify his personal fortune. He owned different types of stores in both the capital and provincial centers, maintained a partnership in a mine, and rented a sugar hacienda which he chose to operate through a company. He paid 3,000 pesos rental annually for five years to the owner of this Cuernavaca estate (another merchant in Mexico City) and turned over its management to an administrator who was entitled to a third of any profits.[14]

Most estates owned by merchants were located either in the Valley of Mexico or in those immediately surrounding it. Several commercial families did have substantial possessions in the provinces of Valladolid and San Luis Potosí; none, however, were found with haciendas in the Bajío or in the great desert North. Most estates produced commodities intended for the lucrative Mexico City market. Those in the northern Valley of Mexico produced pulque, those in Chalco supplied wheat, others in the Valley of Cuernavaca turned out sugar, and yet others in Toluca, Valladolid, and San Luis Potosí raised cattle and sheep.

Investment Patterns of Retail Merchants

Estate ownership was not limited to the great wholesalers. Other more modest traders also engaged in agriculture, though estate ownership did not normally extend down to petty traders or proprietors of only one or two grocery stores. Overall, those retail traders who had one or more cajones or tiendas mestizas in the capital or perhaps in a provincial city had a good chance to acquire an estate in their lifetime.

Probably the most successful such individual in late colonial Mexico City was Joaquín de Aldana, already mentioned in Chapter 4. This native of San Juan Teotihuacán, while still a young man, had purchased two tiendas mestizas in the capital and at least one other located in his home town. He began his activities in the pulque trade when his wife, upon the death of her father, inherited pulquerías and pulque ranchos worth nearly 28,000 pesos. By 1784 he was contracting for the pulque produced on the ranchos of the Marqués de Valle Ameno.[15] In 1787 he entered into a contract with the Romero de Terreros family for the exclusive operation of their vast pulque interests. By the turn of the century, he had begun to diversify his economic activities even further. In 1800 he was in the process of selling one of his stores in Mexico City for 28,000 pesos. In 1801 he sold a wheat hacienda for over 35,000 pesos and a panadería in the capital for 22,000.[16] Aldana is last seen in 1805 with the title of *alcalde de barrio* of one of the cuarteles of the city, discussing the operation of one of his general merchandise stores in the provinces.[17]

Fewer merchants had the vast economic resources necessary to enter silver mining; nonetheless, what is striking is the number of traders who still attempted to involve themselves in it in one manner or another. The smaller traders, none too surprisingly, usually invested in smaller mines outside of the arenas of great silver strikes. Investment in the major mines of Pachuca, Zacatecas, Guanajuato, and the like was the preserve of the most successful wholesalers and wealthy established creole families.

By and large, it seems that merchants did not care to entail their holdings. Of those studied, only Sebastián de Heras Soto, well before obtaining his title, sought to establish a mayorazgo.[18] Few children of traders came into possession of an entail, though occasionally an eldest son would become heir to an ancient, and usually modest, mayorazgo back in Spain. Children typically divided their parents' estate equally among themselves, though some were favored with larger shares. No case was encountered in which one or more offspring were repudiated by their parents. Of course, this does not mean that each actually managed his or her share as a separate enterprise. In fact, the evidence indicates that many chose to turn over control to a single member of the family who would then oversee operations or perhaps arrange a rental to other parties. At this time, people commonly perceived themselves and their possessions as belonging to a broad kin group, and though each member might pursue a different career—estate manager, merchant, lawyer, priest, and so forth—they all endeavored to promote the common good of the family and its investments.

Elite Families and Commerce

At least by the time of the second generation, the family of a successful wholesaler owned and operated a diversified economic empire, consisting of a number of mercantile businesses abroad, in the provinces, and in the capital, estates located in different parts of the colony and producing different commodities, perhaps a mine or at least a share in one, and interests in manufacturing and processing enterprises. Typically, the family did not abandon commerce or even curtail it greatly upon the demise of the founder. A son, an immigrant nephew, or sometimes both would assume control of the family's commercial interests, while other members occupied themselves with other branches of investment.

Ideally, the individual family sought not only to diversify but also to integrate its investments so that the various branches were interconnected and mutually supportive. Estates produced goods that the family trading house marketed in the capital, and the stores in turn supplied needed equipment to the haciendas. Similarly, agricultural products were processed in firms owned by the family or under a long-term agreement with it. Family stores in the mining centers provided necessary items to mines in which the family had an interest and which supplied the silver coin so vital to the efficient operation of the central trading house. Thus the trading house remained vital to the maintenace and proper functioning of the fortunes of the second and third generations of such families as the González Guerra, González Calderón, Vértiz, González Noriega, Ibarrola, and Icaza.

Significantly, even the ennoblement of a family did not diminish its active participation in commerce. It could not, for extensive commercial operations were essential to the survival of the family fortune over the long haul, as essential perhaps as was the acquisition of estates.[19] For these families then, ownership of large estates and continued vigorous participation in commerce went hand in hand. Noble families such as the Apartado, Regla, Vivanco, Jala, Peñasco, Castañiza, Guardiola, and Cortina regularly maintained a member either in the Consulado or otherwise active in large-scale trade.

Investment in Small Noncommercial Business

As already seen, wholesalers were not reluctant to invest in any enterprise, however humble, in the world of commerce, if they thought it might render profits, and, in like fashion, they were willing to invest in modest enterprises in other fields of economic endeavor. When a trader obtained excess capital, he rarely held it inactive but rather inserted it into whatever enterprise seemed then the most promising. When, in 1800, José Ruiz de la Cortina, soon to be consul of the merchants' guild, found himself with a spare 24,000 pesos, he invested it in a company in the three hog slaughterhouses (tocinerías) of Antonio Somera for the period of five years for half of the profits.[20] The large bread bakeries of the capital were equally attractive investments to the large trader. Here though, they seemed more inclined to purchase the establishments outright than to invest in partnership.[21]

Business association with artisans held no stigma for even

the greatest of merchants. Martín Angel de Micháus y Aspiros amassed much of his early wealth through ownership of a large tannery which put out skins to leather-workers. Francisco de Iglesias was successful enough in trade to form his own commercial company with an agent in the Spanish port of Bilbao, to own a tienda mestiza, and to invest in mining. In addition, during this same period, he owned a paint factory, which he managed through a partner who received a third of its profits, and formed yet another company with a master carriage-maker of the capital, who took 2,000 pesos from him in return for a half-share of the profits.[22]

Merchants and Money-Lending

Finally, wholesale merchants constituted the largest group of non-institutional money-lenders in this society. We have already seen that they were periodically able to assemble great amounts of silver coin, and would, if they had no immediate use for it, lend it to fellow merchants for periods of several months up to a year. These loans could total anywhere from 20,000 to well over 100,000 pesos. But generally, merchants did not limit their money-lending to each other; rather, they were continually making loans to estate owners, miners, manufacturers, and other business people. The terms of their loans were similar to those made by ecclesiastical and charitable organizations. The repayment period usually ran anywhere between two and seven years (five years was very common) and was normally easily renewed, so long as the borrower continued to meet the 5 percent interest charges. It needs to be said that though no proof was found in the documentation, there is a distinct possibility that these loans were discounted, making a fiction of the constant 5 percent annual interest rate. Loans were secured by real property, bondsmen, or a combination of the two. Though naturally some merchants were more active in money-lending than others and all found it more attractive at some times than at others, there is no evidence that any of them abandoned commerce in favor of specialization in this banking service. One explanatory factor clearly is the abiding allure of commerce, which, despite periodic disruptions, continued to offer attractive profits. Another is that a person who chose to devote himself exclusively to banking would face two bleak alternatives: either to retain immobile a considerable amount of coin as security against a sudden downturn in the economy or to loan out all his funds and thereby expose himself to ruin if his borrowers could no longer make the interest payments.

Merchants and Urban Property

Neither the wholesale traders, nor most other entrepreneurs of the city, whether creole or peninsular, speculated in urban real estate or rented out buildings. In the 1813 survey of property ownership in the city, only one wholesaler, Esteban (Vélez de) Escalante, owned more than one or two buildings. He was in the business in a big way, with at least twenty-four structures (including an entire city block) which rendered a total annual rental of over 8,000 pesos. The relative stability of urban property values and the greater rewards possible in other fields of the economy combined to place most ownership of buildings, whether residential or commercial in nature, in the hands of charitable and religious institutions and well-entrenched, often entailed, creole families that were content with the 5 percent annual return on the investment.

Though the evidence is far from conclusive, there are some hints that the great traders and the smaller retailers of Mexico City had different attitudes towards home-ownership. Wholesalers were not quick to acquire or build the magnificent houses which still dot the capital. They characteristically erected these status symbols only after they had made their initial fortunes, diversified their investments, and created an enduring base for their wealth and social standing. Retailers, on the other hand, recognized that capital liquidity was not going to elevate their social rank in any appreciable way. They might be able to acquire another store or two in the capital or in nearby towns and perhaps invest in a company with an artisan or rent a small estate for a few years and thereby move into prominence among persons in the retail trade, but there was simply no way that they could assemble sufficient funds and establish the personal contacts vital for elevation to a higher level in the city's commercial hierarchy. More retailers than wholesalers, therefore, strove early in their careers to purchase a modest, but comfortable, residence. It offered them both a degree of security and higher stature among their peers, benefits that the same act would not have provided to an aspiring wholesaler.

Honors and Merchant Eligibility

Merchants actively pursued and often obtained offices and titles which conferred rank and honor on their holders. Table 30 offers an index of some of the honors gained and organizations joined by seventy prominent wholesalers of Mexico City in the period 1770–1826. These individuals were not preselected but constitute those about whom the most comprehensive data were found. If there is error in the table, it is a slight underassessment of honors received. All those cited have been confirmed; however, it is difficult to locate listings of all the recipients of some honors, so a few may have been omitted.

Wholesalers in great numbers joined the officer corps of both the regular army and the militia. Almost half of the seventy held officer's rank, and some were of great prominence. Joaquín de Colla was the colonel of the Urban Regiment of Merchants of Mexico City, and he and his sergeant major, Martín Angel de Micháus y Aspiros, though peninsulars, were detained by the conspirators (some of whom were their troops) for refusing to countenance the 1808 coup against Viceroy Iturrigaray.

While based in the capital, some of these traders also had sizable economic interests in the provinces through marriage and investments in mining and agriculture and were able therefore to become officers in provincial regiments of the army of New Spain. In 1799 Antonio de Pérez Gálvez served as a colonel in the Cavalry of the Prince stationed in the Bajío, while Lorenzo de Angulo Guardamino was lieutenant colonel of the Infantry of Tlaxcala.[23]

Still, many of the most successful merchants of the capital enrolled themselves as common footsoldiers in the capital's regiment of merchants, and though intermixed with owners of small retail shops, they neither complained nor attempted to ascend into the officer corps. An explanation may be that all soldiers of the regiment, not just its officers, were entitled to the military fuero. A list of the men and officers in each company of this regiment was compiled in 1807 because only 399 men were taking their regular shifts at providing security in the streets, although the regiment

Table 30. Ranks and Honors Received by Merchants, 1770–1826

Name	Military Officer	Consulado Officer	Noble	Noble Order	Familiar	Regidor Honorario	Alcalde Ordinario	Regidor Perpetuo
Juan José de Acha	X					X	X	
Tomás Domingo de Acha		X		X	X	X	X	
José Adalid						X		
Diego de Agreda	X	X	X	X		X	X	
Joaquín Alonso de Alles	X	X	X			X	X	
Pedro Alonso de Alles		X	X	X		X	X	
Francisco Alonso de Terán	X							
Antonio Alonso de Terán	X							
Lorenzo de Angulo Guardamino	X			X				
José Joaquín de Ariscorreta	X	X					X	
José Manuel Balbontín	X							
Antonio de Bassoco	X	X		X		X	X	
José María de Bassoco	X		X				X	
José Bernardo Baz	X		X			X		
Juan Alonso de Bulnes Villar	X					X		X
Juan Antonio de Cobián						X	X	
José Pasqual Cobián de los Rios						X		
Joaquín de Colla	X					X	X	
Francisco Cortina González	X	X		X		X	X	
Joaquín Cortina González	X	X		X		X		
José Mariano de la Cotera		X		X		X		
Francisco de Chavarrí		X	X			X		
Juan Díaz González		X					X	

	1	2	3	4	5	6	7	8	9
José María de Echave							X		
Diego Fernández de Peredo	X		X						
Manuel Fernández Sáenz de Santa María		X	X						
Lorenzo García González de Noriega	X		X		X	X			
Manuel García Herreros						X			
Ignacio García Sáenz	X				X	X			
Diego Gómez de Barreda	X				X				
José Gómez Campos							X		
Servando Gómez de la Cortina			X	X		X		X	
Vicente Gómez de la Cortina	X		X	X		X		X	X
Antonio González Alonso			X			X		X	
Juan Ignacio González Guerra	X		X					X	
Pedro González Noriega						X			
Juan Ignacio González Vértiz			X	X	X	X		X	
Gabriel Gutiérrez de Terán			X			X			
Francisco Javier de Heras					X			X	X
Manuel de Heras Soto									
Sebastián de Heras Soto	X		X	X	X			X	
Fernando de Hermosa y Miranda				X		X		X	
Manuel José de Horcasitas	X		X						
Tomás Ramón de Ibarrola						X			
Antonio de Icaza	X		X		X			X	
Isidro Antonio de Icaza						X		X	
Mariano Icaza	X					X			X
Francisco de Iglesias	X								
Francisco Ignacio de Iraeta	X		X		X	X		X	
Gabriel de Iturbe e Iraeta	X		X		X	X		X	
Francisco Maniau y Torquemada						X			
José Martínez Barenque	X				X				

(continued on next page)

Table 30. (continued)

Name	Military Officer	Consulado Officer	Noble	Noble Order	Familiar	Regidor Honorario	Alcalde Ordinario	Regidor Perpetuo
Francisco Martínez Cabezón		X						
Martín Angel de Micháus y Aspiros	X	X						
Manuel Noriega Cortina						X		
Bruno Pastor Morales	X							
Antonio de Pérez Gálvez	X	X	X	X				X
Roque Pérez Gómez	X	X	X					
Francisco Antonio de Rábago		X						
Juan Marcos de Rada	X	X						
Francisco del Rivero	X	X					X	
José Ruiz de la Barcena		X						
Francisco Sáenz de Escobosa	X					X		
José Sánchez de Espinosa							X	
José Miguel Sánchez Hidalgo						X		
Juan de Sierra Uruñuela					X			
Francisco de Soberón y Corral	X							
Simón María de la Torre y Albornoz				X				
Gabriel Joaquín de Yermo		X				X		
Gabriel Patricio de Yermo								X

Military Officer—Officer in either the regular military or the militia.
Consulado Officer—Prior or consul of the Mexico City Consulado between 1770–1826.
Noble—Ennobled, having gained a noble title either through merit, inheritance, or marriage.
Noble Order—Member of a noble order, either Santiago, Alcántara, Calatrava, Montesa, or Carlos III.
Familiar—Familiar of the Inquisition, involving having the purity of the family blood line certified.
Regidor Honorario—Regidor honorario of the Mexico City Ayuntamiento.
Alcalde Ordinario—One of the two judicial officials elected by the ayuntamiento of the city.

contained 929 soldiers, not counting officers, sergeants, corporals, and drummers.[24] While all officers were almaceneros, few sergeants or corporals were. In fact, for some reason, commercial agents (the corredores de comercio) were heavily overrepresented among the noncommissioned officers, even to the point of near exclusivity in some companies. With the exception of a few artisans, the ranks of the regiment were filled by the owners and managers of every type of commercial establishment and by more commercial agents.

The column of Table 30 showing which of the seventy merchants served as an officer of the Consulado is not comprehensive, since not all officers are included (see Appendix A). However, when compared with the other columns, it reveals that few who failed to receive this honor received many others. Rare is the officer of the Consulado who did not also obtain honorary posts or membership in a noble order. Almost as rare was the merchant not a Consulado officer who was graced with more than one honor. Most of the exceptions consist of relatives of noble families who were thereby more likely to gain honors in this society.

Some of the most successful merchants applied for and received ennoblement from the crown. Two points need to be stressed in this regard. First is that many of the most wealthy and prestigious merchant families, the González Guerra, Icaza, Alonso de Terán, and González Calderón among them, did not pursue noble status. Second, those who gained titles by no means constitute all of the most wealthy mercantile families, though they were certainly among them. Ennoblement was just one, not the sole, expression of elevated social status; other families sought honorary posts in the government or high rank in the church, the legal profession, and other organizations.

Some merchants belonged to the long-honored noble orders of Santiago, Alcántara, and Calatrava. Few of them attained membership solely on their own merits; most did so through blood or marital ties with families of recognized quality. Men of commerce were most successful in obtaining entrance into the recently formed Order of Carlos III (ten of the fourteen in noble orders). It sometimes happened that two members of a family belonged to separate orders.

To be designated a familiar of the Inquisition made the individual an official of that organization, though with no actual function or effective power. What was most prized about this title was its commentary on the purity of blood and the virtuousness of the recipient's family. An honor not often bestowed in the colony, the "familiar" designation was rarely bestowed on merchants. Those men of trade who were so cited referred to their distinction at every opportunity.

In the late eighteenth century, the ayuntamiento or city council of Mexico City, along with others in the colony, was reorganized to allow for the entrance of honorary regidores (municipal councilmen), usually six in number, selected by the proprietary members on a rotating basis. Only members of the city's elite were eligible. Therefore, it is not surprising that some wholesale merchants were represented along with members of titled and other landed creole families, plus a smattering of prestigious lawyers. Several from a single extended family would commonly serve over the course of time, though only one at a time.

A new procedure for the selection of the two principal municipal judges (alcaldes ordinarios) accompanied the creation of the honorary councilmen in the mid 1770s. Now a single new judge was elected each year, often from the ranks of the regular and honorary regidores for a two-year term. He would serve the first year as the junior alcalde and automatically ascend to the senior position the following year. Many merchants who became honorary councilmen also became alcaldes, and they were joined in this position by a goodly number of other almaceneros who had not been selected as regidores.

Here as elsewhere in Spanish America, it was harder to become a councilman than an alcalde, and few merchants entered the regular ayuntamiento. That institution remained firmly in the hands of the established creole elite. In fact, most merchants who achieved entrance, whether immigrant or native born, did so during the repeated political shifts which marked the Wars of Independence and the brief imperial regime that followed them. In this period, it was common for an entire city council to be thrown out of office one year to be replaced by another which represented the faction then in control of Mexico or Spain. The next year that council itself might be dissolved and replaced by yet another or even by the one which had earlier been removed from office. Overall, though the scanty numbers make any generalization hazardous, creole merchants more often reached office during liberal regimes and in the post-Independence period, while peninsulars did so after the original council was removed in favor of one believed to be more loyal to Fernando VII.

In general, few merchants below the level of almacenero received any significant honors, but likewise, some of the wealthiest wholesalers never gained such distinctions. For example, José Gómez Campos, Manuel José de Horcasitas, Francisco de Iglesias, and Francisco Martínez Cabezón were all successful in commerce, mining, and agriculture. Though some were members of prominent old families and others were patriarchs of newly emerging ones, none of them accumulated the honors that did other almaceneros who were perhaps even a bit less wealthy than they. It may be that they had some special reason for not soliciting honors or that there were some flaws in their eligibility which do not emerge in the documentation. But given the fact that membership in each of the eight categories (except military rank) was open to at best several persons each year and given the size of the competing body of merchants plus the number of eligible individuals in other professions, it seems possible that there were simply too few traditional honorary positions available to bestow on the many well-to-do wholesalers who emerged in the prosperous climate of late colonial Mexico.

While merchants did not receive honorary appointments to government offices as did prominent members of some other professions and families, some of the most powerful among them were lauded through designation as an honorary commissary of the army.[25] It is not certain if this appellation recognized their role in supplying the military or was given out for other reasons. Antonio de Bassoco did receive appointment as honorary accountant of the military, while Angel Pedro de Puyade, already cited for his marriage to a wealthy creole family, was the sole merchant named an honorary intendant.

Charitable Organizations

Cofradías were popular with every sector of society, and merchants were no exception. Some belonged to sodalities which restricted membership to men of commerce, and some joined others which were less restrictive. Most commonly, they affiliated with one whose patron saint or sacred place was identified with their home province in Spain. It was seen previously that these cofradías regularly functioned as lending institutions, most often to their own constituents and countrymen.

Perhaps because of their business reputations, merchants, following a long-established practice, served often as mayordomos of charitable and religious institutions. As such, they were in charge of most economic matters, deciding on rental or sale of property and goods belonging to the organization and exercising considerable influence in loan-granting decisions. Some of these posts were retained in the same family over generations, with a son or nephew taking over at the demise of his predecessor. In some cases mayordomos were blamed for turning corporate funds to personal benefit. Certain of those accused readily admitted the fact in their wills and instructed executors to settle the matter.

The Second Generation

Children of the most successful wholesalers, as members of the Mexico City elite, understandably contracted marriages and entered professions which would stabilize or enhance rather than endanger their status. There is no evidence that any of them ever married someone not considered Spanish by the society. The sold possible exception occurred when Manuel José de Horcasitas, the peninsular nephew and heir of Francisco Antonio de Horcasitas, married the creole heiress of the mayorazgo of the Moctezuma family.[26] But of course the Aztec emperor's family had been absorbed into the Spanish elite already in the sixteenth century.

We have previously established the frequency with which one or more sons of a merchant would pursue their father's profession, perhaps joined by peninsular cousins. This pattern persisted at every level of trade. Owners of individual stores also trained their sons to take over their businesses.[27]

By no means was the earlier-studied Sánchez Hidalgo family unique when it arranged attractive careers or marriages for all of its children. The four offspring of Francisco José González Calderón further reveal the diverse opportunities open to children of the mercantile elite. The eldest son Tomás was trained as a lawyer, soon became part of the government bureaucracy, and rose to become an oidor first in Peru and then back in his hometown of Mexico City, where he ultimately became dean of the Audiencia. His brother Miguel took over the economic leadership of the family and, while still a young man, established himself as a wholesale merchant and member of the Consulado. Yet another brother, José, opted for an ecclesiastical career and became a prebend of the metropolitan cathedral. The sole sister, Bárbara, married José de Cevallos, an immigrant merchant who himself advanced into the merchants' guild.[28] Both Tomás and Miguel became knights of the Order of Carlos III.

Sons of merchants were well represented in the ranks of lawyers and priests. Many others took over all or part of the family's agrarian interests. Ignacio Adalid, son of José and husband of a daughter of the Conde de San Bartolomé de Jala, reorganized his family's financial affairs after his father died in debt litigation (brought about in part by the bankruptcy of his immigrant cousin Francisco Antonio) and operated his pulque estates and outlets at considerable profit.[29]

Merchants' sons did not normally marry their relatives. There was no compelling reason to do so; sons were already as far inside the family as they could be (thus the binding which was the goal behind so many high-level marriages was unnecessary). Furthermore, consolidation with women on the immigrant side of the family was usually out of the question because there were none on the local scene and that side of the family had less accumulated wealth in any case. However, the situation was totally different for merchants' daughters, who often married immigrant relatives or other men brought into the family businesses. Though these spouses might technically be relatives, they remained outside of the web of trusted creole relatives until their betrothals. Their marriage into the family not only fostered closer integration of inherited family properties but also allied these individuals more firmly to the family by increasing their stake in its overall well-being. In a very real sense, the marriage between an immigrant nephew and a daughter of a merchant was a statement by the groom that he thereby pledged himself to the greater benefit of the extended creole family, while at the same time, the bride's family was stating that he had proved his ability and worthiness and could now be trusted to play a prominent role in the family's economic affairs.

The result of this practice was that some families could become quite inbred. Diego de Agreda first married his cousin, the daughter of his benefactor Francisco Martínez Cabezón. After her death, he married yet another relative, this time a woman from his hometown back in La Rioja.[30] Occasionally, more than one daughter of a wholesaler would marry aspiring merchants, with the result that a pair of men would take over their father-in-law's business and enter the Consulado. In like fashion, a daughter widowed by one merchant-husband might turn around and quickly marry yet another man of trade who was on his way up.[31] Certainly, there was no shortage of aspiring traders willing to use such a marriage to obtain control over a deceased wholesaler's estate.

Perhaps Antonio Velasco de la Torre y Mora, a creole merchant, achieved the perfect integration of interests and careers through the marriages of his son and three daughters. His son Antonio, also a merchant, wed the daughter of an established landed family which owned a seat in the Mexico City ayuntamiento. One daughter married a lawyer who joined the legal staff of the Audiencia of New Spain; another wed a merchant of the capital, and the third exchanged vows with a merchant, but this time one of the important provincial center of Guadalajara.[32]

Few merchants' daughters became nuns; the number was almost negligible. The vast majority married and carried with them significant dowries. And of course, since so many of them wed men who were then attached to the family's economic interests, the dowries often did not pass out of the family's effective control.

Immigrants

Spanish immigrants came to Mexico in great numbers, but few were preordained to take over the businesses of their sponsors. Initially, they had little status in urban Spanish society and competed with each other to see who would graduate from the ranks of employees to those of proprietors. Many never did. These would often never marry or obtain valuable possessions, and would remain dependents of their families or employers in Mexico. Significantly, almost all who came, whether they succeeded in business or not, were true immigrants; that is, they never returned to Spain. In this, they were like most colonial officials from Spain.

These immigrants were not attractive mates for the creole elite until they had proved themselves in the world of business. Characteristically, then, they married well past their youth and to women a good deal younger than themselves. Even at this point though, the immigrants did not take over their families, but were rather absorbed into them. Previously they had been outsiders, in the sense that they lacked the web of friends and relations enjoyed by other members of their new extended families. Their relatives were typically prestigious, prosperous, and ambitious in their own right. They were also often themselves intermarried with other elite families. These newlywed immigrants might not even be the only merchants in the family, since so many creole sons also followed that profession, and other daughters might have wed men of commerce. Most certainly, the wealth and abilities of these immigrant traders were desired and often needed by the families who received them, but the tracing of family histories over several generations manifests a consistent pattern in which the same extended families with the same or similar properties and business interests assimilated into themselves immigrant relatives without great modification of their internal composition or economic orientation.

PART THREE
Manufacturing

Whether in processing plants or in artisan shops, a great many citizens of Mexico City made their living from the refining and elaboration of raw materials into finished goods. Scholars have often ignored this aspect of the city's business life, which provided employment for a large number of people of every social level and ethnic group. The following section will deal with the magnitude and scope of manufacturing and artisan activity in late colonial Mexico City and outline the broad social and economic behavior patterns of the participants in this branch of the economy.

8 Manufacturers

Historically well-known as a commercial-bureaucratic center, Mexico City was also the site of significant manufacturing, enough to employ large numbers of individuals and to render considerable profit to many plant owners. Most industry consisted of processing of raw materials such as grain, meat, wool, and cotton into products of utility to the urban population. Few if any of these goods were exported, and, seemingly, few were even shipped outside of the Valley of Mexico. The market for these products, as for so many others in the country at this time, was Mexico City itself.

Panaderos

SIZE AND STRUCTURE OF BAKERIES. Wheat bread, rather than maize tortillas, was the staple of life for much of the population of the city. It was produced in large bakeries scattered throughout the city; demand was sufficiently great to support fifty-eight such businesses in 1793. These were owned by forty-eight separate individuals, including three women. One person owned four panaderías, two others owned three apiece, and three others each owned two.[1] To maintain price stability and to prevent the industry from falling into the hands of a few persons, the municipal government regulated both the price of bread and the number of retail stores with which a panadería could deal. The bakeries were spread quite uniformly throughout the neighborhoods of the city, and each supplied perhaps five pulperías in a certain area which

187

were chosen by officials. The sale of bread to other stores was forbidden.

An exact description of one of these facilities is provided in an architect's report prepared for a 1790 court case.[2] The two-story building was composed of a main wing measuring 55 by 21¼ varas, attached to an annex of 19 by 13⅔ varas by a connection 6⅓ by 7¼ varas in size, which together constituted a total area of 1,529 square varas. The entry to the building was through a store, with an entryway leading to a stable and a coachhouse containing a well. The structure contained two patios, the large one with a fountain, and three corridors passing through the work area. There was a small salt storeroom and a large granary with a wooden floor. The main patio also contained a large vat with attachments which supplied the hot water needed in baking. There was, quite naturally, a capacious oven room with a woodshed nearby and even a special room where the dough could rise. The rest of the main floor was made up of the barracks-like living quarters of the workers. The second story, reached by a stairwell, consisted of the living quarters of the owner, including a reception room, three bedrooms, and an elaborate kitchen, as well as living space for the administrator of the business and the domestic servants. The entire structure was composed of stone and mortar, with cedar frames around the doorways and windows. The architect placed the value of the entire facility at 16,250 pesos.

This stated value was quite representative of panaderías in general, though considerable range did exist. Table 31 lists the price of bakeries which were sold or inventoried. The large investment required for the building and the necessary equipment is obvious. However, the one exception (726 pesos) bespeaks the existence of some very small operations, whose presence is confirmed by other documentation.

THE WORK FORCE. A review of the 1753 census of the city (which provides accurate data for three-sevenths of the central city) allows greater insight into the organization of these businesses. Twenty-seven panadería-owners were named; of these, fifteen lived on the premises of their bakeries along with the workers. Three of the owners were women. These fifteen panaderías employed 169 laborers (operarios), an average of just over eleven

Table 31.   Listed Values of Panaderías at Sale or Inventory

Year	Value
1790	16,250 (pesos)
1791	3,500
1791	20,025
1792	726
1798	6,000
1800	17,961
1805	19,000
1809	26,860
1811	9,786

Sources: AN, Pozo, May 16, 1791 and Oct. 1, 1791; Burillo, Oct. 20, 1792 and Jan. 16, 1798; Barrientos, Aug. 8, 1805 and March 9, 1809; AGN, Tierras, leg. 1207, exp. 2, Oct. 30, 1790; DM, June 30, 1811; GM, April 2, 1800.

per bakery. There was, however, great variation in the size of the crews. The largest panadería employed twenty-two workers, another eighteen, most between ten and fifteen, and several less than ten. One listed only three workers and another only one. The vast majority of the laborers were Indians, with a few mestizos and mulattoes. Approximately half were married and lived in the building with their families. In a large facility, the number of children could approximate that of workers.

Extrapolating these figures for the fifty-three panaderías reported in 1793, if the same ratios hold, these bakeries employed nearly six hundred persons, whose wives and dependents would have roughly doubled that figure. Thus, perhaps a thousand or so members of the Indian population of the city worked and lived in these bakeries.

An 1805 order issued by Viceroy Iturrigaray gives us even more information about the lives of these bakery employees. He ordered panaderías to eliminate all enclosure of employees deriving from debts owed to the proprietor. In the future, owners were forbidden to make loans to their workers, either in cash or in goods, under penalty of losing the amounts advanced. However, all current debts were to be repaid over the next three months by garnisheeing one-half of the daily salary of the affected workers. Any debts remaining at the end of that time were to be paid off from a third share of the daily salaries. No longer were workers to be locked in the buildings. All workers were to be paid on a daily basis, and no deductions could be made for fiesta costs or other expenses. All oficiales or journeymen were to be paid 2 reales per ovenload of bread, and the salary of bakers (horneros) was to go up by half a real per ovenload. No women were to be allowed to enter. Although bread-making did not commence until 12:00 noon, all workers were to be present by 8:00 in the morning. Youths of every color and caste were to be eligible for apprenticeship in baking, though no more than two apprentices could work in any one bakery. No prisoners were to be assigned to panaderías, and no worker could leave his employment without giving notice to the alcalde of his barrio or to the governor of the Indians.[3] Not all workers, however, were restricted to their bakeries. The 1753 census reveals a scattering of Indian and mestizo workers who lived separately with their families.

As in virtually every other enterprise in which the owner himself did not have to perform technical work, there was a separation between ownership and management of panaderías (even though, as we have seen, the owner often lived in the building). Every bakery studied employed a mayordomo who was eligible, if competent, for advancement to a managing partnership with the proprietor. Of the thirty-two panadería mayordomos in the 1753 census, only eight lived with their employers, the remainder residing either alone or with their families. Every mayordomo was of Spanish ethnicity, and a goodly number of these were born in Spain itself. Many immigrants found themselves entering this or similar forms of employment, which taken together can be seen as composing a single level. All such occupations had the quality of giving the person employed responsibility over workers, servants, or business correspondence as the agent of the proprietor. Mariano Borunda, for instance, in a single advertisement sought a position as a copyist, a concierge, or as a mayordomo of a panadería, stating that he had experience in all three fields.[4]

THE PROPRIETORS. The owners of bakeries were also exclusively Spanish by ethnic grouping, and again peninsulars were notable among them, though not in the same numbers as among mayordomos. Some panaderías, it is true, were owned by convents, which regularly rented them out. But the renters tended to be the same types as actual owners. By and large, panadería owners had no outside economic interests; surprisingly, no proprietor had any rural estates to supply his bakery. There is evidence that some panaderías stayed within a family for generations, since a few families in the business in the 1753 census were still involved at the end of the century. Overall, however, as will be argued below, these bakeries did not provide solid foundations on which to erect enduring family fortunes; some were chronically plagued by debt and the need to negotiate new loans to pay off old ones which had come due.

Most large merchants and important professionals avoided ownership of or even investment in these businesses. Most panaderías seem to have been acquired by individuals who had built up a little capital from small-scale commerce or other means or had been able to obtain a loan from an ecclesiastical institution. This initial capital notwithstanding, most purchasers were forced to pay for their new businesses in installments. Thus, the new owner might well find himself initially in debt to two separate parties: the seller and the institution that loaned him the down payment.

While some persons entered the business in order to abandon retail commerce, yet others continued their involvement in retailing after acquisition of a panadería. Notable in this latter category was Joaquín de Aldana, whose career in the retail and pulque trades has already been outlined. He, like so many other bakery owners, turned to a company agreement to manage his business. His manager, Ignacio de Paz y Pérez, a native of the capital, in 1807 listed his worth at 35,000 pesos, and by his own statement all of it, except for 1,400 pesos inherited from his father and 4,000 pesos left him by his partner's late wife, derived from his company with Aldana.[5]

This is just one example of the many company arrangements that typified the bakery business. Though they had many different origins and derivations, almost all of them involved one party investing all or the bulk of the capital and the other managing the enterprise, usually with an equal division of the profits. Pedro José de Berazueta and Miguel de Aristegui together acquired a panadería for 3,500 pesos and formed a company in it for the term of five years. However, Berazueta ultimately put up 10,000 of the total 12,300-peso investment, and Aristegui agreed to manage the business, with the help of a mayordomo he would select, for half of any profits.[6] Antonio Maque and Alvaro del Casal also formed a company in a panadería immediately upon acquiring it. In an agreement of the greatest simplicity, they stipulated that during the company's nine-year term Maque would supply all the capital and Casal would serve as the administrator, with an equal division of all profits.[7] Some companies existed informally for extended periods before they were set forth in formal contracts.[8]

THE TERMS OF TRADE.   The bakery business demanded periodic influxes of capital to pay for needed grain. Owners used a variety of means to acquire their principal raw material; often they had to borrow money for the purpose. They could not always count on having sufficient capital on hand from the sale of their product to the pulperías of the city, since, although they delivered the bread daily to these stores, it appears that they were paid only periodically. Antonio María Jiménez, the administrator of a panadería, reported that he delivered bread daily to the tienda mestiza of the widow Gertrudis Soriano in Xochimilco and that she paid him monthly.[9] Jiménez, however, made this statement before the Consulado in a suit against the woman for nonpayment. In a case before the civil court of the Audiencia, Juan José del Castillo, the owner of a panadería, sued the estate of the deceased Tomás Moreu for the sum of 161 pesos owed him: 100 pesos he had loaned him for the development of his store in the barrio of Necatitlán and 61 from the purchase of bread.[10]

We have already seen in Chapter 5 that the small general stores were themselves reliant on credit sales, often having to accept pawned items in payment. Thus the dependence on credit transactions worked its way out from the sphere of retail trade into that of actual production. Whenever a demand for immediate payment occurred in any point in the economy, it sent immediate reverberations all along the credit chain, sometimes driving the effected business and any number of affiliated ones into a crisis situation or even bankruptcy.

Lacking the ready capital to pay cash for grain and other needed supplies, the bakery-owner might solicit a loan from an individual or an institution; in some cases, the lenders translated the act into a company arrangement. Needing 5,000 pesos, José María Vázquez in 1797 agreed to a company for the next five years with Pedro Caso, a merchant of the city. Vázquez would continue to administer his panadería and could extract enough money to see to the daily needs of himself and his family, but ultimately all profits were to be divided in half.[11] Pedro Pablo de San Julián turned to the almacenero Leonardo María Calo when he needed 5,000 pesos in 1789. He retained total control over his business, but entered into a two-year contract that gave Calo a half-share of all profits.[12]

Some bakery owners remained in financial straits for extended periods and depended on the good will of other individuals to keep out of bankruptcy proceedings. In 1804 José Lucas Pérez Hernández formed a company in his panadería for the period of eight years. His partner invested 12,000 pesos for a half-share of the profits.[13] Ten years later, when he dissolved a company he had maintained for only a year with yet another person, he stated that it was through kindness that his former partner was letting him retain the building and equipment, valued at 5,000 pesos, as a loan for four years at the standard 5 percent rate of interest; Pérez Hernández, however, was required to put up some jewels as collateral.[15]

More commonly, however, loans were not translated into company agreements, but simply remained as debts of the bakery. Thus a business with a substantial list value could have many outstanding liens against it. When Juan de Arredondo acquired a bakery for 20,025 pesos at a bankruptcy auction, he also had to assume the 16,000 pesos of liens against it. He did so by recognizing them as a loan at 5 percent for the term of five years, the customary procedure when a property with debts was transferred.[16] In 1805 Francisco Orduña bought a panadería for 19,000 pesos; four years later, the business had a list value of 26,860 pesos, but Orduña found it necessary to borrow 8,000 pesos for nine years from the Franciscans to redeem the 7,000 pesos of urgent debts his business had generated.[17]

José de Arechaga was one of those who found himself without the funds to buy needed wheat; he therefore borrowed 6,000 pesos for one year from a private individual, putting up the panadería itself as collateral.[18] Some owners had to keep taking out new loans to refinance old ones. Mariana García de la Carrera, a widow, had run a panadería by herself for fourteen years when in 1787 she found it necessary to borrow 2,000 pesos for three years from Bárbara Cortés, a spinster, pledging two houses in the city as collateral. Within a year, in order to pay the 2,000 pesos debt earlier contracted, she borrowed 4,150 pesos for five years from Doctor Andrés Ambrosio de Llanos y Váldez, again putting up the two buildings as collateral and adding a guarantee by her son. Less than three years later, she had to put up all of her worldly goods to secure a 4,000-peso loan for five years from Juan Manuel Echeveste.[19]

Of course, contracting loans did not always signify a weak economic condition; it might instead mean business expansion. The brothers Félix and Gerónimo Prieto reported that they had often managed panaderías for their owners, but because they had always had to divide the profits with them, they had never been able to gain the maximum from their work. Finally, in 1791, they arranged to borrow 12,000 pesos for three years from Josefa de Sandoval y Rojas, who herself had been the owner of a panadería, and use this money to establish themselves independently for the first time.[20]

OBTAINING GRAIN. The major concern of bakery-owners was obtaining a steady supply of grain, and to this end they used a variety of tactics. Some evidence indicates the existence of wheat merchants, who acted as middlemen between the growers and the bakers. Several individuals who identified themselves as merchants were found with no other mercantile activity than the sale of wheat. As with so many other transactions, grain purchases were normally made on credit and paid off in installments. The merchant Manuel de Menoyo declared that he was owed 956 pesos by Domingo de la Cotera and that the debt derived from the sale of 237 cargas of wheat at 6 pesos per carga. De la Cotera agreed to pay off the amount with 60 pesos twice a year over the next eight years.[21]

Some owners had standing agreements with certain mills located near the capital. José Manuel Barreda, for instance, regularly received flour on credit from the mill owned by the silver merchant and agriculturalist Juan José de Oteiza. By Barreda's own statement, bad economic conditions had left him still owing 970 pesos. However, there was no long-term difficulty, for Barreda himself had 5,600 pesos loaned out to three different parties and would be able to pay off the debt once he himself was paid back.[22]

Others purchased grain directly from estate owners. In 1805 José María de Benavente made two such transactions within four months of each other. He first contracted to buy 700 to 800 cargas of wheat from the regidor Joaquín Romero de Caamaño at the price of 9 pesos 4 reales per carga, paying 2,000 pesos immediately, another 2,000 pesos in a month, and the remainder after two months. In the other agreement, he bought 1,000 cargas from three estates in Toluca owned by Francisco Emeterio Elorreaga of Mexico City; the seller was to deliver 200 cargas each month between August and December to three mills located near the capital, at the price of 8 pesos 2½ reales per carga. Benavente had already paid 4,000 pesos and would pay the remaining amount upon delivery of the final shipment.[23]

Finally, some bakery owners made loans directly to estate owners with the express stipulation that repayment was to be made in the form of grain delivered to their premises.[24] Pedro La Farga loaned 2,000 pesos to Manuel Enderica for the cultivation of 38 cargas of wheat already sown on his hacienda, the loan to be repaid at the time of the harvest.[25]

THE SOCIAL POSITION OF PANADEROS. Panadería owners were never able to contract a marriage that would elevate their status measurably; like others at their level, they were usually unable even to command a dowry. Few if any were able to make the leap into commerce, certainly not on any significant scale. They were devoid of honors from the municipal and colonial governments and from the church. Few of their children achieved any notable upward mobility; rather, they moved into retail commerce or the more prestigious artisan crafts. Some few sons did become clerics, but did not ascend to high office.

Bakery owners, along with the other manufacturers of the city, did imitate the merchants in one respect: their fascination with the military. But indicative of their relative stations in society, while many merchants gained officer rank, few proprietors of panaderías rose above the rank of sergeant or álferez (ensign) in the militia squadrons of the capital.

Tocineros

THE SCOPE OF MEAT PRODUCTION.   In the late colonial period, Mexico City, having a large, heavily-hispanized population with regular access to money, consumed great quantities of meat of every variety. Humboldt reported that in 1791 alone the capital went through 16,300 cattle, 278,300 sheep, 50,600 hogs, 24,000 kids and rabbits, 1,255,000 chickens, and 125,000 turkeys.[26] The city council presided over an annual auction in which private citizens bid for the right to supervise the slaughter and wholesale of beef and mutton for the entire city (the abasto). The person designated became merely the overall administrator of a rather decentralized system of meat distribution and was entitled to a fee from every wholesale meat transaction in the city. He was by no means responsible for supplying all the livestock from his own herds, nor did he gain an effective monopoly over the city for that year.[27] Some of the actual slaughterhouses were owned by convents and other ecclesiastical and charitable institutions, which derived an income from renting them out to private parties.

Neither the supply nor the marketing of beef or mutton will be discussed here. As both were provisioned through municipal contracts, documentation concerning their sale and distribution was not abundant in the notarial and court archives examined.

PARALLELS BETWEEN MEAT AND BREAD PRODUCTION.   Hog slaughterhouses were part of this business, and a number of these plants were scattered across the city, some quite close to the central business district. An examination of their ownership and operation reveals that their value was roughly similar to that of panaderías, that they were managed in similar fashion, and that they were owned by persons from similar social backgrounds. The parallels between the two industries were numerous.

The great majority of workers were poorly paid Indians. There is, however, no indication that they were bound to the plants in the same way as bakery employees. Ethnically, the owners were all Spanish; again, there was a healthy sprinkling of peninsulars among them. Newly purchased tocinerías were often paid for in installments, or the sale price was recognized as a loan to be repaid with interest after a set number of years. There was again separation between ownership and management, slaughterhouses being normally run by administrators who were often peninsular by birth. They were often operated by partnerships, many of which derived from the owners' chronic need for capital with which to purchase necessary livestock. Bankruptcy was an unfortunate reality for far too many of them.

THE PROPRIETORS. The owners were usually men who had obtained their businesses with limited savings or with loans from ecclesiastical institutions. Several government officials and prominent clerics owned tocinerías at one time or another, but they never constituted even a significant fraction of proprietors and were rarely active in the operation of their properties. Most owners moved into the business from retail commerce and might well retain some affiliation with it. None of those studied ever owned or rented a rural estate of any kind and were therefore unable to supply themselves with livestock. Bartolomé González y Obin, a native of Asturias, initially owned a retail store in the capital, valued at around 4,500 pesos. When he married, he gave arras of 500 pesos but received no dowry. Eventually, however, he divested himself of the store and purchased a tocinería at public auction. When he made out his will in 1782, the slaughterhouse was his only business; he even lived in the building. Apparently a good businessman, he declared himself free of debt.[28] His widow, María Magdalena Orihuela, was not able to give her daughter a dowry when she married, but did turn over management of the tocinería to her son-in-law.[29] When she died in 1800, the business was valued at 16,850 pesos.[30]

Some proprietors involved themselves in other undertakings, though always on a small scale. Manuel de Caso repeatedly went into companies with his brother and a cousin to engage in the sale of mules.[31] Pedro José Enríquez rented a mill in Tacuba for seven years for 2,000 pesos (apparently the total rather than the yearly rental) to be paid monthly, with a guarantee from the Conde de Santiago, who agreed to complete the terms of the contract if Enríquez died while it was in effect.[32] Strangely, some tocinerías were owned jointly with contiguous roominghouses (perhaps the residences of the employees), and the establishments were normally sold as a unit.[33] As with bakeries, many owners lived on the site of their businesses.

THE CHRONIC DEBT STRUCTURE.   As shown in Table 32, tocinerías themselves could be worth a great deal of money, but large sums were still needed periodically to acquire livestock. The slaughterhouse owners themselves had to sell their products on credit to retailers who were unable to assure them a reliable cash flow. They were therefore usually on the lookout for extra capital, either as loans or as investment from financiers who wished to become partners. As a result, many tocinerías suffered from liens which could total most of their listed value and even force their owners into bankruptcy.

In 1800 Antonio Somera decided on a major refinancing of the three tocinerías he owned in the city and agreed to a five-year company with the prosperous merchant José Ruiz de la Barcena. Somera retained management of his plants and invested their value, nearly 6,000 pesos in cash, plus 9,000 pesos in goods. Ruiz de la Barcena, for his part, put in 24,000 pesos cash. Somera was permitted to pay for his own and his family's subsistence from the company's general fund, but he could not act as a bondsman or enter into any business outside the company. All profits were to be divided equally and paid in cash.[34]

In several instances, slaughterhouse owners handed over their businesses to administrators only when the latter themselves agreed to make a direct investment. In 1796 Juan José de Ojeda was renting a tocinería, valued at 4,800 pesos, for 400 pesos a year. Declaring that he could no longer manage the business by himself, he accepted Bruno Desa as his partner and administrator, but only if Desa invested the money needed to raise the capitalization to 5,000 pesos. This done, Desa was entitled to one third of the profits plus 25 pesos a month for the maintenance of himself and his mayordomo. The company would last as long as the two partners so desired.[35]

In 1811 Manuel Fernández de Peredo owned a tocinería valued at 19,649 pesos, of which 14,000 pesos was his own money. He formed a company with Francisco Sánchez, making him the managing partner provided he also invested 7,000 pesos. Fernández de

Table 32.   Listed Values of Tocinerías at Sale or Inventory

Year	Value
1796	5,000 (pesos)
1800	16,850
1801	15,000
1802	4,500
1804	13,150[a]
1806	7,300
1808	13,520[a]
1809	42,782
1809	60,930[b]
1809	21,650
1811	19,649

[a] Including a casa de vecindad.
[b] 40,930 pesos for the structure, 20,000 pesos for the goods.
Sources: AN, Burillo, May 10, 1796, Oct. 9, 1801, March 20, 1802, Feb. 18, 1804; Tomás Hidalgo de los Reyes, Nov. 11, 1811; GM, Feb. 8, 1800, Jan. 11, 1809, and Aug. 8, 1809; DM, June 19, 1806 and Nov. 20, 1808.

Peredo was owner of the building containing the business and demanded an annual rental of 1,500 pesos from the company's general fund. Sánchez and his family were allowed to live in the building at no expense. The agreement was for five years and stipulated an equal division of the profits, with Sánchez receiving payment in cash. The contract also stated that Sánchez had first option if his partner decided to sell.[36]

Sons were not at all reluctant to follow in their fathers' footsteps, even in a business as risky as this. In 1795 Antonio de Orihuela reported that his son, also named Antonio, had worked for him for years without pay and had showed himself to be intelligent in the business. The father agreed to loan 3,000 pesos to the son, who thereupon set up his own slaughterhouse in a building belonging to his father in Chalco. Indeed a good businessman, he soon made enough profit to pay back his father in full.[37]

Marriage never raised a slaughterhouse owner to the social heights, nor did any owner ever construct an economic empire based on his business. Tocineros never received any major honors from the society, and their children did not enjoy remarkable social mobility. Finally, like bakery owners, they too were quick to enter the military, but only rose to the middle ranks.

Obrajeros

SECURING LABOR: THE ENCLOSURE QUESTION.   Though not famed as a center of textile production like the cities of Puebla and Querétaro in the late colonial period, Mexico City nonetheless contained a number of obrajes. A partial listing of obraje owners for the capital in 1798 included thirteen names.[38] The plants themselves do not seem to have been very valuable. In 1787 the Juzgado de Capellanías advertised its intent to auction off the obraje left by the death of José Razo, which was valued at 14,000 pesos but encumbered with capellanías of 8,000 pesos.[39] Upon the death of Manuel de Otero y Araujo in 1785, his three children declared the worth of his obraje to be 10,650 pesos and that of the house next to it to be 5,600, but the two together suffered from liens totally 6,400 pesos.[40] However, not all cloth weaving was done in obrajes. As we shall see in the following chapter on artisans, great numbers of weavers of every variety practiced their craft independently.

In contrast to the situation in bakeries and slaughterhouses, the problem in obrajes was not supplies but labor. In 1807 Manuel Durán de Otero, by his own statement the owner for over forty-five years of the oldest obraje in greater Mexico City, wrote an extensive letter to a government official detailing his labor difficulties. He claimed that his troubles stemmed from the two-year-old viceregal order forbidding the enclosure of workers for the entire week. Extrapolating from one of his statements, it appears that it was still all right to confine obraje workers during the work week, but they had to be freed on Sundays and holidays. They could no longer be bound to the factory through debt. Although he averred that he was owed over 4,000 pesos by his employees, Durán de Otero argued that he was unable to collect the money or to use the debt as an excuse to bind his workers to their tasks, for he could no longer advance them more than four months' salary and could only garnishee two-thirds of their pay for reimbursement. But this was not his biggest complaint; it was rather that other obraje owners were violating the order by giving money to his inebriated workers on holidays and then locking them up in their own plants to pay off the debt in labor. Characteristically, he blamed the entire problem on the personality of the plebeian sector of the society, stating that its members immediately got drunk when freed from the confines of an obraje and then pestered the owners for advances to buy yet more liquor when their own money ran out. Although Durán de Otero requested the official to inspect these other obrajes and to return his workers held there, the tone of the document makes it clear that he was actually militating for the repeal of the order.[41]

SECURING LABOR: INCARCERATION OF DELINQUENTS.   Since obraje labor was unpopular even among the most impoverished in the society, the municipal court regularly ordered delinquent and idle youths into the locked shops (oficinas cerradas) as apprentice weavers for four, five, or as many years as was necessary to make them qualified journeymen. Supposedly, at the end of the term, they would emerge fully trained with 30 pesos in their pockets. At the beginning of the judicial process, orphaned, disobedient, or criminal youngsters, usually between the ages of twelve and sixteen, appeared before the alcalde ordinario with charges laid against them. However, specific charges were not always necessary. A boy might be sent to an obraje simply for being idle and homeless, or if his guardian testified that he was no longer able to keep him in line. The boy would thereupon be sentenced to a term of training in an obraje and put under the supervision of one of the procuradores of the city. In 1794 Francisco Lostre, the owner of the obraje named Panzacola located in the outskirts of the capital, received an eighteen-year-old who could no longer be handled by his uncle and a fourteen-year-old who had fled from all of his apprentice positions.[42] In 1797 he received a twelve-year-old who had run away from his parents when he had been apprenticed out, a youth who had seduced a minor (she received 25 lashes and was returned to her parents; he also got 25 lashes before entering the obraje), a seventeen-year-old apprentice who had tried to rape the nine-year-old daughter of his master in her sleep, and two vagrant orphans.[43] Nearly all of these boys were Spanish.

A FAMILY BUSINESS.   The obraje Salto del Agua was purchased in 1777 by Manuel de Otero y Araujo from the estate of the late Diego Soto Troncoso.[44] When the purchaser himself died in 1785, he left the obraje, an adjacent house, and apparently little else to his three children. His only son, also named Manuel, was the administrator of the obraje.[45] That same year, the son, in his own name and as apoderado of his two sisters, borrowed 3,000 pesos for five years to use in the business. Also that year, he recognized the obraje's debt of 3,240 pesos (consisting of 2,640 pesos loaned to the establishment without interest, and 600 pesos for a shipment of dye) to Francisco Javier de Iturriaza, a merchant of the city, and pledged to pay it in less than a year, offering the obraje and house as collateral.[46]

In 1806 Mariana de Otero, one of the two sisters, twice a widow, and now the owner of the obraje, made arrangements to rent it out to another person. She turned over the business for the next ten years to María Josefa Saldaña, who agreed to an annual rent of 1,000 pesos and to the payment of an additional 3,000 pesos for materials already there. In fact, she paid the entire 13,000 pesos in advance. Otero promised not to sell the business during the term of the rental, and Saldaña committed her inheritors to the completion of the contract if she died during its term.[47]

Ownership of an obraje seemingly bore no social stigma. Persons decided to invest in one or not according to economic, not social, criteria. In 1810 no less a family than the Marqueses de Selva Nevada forced a certain Agustín Sáenz de Santa María, who owned the obraje named Mixcoac on an estate of theirs, to sell the plant to them by threatening to shut off its water.[48]

Owners of Other Manufacturing and Processing Firms

SMALL FACTORY OWNERS. Certain other mass-consumed items were passing from solely artisan manufacture to factory production at this time. Shoes and hats, once produced almost exclusively by artisans, were now being turned out also in obraje-like installations. José Tomás Palma actually called his shoe factory an "obraje de zapatos," kept his workers locked in, and accepted delinquent youths from the municipal courts to be taught the craft.[49] However, just as the existence of cloth obrajes did not drive independent weavers out of the business in this period, so too artisan shoemakers and hatmakers lived in uneasy coexistence with these nascent industries.

Some of these plants, in fact, seem to have been little more than moderately expanded artisan shops. Julián Pila, a native of Turin, owned a fábrica de sombreros (hat factory) but also retailed hats purchased from international merchants of the city.[50] Other enterprises, like those of paint manufacturers, more closely resembled factories in their organization and scale of production.

PRINTERS. Several printing presses operated profitably in the city, turning out newspapers, religious works, official publications, and great numbers of flyers, leaflets, and broadsides. Licenciado Francisco de Noriega, the editor of the *Gazeta de Gobierno* in 1810, had run the paper through a company with its two printers, he and they each getting half of the profits. But that year he decided to travel to Spain, and it became necessary to name a new editor and devise a new business arrangement. Ignacio Alvarez, one of the printers, and Juan José de Oteiza, a renowned scientist and cleric of the city, were chosen the new coeditors in Noriega's absence, with a salary to be worked out to their mutual satisfaction. Noriega was still entitled to a share of the profits while away. The contract expressly stipulated that he would be paid 500 pesos initially and then 200 pesos a month beginning that June. As profits increased, so would his income, the reverse if they decreased.[51]

Two generations of the Zúñiga y Ontiveros family—the father Felipe and the son Mariano José—made their livings as publishers and surveyors. The father, a native of the capital, was the founder of the invaluable *Guías de forasteros* and publisher of the *Gazeta de México* until his death in 1793. The son, who never married, published the *Diario de México* in 1815–1816. Previously, it had been published at the press owned by the Fernández de Jáuregui family. A man of considerable wealth and of diversified economic interests, Mariano José owned a bookstore—as did many publishers—and also invested 40,000 pesos in partnership with a merchant to acquire a large sugar refinery and estate near Cuernavaca. The entire enterprise was purchased for 140,000 pesos, with 40,000 pesos down and the remainder recognized as a loan at interest. The two investors hired a third man to manage the business, and all agreed that one eighth of all profits would be reinvested, with the remainder divided among the three equally.[52]

MILLERS. The city was ringed by flour mills. Many of them

were owned by prominent agricultural families who wished to control the refining of their own products. Others were purchased by merchants, professionals, and persons with excess capital who were looking for attractive investments. Most individuals studied who had anything to do with the ownership or even the management of mills made their fortunes and careers in other occupations. Mills seemed to change hands with some frequency, although, of course, some of the great agricultural families held onto theirs for many years. The miller, that is to say the person who actually supervised the grinding of the grain, does not seem to have been active in the commodities market. That was reserved for merchants and the agents of agricultural interests. Millers merely performed their tasks and, by and large, stayed out of other enterprises.

THE CONSTRUCTION INDUSTRY. Regrettably, little usable information was gathered about the immense construction industry in Mexico City at this time. The various censuses of the eighteenth and early nineteenth centuries reveal the presence of great numbers of Indian laborers, mixed-blood craftsmen, and Spanish supervisory personnel who undoubtedly were employed in this industry. The city itself was expanding, and with the general prosperity of the period, both private individuals and official bodies were constructing new and opulent buildings, some of which may be seen to this day.

ROCK QUARRIES. The construction boom of late colonial Mexico City created considerable demand for *tezontle*, the red volcanic stone which was used so often as the primary building material. One result was a series of business agreements to quarry the substance from nearby upcroppings. In 1804 Pedro Elosúa Abarrategui, a merchant of the city and the owner of a rancho in Coyoacán, rented out a hill located on the rancho for one year for 500 pesos to José Antonio Machón. This payment gave Machón the right to quarry all the tezontle that he wished from the hill, but he was forbidden to touch any other part of the property, except to graze his mules there without charge. Elosúa Abarrategui also retained the right to quarry, provided only that he not do so on the same site as Machón.[53] In an earlier transaction, as part of a comprehensive contract regulating the exploitation of a rancho which encompassed a peñón (outcropping) of volcanic rock, the proprietor, an attorney, and the manager, an Indian cacique, agreed to divide equally all profits derived from production of tezontle and from all the other enterprises on the estate.[54]

THE CIGAR AND CIGARETTE FACTORY.   The immense factory located in the heart of the city, owned and operated by the royal tobacco monopoly, unfortunately was outside of the scope of the documents examined. The plant was huge, employing around 7,000 workers of both sexes (in two separate divisions), with a total annual salary in the 1780s and 1790s of perhaps 750,000 pesos. Most of the common laborers were Indians and castas, but some were Spaniards. Given the size of the work force and the fact that they were paid in cash, it is understandable why ambulatory vendors frequented the establishment.[55]

9 Artisans

THE HIERARCHY OF CRAFTS. In the Mexico City of late colonial times, a large portion of the population—primarily but not exclusively male—were skilled artisans, members of the many craft guilds of the city. Clothing, jewelry, buildings, furniture, fabrics, and leather goods were all made predominantly by craftsmen. Much artisan activity involved the elaboration or finishing of materials, natural and manmade, which were brought into the city from abroad or from the provinces.

The crafts themselves were ordered in a traditional hierarchy based on prestige, the worth of the goods produced, and the income that a master craftsman might earn. Some members of the highest-ranked guilds (silversmiths, goldworkers, coachmakers, and saddlemakers among them) could live very good lives indeed, drawing an income and enjoying social status similar to that of retail merchants and lower-ranked professionals and bureaucrats. Even in lower-ranking crafts, the most successful could expect to maintain themselves comfortably and to expand their economic interests beyond their particular crafts.

SOCIAL TRANSITION IN THE ARTISAN SECTOR. It is at the artisan level on the occupational scale that we witness two important social phenomena: first, the disappearance of the prefix *don* before the names of some of the personnel; and second, the massive presence of non-Spaniards in virtually all the crafts, though, of course, to a lesser extent among the most prestigious ones.

While virtually every person mentioned by name in the previous chapters had "don" or "doña" consistently placed before his or her name in all types of documentation, such was not the case with all artisans. Though some flexibility did exist, as a general rule a master of a guild was addressed with the "don" prefix and his wife with the "doña," while a journeyman was not and likewise his spouse. This was the case among artisans whether they were Spaniards, castas, or Indians. Journeymen of prestigious crafts (silversmiths and coachmakers for instance) might at times be addressed with the prefix, while masters of less-esteemed guilds (such as carpenters and tailors) might be addressed by their unadorned name.

The 1753 census of the city, corroborated by other evidence from the later colonial years, reveals the overwhelming presence of castas and Indians in the guilds of the city. Non-Hispanics could be found in every one, regardless of legislation specifically designed to exclude them. The silversmiths and goldworkers guilds were by law restricted exclusively to those who could prove their purity of descent. Every youth applying for an apprenticeship in these crafts had to undergo an examination by the head assayer of the royal mint to certify his Spanish heritage. Yet despite the regulations and examination, persons recognized by the society as non-Hispanic regularly entered these guilds. The 1753 census contains the names of silversmiths who were mulattoes and apprentices in that craft who were Indians. Mestizos and mulattoes regularly qualified as goldworkers, with apprentices coming from a variety of ethnic backgrounds. Thus even the most exclusive guilds did not remain purely Spanish. All others invariably embraced members from every ethnic group in the colony, though none lacked a considerable portion of Spaniards, perhaps even a majority, especially among the masters. Thus, outside of the precious-metal workers, no member of a guild could consider himself as belonging to a predominantly Spanish institution. Finally, peninsulars could be found among the Spaniards in virtually every guild, whatever its status; their careers were largely indistinguishable from those of their creole counterparts.

THE TYPES AND NUMBERS OF ARTISANS.   The 1788 census of Mexico City's guilds, laid out in Table 33, expresses the number and

Table 33.   Membership in the Craft Guilds of Mexico City in 1788

Guild	Masters	Journeymen	Apprentices	Total
Arte de Leer				
(Primary School Teachers)	16		1,327	1,343
Arte de la Seda				
(Silk Weavers)	30	50	23	103
Tejedores de Seda de lo				
Angosto				
(Tight-Stitch Silk Weavers)	62	654	38	754
Mujeres Hiladores de Seda				
(Female Silk Spinners)	23	200	21	244
Hiladores de Seda				
(Silk Spinners)	19	146	21	186
Sayaleros				
(Sayal Cloth Weavers)	75	370	39	478
Algodoneros				
(Cotton Weavers)	57	300	40	397
Obrajeros				
(Textile Mill Workers)	10	697	298	1,005
Bordadores				
(Embroiderers)	16	50	10	76
Sastres				
(Tailors)	94	698	423	1,215
Pasamaneros				
(Lacemakers)	22	102	13	137
Ojalateros				
(Buttonhole Makers)	30	42	17	89
Listoneros				
(Ribbon Makers)	17	63	30	110
Cordoneros				
(Cord Makers)	28	195	43	266
Jarcieros				
(Cordage Makers)	16	51	18	85
Sombrereros				
(Hat Makers)	142	48	3	193
Tintoreros				
(Dyers)	11	25	5	41
Plateros				
(Silversmiths)	36	190	44	270
Bateojas				
(Silver Sheet Makers)	7	52	10	69

Table 33.   (continued)

Guild	Masters	Journeymen	Apprentices	Total
Tiradores de Oro (Gold Wire Drawers)	12	69	14	95
Doradores (Gilders)	26	79	10	115
Fundidores (Smelters)	5	3	1	9
Herradores (Farriers)	28	50	12	90
Herreros (Blacksmiths)	53	214	50	317
Agujereros (Needle Makers)	11	30	13	54
Calderos (Kettle Makers)	18	44	26	88
Espaderos (Sword Makers)	9	10	3	22
Carpinteros (Carpenters)	170	498	157	825
Tonaleros (Coopers)	6	8	4	18
Loceros (Potters)	16	62	5	83
Cereros (Wax Workers)	17	39	15	71
Veleros (Candle Makers)	37	138	12	187
Curtidores (Tanners)	30	90	47	167
Zurradores (Curriers)	25	92	7	124
Zapateros (Shoe Makers)	37	168	32	237
Silleros (Saddle Makers)	20	82	18	120
Carroceros (Coach Makers)	20	105	39	164
Coheteros (Fireworks Makers)	39	42	11	92
Arquitectos (Architects)	11			11

Table 33. (continued)

Guild	Masters	Journeymen	Apprentices	Total
Albañiles (Masons)	a	810	1,205	2,015
Canteros (Stonecutters)	a	405	150	555
Empedradores (Pavers)	35	428		463
Cañeros (Pipe Layers)	9	87		96
Escultores (Sculptors)	52	135	73	260
Músicos (Musicians)	27	189	93	309
Barberos (Barbers)	315	422	97	834
Peluqueros (Hair Dressers)	45	98	57	200
Confiteros (Confectioners)	23	36	7	66
Boticarios (Pharmacists)	141	219	83	443
Fonderos (Eating Stand Owners)	33	65	30	128
Cargadores (Carriers)	a	1,209		1,209
Aguadores (Water Drawers)	a	610		610
Cocheros (Coachmen)	a	967		967
Lacayos (Grooms)	a	513		513
Totals	1,981	11,949	4,694	18,624

[a] Though organized into guilds, these occupations did not require specialized training or the passing of exams for entrance; therefore, no "master" category existed.

Source: BN, ms. 1388 (451), "Relacion de los Gremios, Artes y Oficios que hay en la Novilisima Ciudad de México," 1788.

variety of artisans in the capital. The total figure of 18,624, which embraces masters (including the heads and inspectors of guilds), journeymen, and apprentices, subsumes the membership of some occupations best considered under other headings (teachers, architects, pharmacists, and obraje workers), as well as others (carriers, water drawers, coachmen, and grooms) which required no special training but involved housework or unskilled labor in the marketplace. (The great number of "apprentices" under the heading "Arte de Leer" refers to the students of the teachers in the Guild.) Yet when the persons under such headings are deleted, over 10,000 true craft-workers still remain. In virtually every guild, journeymen outnumber masters by ratios between 2 to 1 and 7 or 8 to 1. The number of masters tended to be fairly close to that of apprentices, though some glaring exceptions can be noted (tailors on one extreme and hatmakers on the other). When we consider that the 1790 census put the population of the entire city at 113,234 persons, it seems likely that the crafts supported between a third and half of the inhabitants.

Silversmiths

SOCIAL POSITION.   The social characteristics of master silversmiths often were indistinguishable from those of most retail merchants, small manufacturers and processors, and low-level professionals. The vast majority of these artisans were creoles, although peninsular-born members were present in appreciable numbers. Neither they nor their offspring enjoyed dramatic social mobility. Some sons went into retail commerce, others the professions, while yet others followed in their fathers' footsteps. Sons of retail traders and nonelite professionals also trained to be precious-metal workers. In 1808, for instance, Antonio Cervantes, the head assayer of the royal mint, apprenticed his son with Ventura Alamillo, a goldsmith of the capital.[1]

Marriage did not give the precious-metal workers any great boost up the social ladder. As with tocineros and panaderos, many could not command a dowry, while a few did obtain considerable amounts. Miguel María Martel, a native of Ceuta, married a daughter of the physician Doctor Miguel Fernández de Sierra, and her grandfather, former president of the Protomedicato Doctor

José Maximiliano Rosales de Velasco, provided a dowry of nearly 7,000 pesos.[2] When José Guzmán married Ildefonsa Verástegui, she brought him a dowry valued at 2,183 pesos, consisting entirely of clothes and jewelry.[3] Perhaps typifying the career cycle of a silversmith, Bartolomé Barreda, a native of Mexico City, possessed no wealth and received no dowry upon his first marriage, but had an estate valued at 6,000 pesos and obtained a dowry of 1,730 pesos upon his second. At the time of his third marriage, he owned both his own shop and a coppersmithery.[4]

BUSINESS OPERATIONS.   Economically too, master silversmiths closely resembled the owners of retail stores and processing plants. Each silversmith aspired to ownership of his own shop and to eventual expansion into other forms of trade and enterprise, often through the use of partnerships. Some proprietors entered into companies in which unaffiliated masters of their craft managed their shops for them; these could take the form of a single long-term contract with a particular individual or a series of agreements with different managers. Silversmiths were quick to seek loans, from both individuals and institutions, and to form companies in their own shops with outside investors. At times they turned directly to the almaceneros of the city for major purchases of jewels and metals; at other times they bought from colleagues who had become involved in the marketing of precious materials to fellow silversmiths, seemingly as representatives of wholesale merchants. For these artisans too, bankruptcy was an unpleasant reality they sometimes had to face.

José Mariano de Avila, himself the son of a silversmith, experienced varying economic fortune, and his career exemplifies the types of company agreements common to the trade. In 1784 he managed his father's shop located on the street of silversmiths, which led into the central plaza of the city from the east. (Most silversmiths had their shops on the two blocks nearest the plaza; those who did not normally had them on adjacent streets.) As manager, Avila maintained a company with three women who had invested a total of 25,000 pesos in the shop, one having put in 21,500 pesos, another 3,000, and the third a mere 500 pesos. This arrangement had yielded good profits in the past; now the partners modified the contract to include yet another investor, José Monterde, who added 25,000 pesos of his own money. The new company was for only one year but was renewable. Avila was forbidden to accept further financing from any other source, even from his wife. Profits were to be divided into equal thirds between Avila, Monterde, and the women, who would divide their share among themselves according to their investment.[5] Fortune seemingly did not smile on Avila, for eleven years later, stating that he was currently without a post, he entered into a two-year company to manage the shop of another silversmith, Eduardo Calderón, for two thirds of the profits. He was required to contribute only his skill and intelligence; Calderón provided all the goods and money. Finally, though Avila was in charge of daily operations, Calderón retained ultimate authority, including the right to hire and fire.[6]

Avila's first company was very heavily capitalized when compared to other silversmith shops and companies found in the documentation. More typical was the arrangement between the silversmith José Manuel Infante and Acensio Ruiz in 1791. Ruiz invested 1,000 pesos in return for a third share of the profits over nine years.[7] In 1808 Fernando Sámano, another silversmith, related how eight years earlier he had accepted 1,100 pesos from Diego Fernández de Celís for a full half of the profits. The informal oral agreement was so pleasing to both parties that after these many years they decided to formalize the company under the same terms. It was to last as long as both parties so desired.[8]

From all indications, the value of the shops and their equipment was quite small. Francisco Orozco sold his shop and tools to José Manuel Infante for 300 pesos.[9] (Typical of this money-short economy, Infante could not pay even this small amount in cash and agreed to pay 100 pesos in each of the next three months.) In 1810, when a court ordered Miguel Picazo to action off his shop with all its equipment to satisfy a law suit, its total value was put at a mere 519 pesos.[10]

As in commerce, the entire craft system was based on the necessity of credit and installment transactions from individual retail sales up to wholesale purchases and even to the sale of the shops themselves. In a typical case, the attorney Licenciado José Antonio López Frías bought three items of jewelry from Pedro Castro for 950 pesos and pledged himself to pay within six months, offering his estates in Coyoacán as collateral.[11] Silversmiths, in turn, bought necessary materials on credit from others in their craft and from merchants in the city. In 1809 José Vera purchased pearls valued at 8,000 pesos from the merchant Juan Manuel de la Lama, paying 3,800 pesos in cash and promising the remainder in the following month, with two roominghouses as his collateral.[12] José María Rodallega acquired jewels on credit from both José Gómez Campos and the Conde de Agreda.[13]

Silversmiths who wholesaled to others in their craft may well have been acting as agents of regular merchants; international traders were undoubtedly the ultimate source of supplies. At times, artisan wholesaling could extend into the provinces. In 1785 a silversmith of Valladolid, Michoacán owed 870 pesos to the Mexico City silversmith Bartolomé García Díaz from an account that they had maintained over a number of years.[14]

Needing funds with which to purchase materials, silversmiths had frequent recourse to loans from institutions and private individuals. And, of course, some borrowers, unable to redeem the debts, found themselves confronting bankruptcy. José Fernández admitted to debts totalling 2,468 pesos and further stated that he could redeem them all if forced to sell his holdings. However, he petitioned the court for esperas of five years so that he might pay off the creditors from his income and still retain his properties.[15] José María Bernal, who fell deeply into debt from his artisan activities and from other investments, had his property embargoed for two years and was himself imprisoned for nine months before his creditors agreed to release him and give him back his tools so that he might gain the necessary revenue.[16] José María Rodallega had no such luck; in 1815 he was in bankruptcy proceedings, and the court ordered the auction of his shop and tools to cancel his debts.[17]

ECONOMIC ACTIVITIES OUTSIDE OF THE CRAFT. Feeling no compulsion to limit economic activity to their craft, master silversmiths regularly involved themselves in all sorts of undertakings in retail commerce and other fields. Extremely few artisans, either in silversmithing or in any other craft, were able to acquire even moderately sized rural estates, but the fact that even a few did denotes the economic possibilities that were open to the most successful among them. Ramón Sánchez de Almazán in 1800 agreed to rent some of his land near Toluca to a priest with a neighboring estate and to loan him money until the harvest.[18]

Many masters with their own shops, the elite among silversmiths, could afford to own houses in the capital. Some, in fact, invested in urban real estate, especially in roominghouses, which they were prone to offer as collateral when contracting loans. At least one silversmith had a female slave as a domestic.[19]

The most popular outside economic investment of silversmiths was retail commerce. We have already referred to Bartolomé Barreda's ownership of a coppersmithery. José María Bernal owned and managed a ceramics shop (tienda de loza) which represented a personal investment of 2,300 pesos. In 1795, needing additional capital, he formed a company in it with José Leandro de la Peña, who invested 2,000 in cash in return for profits in proportion to his investment. Bernal retained management of the store, and the company was to endure so long as the two partners wished.[20] It should be noted, however, that Bernal still owed de la Peña the 2,000 pesos some six years later when he was in debt proceedings and was able to get out of jail only by recognizing the amount as a loan at the standard rate of interest.[21]

José Manuel Infante (who in 1791 accepted an investor as a partner in his shop, then in 1798 bought the shop of another silversmith) in 1802 brought to an unsuccessful conclusion a company he had managed in the pulpería of María Antonía Montalvo y Cuesta. In the original agreement, he had agreed to manage the store for half the profits or losses. He did not supervise daily operation in person but had hired a cajero for that purpose, restricting himself to overall administration. He failed miserably. In 1802 the two partners admitted that they had each lost over 265 pesos during the existence of the company; unfortunately, neither the value of the store nor the duration of the arrangement are known. The entire affair entered the courts when Montalvo y Cuesta sued Infante for mismanagement.[22]

JOURNEYMEN.   A document of 1793 affords us a rare glimpse of some aspects of the lives of journeymen.[23] In a survey conducted by the guild, the names of 77 journeymen silversmiths are given; 68 of these entries have additional data. The 1788 census of all

guilds lists 190 journeymen silversmiths, so a good portion of the
total is included in this report. Interestingly, all the names are pre-
fixed with "don." Of the 68 whose vital statistics are given, only
two were 50 years of age or older, eight were in their forties, and
14 were in their thirties. The bulk, 40 journeymen, were in their
twenties, and four were 19. Most of them had begun their training
in their midteens, with a few starting later than that. A significant
minority started at the ages of 11 and 12, and a few even earlier;
one man declared that he had begun at the age of six. The vast majority had entered their apprenticeships on the basis of informal
oral agreements. Some did have written contracts of the type
which will be examined below. Forty-three of the sixty-eight were
married; a large majority of these wed between the ages of twenty
and twenty-five, though one married when just fourteen and another at sixteen. Forty-one of these journeymen had married by
the age of twenty-five. Only sixteen of the forty-nine who were
twenty-five or older had not married by that age, and some of
them did so in later years. Of the twenty-four who were thirty or
older, only four were still single.

    APPRENTICES.   In the 1788 census, thirty-six master silversmiths
had forty-four apprentices. According to a 1792 count of apprentices in the guild, thirty-three masters had fifty-six apprentices,
several of them their own sons.[24] One master had five apprentices, another four, three had three, ten had two, and eighteen had
just one.

    Many parents and guardians, to give added weight to appren-
ticeship contracts, went before an alcalde of the city, who would
duly record the agreement reached between the adult and the master craftsman.[25] Each contract followed a set format. The sponsoring adult would first identify him or herself and then give the
name and age of the youth, usually with a brief description of
the relationship between them. He would then state that to give
the child proper training and direction in life, he had contracted
with a craftsman identified by name to take the child in for a
set number of years, normally three to five, during which time
the artisan would feed and maintain the youth; however, he would
not be responsible for extraordinary expenses in case of prolonged
illness or some other calamity. The child was placed under the

charge of a procurador of the city for the duration of the training. He was to be educated in the craft and was to emerge at the end of the set period, or however much time was needed, qualified to pass the journeyman's exam and with 30 pesos in cash, or sometimes a suit of clothes, or both. The artisan committed himself to train the lad to pass the exam no matter how long it might take, and if it took longer than the set number of years, he had to continue to train him as an apprentice while paying him the salary of a journeyman. With this rule, artisans must have examined youths with some care before agreeing to take them on. The individual artisan did not always stipulate the same period of training for all of his apprentices; some contracts were for shorter terms, others for longer.

Coachmakers

The manufacture of coaches was, along with the making of jewelry, far and away the most heavily capitalized artisan craft. Actually, coachmaking required a heavier initial outlay for equipment and facilities than metalworking, but lower expenditure for materials. Coaches were of rather moderate price and could be made quite quickly. For example, Antonio Banineli, a coachmaker, paid 500 pesos for a used coach. When he signed a contract to make some of his own, he stipulated a period of forty days for the manufacture of each one. The manufacturing shops were sometimes affiliated with coach-renting services. Ignacio José de Echagaray priced his carrocería (coachmaking shop) at 6,720 pesos.[26] Another was purchased for 4,527 pesos, and a combination coachmaking and coach-renting facility was sold for 5,897 pesos.[27]

Given the heavy capitalization of the shops and the kind of expenditures involved in the construction of relatively few large-sized units, these craftsmen often found it necessary to seek out loans and to enter into companies with outside investors. In 1806 Antonio Banineli made a coach for José Mariano Frenero; the latter then contracted with him to make six more vehicles for sale. Frenero gave Banineli an initial 2,000 pesos and promised to pay him 500 pesos upon the receipt of each completed carriage, plus another 1,000 pesos after the sale of the six.[28]

José de Blancas, another coachmaker, formed a company for

three years with Bachiller Juan José Nicolás de Sevilla, the curate of San Agustín de las Cuevas; the priest agreed to invest 4,000 pesos for a third of the profits, giving Blancas an additional year at the end to return the capital.[29] Coachmaker José Roldán, declaring that his shop was not earning money because of undercapitalization, contracted a company for two years with Francisco de Iglesias, who put in 2,000 pesos for half of the profits.[30]

The municipal government sanctioned a system of coaches (coches de providencia) for daily rentals, and this enterprise attracted its share of businessmen. Manuel Prieto and the lawyer Licenciado Mariano García de Aguirre, both owners of some coaches, had jointly purchased a corral and small shop for 500 pesos (plus an additional 52 pesos for improvements). When the lawyer decided to remove himself from the business, he sold Prieto his two coaches and his share of the rental firm for 1,250 pesos. The coaches alone were worth 698 pesos. Prieto agreed to pay him off at 110 pesos a month, pledging his revenue from the rentals toward that end.[31]

There is evidence that professionals and government officials occasionally purchased coachmaking shops, which they presumably then entrusted to master craftsmen.[32] As in other crafts, it was not unusual for more than one member of a family to enter the trade and to pass it down to the next generation. Andrés, Agustín, and Pedro Sánchez de Vargas were brothers, natives of Mexico City, and master coachmakers, as was their nephew Manuel del Castillo.[33] To all appearances, they worked together.

In 1801 some of the officers of the coachmakers' guild decided that it would be a good idea to stay on the best of terms with Joaquín Romero Caamaño, the regidor of the city entrusted with supervision of gremios. Miguel Gallardo therefore built a coach for him gratis in honor of his saint's day.[34] A dispute within the guild brought the act out into the open and turned it into a lawsuit, the resolution of which remains unknown.

Blacksmiths

In late colonial Mexico City, at least some blacksmith shops had evolved into very large enterprises containing a number of forges and valued in the thousands of pesos. Most of these businesses were managed through companies of one form or another. The supply of such shops and the sale of their finished products were closely intertwined with the regular commercial life of the city, so much so that many of the salient features of the organization of these businesses can be brought out through the examination of the career of one merchant, Juan de Dios Martínez.

In 1802 Martínez sold, for 6,000 pesos, the building and equipment belonging to a company he maintained with Cayetano Urrutia, a master blacksmith.[35] The purchaser was himself a merchant, Manuel de Ordóñez, and he immediately contracted a new company with Urrutia. The agreement, for the term of five years, stipulated that neither party could withdraw prematurely without paying damages. While Martínez's company with Urrutia had included a vinatería, the new one concentrated exclusively on ironware made in the shop. Urrutia would take charge of the shop and equipment (valued as we have seen at 6,000 pesos) and also receive 500 pesos in cash and 1,500 pesos of iron plate from his partner. He would get half of the profits plus 2 reales a day for subsistence. For his part, Urrutia invested his seven forges and personal skill and agreed to purchase iron from Ordóñez whenever the latter had some from abroad, but always at the prevailing price. Ordóñez had the right to approve all purchases over 25 quintales.

Juan de Dios Martínez did not abandon involvement in the blacksmith trade when he left the above company. By 1808 he had signed a contract with yet another master, José Algarín. The previous year Algarín had entered into a separate agreement designed to bring another blacksmith into the business. Though a master, Francisco Prieto did not yet have a forge of his own and sought to acquire one by contracting to work for Algarín for five years. He bound himself to work daily at a forge in Algarín's shop and to oversee the work of the journeymen there employed. In return, Algarín agreed to supply all material and equipment and to pay Prieto 12 reales for each piece that he turned out, plus an additional 100 pesos annually for supervising the journeymen. It was expressly stipulated that Prieto could terminate the company whenever he had sufficient funds to purchase his own forge.[36]

From all indications, Algarín had contracted with Prieto while himself a partner of Martínez. It was required by guild regulations that a master blacksmith oversee all work performed by journeymen, and Prieto well suited this task. However, he departed within a couple of years, and the partners obtained his replacement by yet other means.

In 1808 Martínez and Algarín sold three hundredweight of iron on credit to the master blacksmith José Francisco Arizaga, who promised that he could work for them to pay off the 126-peso purchase price if he could not redeem the debt within a certain period of time.[37] Such was to be the case. In 1810 the partners reported that they had employed Arizaga to supervise their forges for this very reason and that they now wished to include him in their company to continue this work. The agreement was for nine years. Arizaga was to attend the forges daily and to be responsible for all repairs. He further committed himself to work exclusively for Algarín and Martínez. In return, the two owners would supply all equipment and material. Arizaga was entitled to any profit from the forge that he himself worked, but would gain nothing from those that he supervised on behalf of the owners.[38]

The social status of beginning blacksmiths prevented them from making a marriage that would improve their social standing or give them substantial dowries. A beginning blacksmith, even a master such as Arizaga, might be at such a modest level as not to merit a "don" before his name. But because some of them were able to expand their businesses and earn good profits, the most successful were later able to invest in other forms of enterprise and, in a few cases, even acquire landed estates.

When Manuel de la Vega, a native of Seville, married for the first time, he was unable either to claim a dowry or to allude to any wealth of his own. However, at the time of his second marriage, he received a dowry of 2,800 pesos and could himself give arras of 300 pesos. In his 1789 will, he listed his major holdings as a fully equipped blacksmith shop and two horses. He had also diversified his economic interests and was renting three inns in the city.[39] José Ramón de Guitara, another blacksmith, did well enough to purchase a wheat rancho from a notary of the city.[40] José Saturnino Frías was not able to command a dowry in either of his two marriages; however, all three of his sons became master blacksmiths in their own right. And in 1793, now of advanced years, Frías owned his place of residence, which included his fully equipped shop.[41]

Tailors

The great many tailors of the capital made up a multi-leveled occupational unit, but the considerable diversity within the craft was not well reflected in the documentation examined. The best off—those who were purveyors of elegant ware to the rich—do not appear in appreciable numbers. Therefore, the discussion which follows by necessity concentrates on the large number who struggled just to make a living. Very probably the practice of tailor-shop-owners forming companies with unattached craftsmen was more prevalent among the most successful than among those treated in this section, and, of course, the terms of the agreements probably differed, reflecting the different stations of the contracting parties.

Tailorships required minimal capitalization, so their owners did not normally take out loans of any size nor form companies with investors. When tailors did contract companies, it was with others in their trade, and not in order to separate ownership from management but to provide for continuity of operation while the owner was absent or incapacitated. In 1800 Juan Burgechán, a master tailor, decided to travel to Spain and therefore formed a company with another master, Angel Albia, who would use the shop in his absence. Indicating the low value of the operation, Albia had to pay Burgechán a total of only 100 pesos as rental and as compensation for profits lost during the trip to Spain. To avoid being immediately kicked out upon Burgechán's return, Albia obtained a stipulation that the company would continue for three more years after his return, with an even split of the profits.[42]

Francisco Ayusto, another owner of a tailor shop, by his own admission suffered from broken health, and for that reason entered into a four-year company with another master tailor, Joaquín Botello. Ayusto invested his shop plus whatever capital was required to purchase materials, as it was customary for clients not to pay until receipt of their completed articles. Botello, who brought only his skills to the company, received an equal share of the profits. Finally, both partners agreed that their previous customers now came under the company.[43]

Weavers

The many independent weavers of the city were organized into guilds and operated their own shops unaffiliated with any obraje. The 1788 census identified fifty-seven masters, three hundred journeymen, and forty apprentices in the cotton-weavers guild. Two other censuses prepared by the guild itself reveal a bit more about these people. In 1796 guild-inspectors took a count of the total number of looms operated by the members; the results are summarized in Table 34. Masters with their own shops (despachos) owned 150 of the 353 looms. Less than a fifth of the masters did not have facilities of their own, and even these normally owned several looms. Widows of masters typically did not abandon the business but continued operation of the looms. Some unlicensed outsiders (intrusos) were present, but handled only about a tenth of all looms. A few journeymen had several looms, but most had only one. All masters and widows of masters were listed with "don" or "doña" before their names, while none of the journeymen had titles before theirs.[44]

In an 1805 count taken to determine who would be required to pay increased dues based on the number of looms owned, the forty-two masters were again addressed as "don," and the journeymen as "señor" and "señora"—for some women were included in their ranks.[45] The presence of women is not surprising. In 1788 women silk-spinners were organized into their own guild with twenty-three masters, two hundred journeymen, and twenty-one apprentices. Women weavers can also be found in the 1753 census, and by no means are all of them widows who had taken up their late husbands' trade.

As with so many artisans, a major problem for weavers was the undercapitalization of their shops. They were therefore often in pursuit of investors, but the amount of capital that they required was comparatively small. In 1783 Antonio Sánchez Recuenco, a master weaver of sackcloth (sayal) and an inspector for his guild, stated that though he owned five looms, he lacked the funds neces-

Table 34.   A Summary of the Membership of the Guild of Cotton
Weavers of Mexico City in 1796 With the Number of
Looms That it Controlled

		Total Number of Looms	Single Highest Number of Looms
Masters with Offices			
(*Despachos*)	38	150	12
Masters without Offices	7	20	5
Widows	5	21	9
Outsiders (*Intrusos*)	9	36	14
Journeymen (*Oficiales*)	77	126	5
Totals	136	353	

Source: AGN, Industria y Comercio, leg. 21, exp. 4, "Lista de los Maestros y Numero de Telares que se hallan existentes hasta este presente año de noventa y seis."

sary to use them fully. He resolved the situation by entering into a three-year company with two unwed sisters, who agreed to put in 400 pesos in return for a half-share of the profits.[46] Sánchez Recuenco offered his looms and equipment as security against the money and promised not to use the funds as a guarantee against any debt he might contract. Profits were to be paid the sisters on a weekly basis, and they could leave the company prematurely if dissatisfied.

Other Craftsmen

Various artisans in other crafts also prospered and typically thereupon diversified their interests. When they did, it was usually through investment in retail trade (pulperías, vinaterías, and the like) or other artisan trades. Acensio Ruiz, a native of Amecameca and a maker of brooms and brushes (escobillero), belonged to five cofradías, but never obtained a dowry from any of his three marriages. When he made out his will in 1792, he reported his purchase of the building containing his shop.[47] Furthermore, the previous year he had invested 1,000 pesos in a company with a silversmith for a third of the profits.[48] When he and his wife died in 1799, they left behind four houses, of which two contained escobillerías and a third was a roominghouse; together they were valued at 9,380 pesos.[49]

Saddlemakers were relatively few in number, only twenty masters in 1788, but their shops, because of the tools and equipment needed, were usually worth thousands of pesos. In 1795 the saddlery (talabartería) of José Espinosa y Segura was valued at 11,222 pesos.[50] It had been under the management of José Ignacio Góngora, who had administered it on salary until Espinosa y Segura made him a full partner. The partnership soured after only a year, and in the suit he filed, Espinosa y Segura claimed that Góngora owed him nearly 750 pesos. This bad experience, however, did not turn Espinosa y Segura against the company form of management. By 1801 he owned a cajón in the Parián, with a stock of saddles and harness worth 13,828 pesos, and that year he contracted with José Buendía to manage it for a period of five years for half the profits.[51] Buendía had complete control over the business; the contract stipulated that Espinosa y Segura could not interfere in its operation. Both partners were entitled to use the store as collateral in credit transactions.

José Agustín López, likewise a master saddlemaker, owned his fully equipped shop in the capital as well as three houses in his hometown of San Miguel el Grande. Leatherworkers dealt extensively on other items besides saddles and harness, and López had a standing contract with a master coachmaker to do the leatherwork required on his vehicles.[52]

Tanners also operated large establishments which were closely tied into provincial and even intercolonial commerce. Some merchants—Martín Angel de Micháus y Aspiros is the most notable example—made fortunes trading in hides. Bernardino de Cuevas, a native of Cuernavaca, operated two tanneries, one in Mexico City and another, under the direction of his brother, in his hometown. When he died in 1799, his Mexico City plant alone was worth 4,500 pesos.[53] The necessity of procuring hides drew tanners into the acquisition and leasing of rural estates and into the purchase of livestock from the provinces.[54] In 1788 Domingo de Vargas bought a tannery in the city from a priest. By the following year, he was formulating plans to market part of his product in Havana, and to that end, he empowered José Joaquin de Ariscorreta, one of the great wholesale merchants of the capital, to act on his behalf.[55]

Clearly not all crafts could be discussed in this chapter. But the forms of economic organization and behavior characteristic of other fields of business were fully in operation at this level too. The less abundant material available on other crafts shows that they were not exceptions.

10 Conclusion

The greatest urban conglomeration in the Americas until the mid-nineteenth century, Mexico City prospered not only as the civil and ecclesiastical center of the country but also as a commercial entrepôt and manufacturing center. As much of its large population received cash incomes, the city itself was a major consumer both of the goods which it produced and of those commodities, raw materials, and manufactured items which it brought in from other parts of the country and from abroad. Much of the production and marketing of goods from the provinces intended for the capital was directed by businessmen of the city. But the businessmen of Mexico City never restricted their market just to the capital and its environs. Mexico City occupied a primary position in the economy of the colony at large, dominating much economic activity in the provinces, especially the most lucrative aspects. The capital served as the residence of most families which made great fortunes from mining, agriculture, or commerce in the provinces; beyond this, businessmen of the capital financed and assumed partial or total control over many enterprises in the hinterland. They also maintained a long-standing domination of most interprovincial commerce against challenges from other cities.

The true elite of Mexico City were a number of frequently intermarried extended creole families, which typically had enjoyed such status for at least several generations and in some cases for much longer. No matter how their wealth originated—from commerce, agriculture, mining, or government service—at least by

227

the second generation these families took steps to diversify their investments in different fields of the economy to ensure themselves against collapse in any one of them. Intermarriage was promoted to avoid loss of status from association with people of inferior status and to prevent excessive fragmentation of holdings through divided inheritance.

But the elite should not be perceived either as static in its composition or as nonentrepreneurial in its economic behavior. Most families attempted to combine safe investments, which yielded a small but guaranteed income, with more speculative enterprises—usually in commerce or mining—which promised substantial profits if successful. Each generation repeated this pattern of investments.

Rural holdings, either in ranching or agriculture or some combination of the two, always composed a significant part of an elite family's economic portfolio. Such investments normally provided a meaningful income and sometimes offered spectacular returns. Landed estates also constituted the only form of property or enterprise which was easily divided and transferred across generations. Agriculture as practiced by the elite meant much more than the simple raising of crops and animals. It involved the vertical integration of the entire production and marketing system, often including not just the commodities from the family holdings but also those from surrounding properties belonging to other parties. Traditionally the most stable component of the colonial economy, agriculture did not suffer quite the same violent fluctuations as commerce and mining. As a consequence, few cases of economic collapse among agriculturally based elite families were found.

But there was turnover in the elite. Its members could not retire from the business world. Fresh undertakings were usually required to maintain one's position, and some families did fail in their efforts. Most replacements came from the ranks of the colony's wholesale merchants, with some lesser representation from high-level government officials and mining and agricultural entrepreneurs. No person ascended into the elite solely through his accomplishments in any of the professions; wealth was a necessary prerequisite to elite membership, and none of the professions in themselves provided sufficient income. Nor, for that matter, did any professional activity provide the status and honors normally associated with elite standing.

The elite received a great many distinctions, including honorific or noble titles, from the crown and the church. Its members also held many appointments, both sinecures and actual functioning positions, in the colonial and municipal governments. They also were well represented among the officers of most professional organizations, being chosen to serve because of their elite status and not specifically because of any achievements within the profession.

The world of commerce was multileveled—sometimes with the same personnel active on several different levels simultaneously—and provided the primary occupation of many hundreds of people, both creole and peninsular. The international traders were the most powerful and wealthy of the merchants. Organized into the Consulado, roughly two hundred men headed trading houses which dealt regularly with other firms scattered across both oceans and in other colonies of Spain. Over the course of the colonial period, the great merchants of the capital, exploiting their access to silver, had become increasingly autonomous of Spanish mercantile firms. By the end of the era, many Mexico City commercial houses were locally controlled, no longer subsidiaries of Iberian interests. This greater independence was undoubtedly abetted in the eighteenth century by the incipient Industrial Revolution and the continued maritime weakness of Spain. However, these factors merely speeded up a process which continued at differing rates down to Independence. Unfortunately, good studies of this dimension of the economy exist only for the beginning and the very end of the colonial period and therefore cannot pinpoint the growth of autonomy in the intervening years.

Furthermore, the exact relationship between Spanish merchant houses and their Mexico City counterparts in the late colonial period is a matter calling for further research. The evidence presented in this study and others is, in sum, ambiguous. Clearly certain firms in Mexico City were free agents, while others were overt branches of Spanish commercial houses. It now appears that a comprehensive exploration of the character of this relationship cannot be achieved primarily from work in the archives of Mexico. The answer must be pursued in Spain itself, especially in the records of individual trading firms.

Nonetheless, the mechanisms used by the autonomous international trading houses of Mexico City to maintain their dominance over the importation of goods into the colony in the half century before Independence are well understood. Some wholesalers dealt directly with ship captains sailing into the port of Veracruz, utilizing their access to silver coin to ward off challenges from emerging commercial centers. Others dispatched agents, usually attached to the Mexico City firms through company agreements, directly to Spain to buy merchandise there for shipment back to Mexico, all under the ultimate direction of the commercial house in the capital.

The Mexico City trading houses did not concentrate solely on the acquisition and sale of manufactured goods from Europe. Great attention was paid to the China trade, conducted annually through the Manila Galleon dispatched to Acapulco, and to the importation of cacao from Spanish South America. In these aspects of overseas commerce, the firms of the capital remained unchallenged by traders from other cities of the colony.

Until the mid-eighteenth century, silver had been the overwhelmingly dominant export from Mexico to Europe. In the late colonial period, however, silver exports were supplemented by shipments of cochineal and also of sugar. Again, it was the merchants of the capital who led the way in this development. They maintained their domination over the trade of these and other commodities in the final years of the colonial period despite the challenge of expanding provincial and port cities. They were able to do so because they controlled much of the specie refined in Mexico and the distribution systems which supplied retailers across the country.

Every aspect of the Mexican economy, and certainly of its commerce, was dependent on credit transactions. An anomaly of late colonial Mexico—one beyond the scope of the present study—is that this region which produced more silver coin than any other at the time was itself chronically short of coin and had no other generally accepted medium. As a result, every transaction, from the acquisition of a business to the purchase of a single retail item, was characterized by credit. Buyers ranging from the highest elements of the society down to the poorest had to pawn personal items, set up payment schedules, or offer bondsmen in guarantee of payment. Credit purchases were so pervasive that any sale made for cash was extraordinary. Thus every individual and business was normally both creditor and debtor. The economy was marked by chains of credit, and if a major business suddenly folded, the act sent a shock wave up and down the economic ladder, bringing down individuals and smaller firms in its wake.

In this specie-short economy, the person with access to coin was in a very favorable position. The commercial houses of the capital sought to obtain this advantage by regularly financing mining operations and moving actively into actual ownership of mines. In every type of agreement between a miner and a merchant, the latter invariably insisted that all silver produced by the mine be handled by his trading firm. Merchants were thereby able to secure coin for purchases of imported goods and to resist any attempted takeover of provincial trade by mercantile enterprises in other cities. Mexico City merchant houses also maintained an effective monopoly over silver shipping throughout the country. It appears that at any one time, perhaps only two silver-shipping firms would be in operation, bonded for hundreds of thousands of pesos and willing to transport metals throughout the country and to any port, all for a fee based on the value of the shipment.

It was this access to specie, plus the large scale of their operations, which enabled the wholesalers of the capital to dominate interprovincial commerce. These merchants frequently opened up branch stores in important provincial and mining centers, placing them under the supervision of managing partners who normally received a third or half of any profits. Equally important was the maintenance of correspondence accounts with provincial shopkeepers. In these agreements, the Mexico City trading firm supplied goods to the shopkeeper, extended him credit, honored all drafts issued against him, and provided other necessary banking services in return for exclusive supplier status and all the silver coin which the retail store might receive. These provincial stores were totally dependent on their Mexico City suppliers. They themselves lacked the coin and the volume of trade necessary to buy directly from ships and foreign concerns. Because of their own dependence on credit dealings with their customers, they would likely fail if unable to obtain lines of credit from their suppliers. And only Mexico City merchant houses were large enough to offer lines of credit to different retailers, for they dealt with enough provincial storekeepers that they were always receiving some payment from one or another of them.

While branch stores and correspondence accounts were the major vehicles used by merchant houses of the capital to control interprovincial commerce in major regional centers and mining towns, these firms turned to several other methods to gain access to trade in yet other areas. Traders continually entered into formal and informal commercial agreements with officials in charge of Indian districts and certain government monopolies. This practice was not effectively curtailed by any reform enacted by the crown during the colonial period. Towns and villages off the established trade routes were supplied through viandantes, itinerant traders who were not affiliated with any larger commercial firm and who entered into one-time credit contracts to take goods into the countryside. These peddlers were marginal to the world of commerce and to the society of the capital; they never ascended to positions in larger firms and rarely even became managers of small retail stores in the capital.

Finally, capital-based merchants often bypassed all intermediaries and dealt directly with producers: hacendados and miners. Again, transactions were conducted on credit, but the merchant normally accepted final payment in silver from the miner or in commodities from the hacendado. We have already seen how useful specie was to the wholesaler; he was also willing to accept agricultural produce because he was often active in the supply of raw materials to the different types of processing and manufacturing plants in the capital and because it was incumbent upon him always to seek out new markets and new products in which to deal. Given the character of commerce in this society, not to expand was to risk eventual failure. This is not to say, though, that these merchants were exclusively commodity traders. Dealing in produce was only a side activity, perhaps necessary, but still merely supplemental. Only sugar was sufficiently lucrative (being of such high unit value) to support exclusive dealers (and even then other merchants dealt in it with regularity). In every other case examined, any merchant who attempted to specialize in commodity trading ultimately went out of business.

Retail trade in Mexico City was multifaceted, with a number of large stores which specialized in imported merchandise, a variety of specialty shops, and several types of general-merchandise and grocery stores which saw to the needs of the populace, plus an assortment of liquor stores which catered to different clienteles. Even this level of commerce, like those above it, was characterized by the separation of ownership from management. Retail stores were normally run by managers who either received a salary or a designated share of the profits as partners of the proprietor. Some owners had several stores (perhaps each a different type), each of which might be managed by a separate individual under a separate and distinct company agreement.

Kinship often linked managers and proprietors. Sons, cousins, nephews, and even daughters might work as store managers, thus earning some income and, more importantly, learning the business in preparation for eventual ownership. But even managing partners who were not kin of the owners were in a prime position to acquire the establishment sometime.

The wholesalers of the city were quite willing to acquire small neighborhood grocery stores, but while they might train the managers and commercial apprentices of their larger retail establishments for higher positions in the commercial firm, no managers of neighborhood stores were permitted into such programs. There existed a distinct social division in the world of management between administrators of large stores which sold imported items and of specialty shops and those of neighborhood grocery stores.

Unlike the wholesalers, the owners of one or several retail stores could not entertain notions of elevation into the elite or even the acquisition of sizable rural estates. Some did manage to purchase moderate-sized estates near the capital, but more commonly they would expand their retail operations through purchase of another store either in the capital or in a nearby town. Some also moved into processing of foodstuffs. The owners of liquor stores were also occasionally able to obtain small rural holdings, but more often they built distilleries to supply their stores. The owners of individual grocery stores could not aspire even to this. Most were content to buy a modest home if they could.

The pulque trade was controlled by the creole elite, who owned the bulk of the pulque ranchos producing the intoxicant and a large number of the pulquerías which sold it. Here, as in so many other cases, owners separated themselves from day-to-day management of their operations, leaving it to specialists who received a share of the income or who leased the operations for a set number of years, committing themselves to the purchase of all or a significant part of the pulque produced on the ranchos of the proprietors.

Commerce and virtually every other form of enterprise in this society was characterized by company agreements, most commonly between ownership and management. Such a partnership provided ample benefits to both parties. It enabled the financier to increase the number of his holdings in commerce and also to diversify into other economic fields, all the while ensuring him of competent management of daily affairs. The arrangement gave the managing partner an opportunity to earn much greater profits than he could ever hope to receive as a salaried employee. It also entailed greater responsibility for the manager and brought him closer to a possible move into ownership. Many managers eventually acquired the businesses they once administered. If the owner was not willing to sell out, his partner might be able to take some of his earnings, perhaps combine them with borrowed funds, and assume ownership of another commercial enterprise.

Only ownership of property or of a business enterprise could lead to great wealth in this economy. No person who remained a manager, no matter how advanced, earned more than a comfortable living. A considerable social gap existed between managers—even the most important—and owners of businesses, even those with fairly modest enterprises. A manager still worked for another person, no matter how much responsibility he had and how much he might make, and for this reason simply lacked the status of an independent proprietor who could hire other persons rather than seek employment for himself.

The term *cajero* always referred to a commercial employee, but depending on the context, it could signify the head administrator of a substantial enterprise or a lowly apprentice or clerk. No cajero owned substantial property of his own or even his own residence. He was always dependent on the beneficence of his employer, whether a relative or not.

Many merchants did employ webs of kin, from both their own and younger generations. Two brothers might well set themselves up as equal partners in a major commercial company and train their sons and nephews (the latter typically brought over from Spain) to move into independent commercial businesses, but only if they had the ability. Most commercial apprentices, whether kin of their masters or not, never rose to the level of independent owner of a merchant house. Some remained shop employees their entire lives; others came to own modest stores which were closely affiliated to a commercial house; yet others became independent proprietors of substantial stores; only the most fortunate and talented ascended to the pinnacle of success and headed a major trading firm.

While there can be no question but that the great majority of trading houses in Mexico City were headed by peninsulars, in some cases the latter were overseeing the commercial affairs of a diversified creole family fortune. Furthermore, a significant number of creoles—some sons of merchants and some not, some with noble titles and some not—headed major trading firms on their own. These men typically directed enormous, family-run enterprises. They had utilized the birthright of the creole elite—the freedom to choose whatever profession seemed most attractive—and had chosen to enter commerce. These creole merchants sometimes journeyed to Spain to learn the business, cultivating the important personal contacts which were vital to the operation of every trading house throughout the colonial era.

Given the practice of several members of a single family involving themselves in wholesale commerce and the frequency with which powerful mercantile families intermarried, it is no surprise that the Mexico City Consulado was dominated by powerful extended family groups. At times, a single member of the merchant's guild could be surrounded by four or five blood relatives and by several other wholesalers who had married into his immediate family.

Successful merchants frequently married the daughters (or widows) of other merchants and thereby came into control of all or part of their businesses. This promoted consolidation of commercial enterprises, giving newcomers access to established firms and preventing overexpansion at the wholesale level of trade. Merchants of the same type also wed into elite creole families and used their commercial contacts and business skills on their in-laws' behalf. Some married the offspring of prominent government officials. While high court judges would themselves marry only into established creole elite families, they would sometimes offer one of their daughters in matrimony to a wholesaler.

Every mercantile family of substance entered into rural-estate ownership by at least the second generation after attaining prominence and often in the first.[1] Such properties provided prestige, certainly, but more importantly, they represented a relatively secure form of investment in an economy marked by erratic and dramatic fluctuations. Estate ownership was a source of financial stability and regular profits and constituted the only form of wealth which was easily subdivided and passed along over generations. Merchants used both matrimony and outright purchase to acquire estates. That they saw agriculture as a profit-making endeavor is demonstrated by the frequency with which they leased rather than purchased properties from their owners.

But the fact that mercantile families moved quickly into agriculture should not be taken to mean that they left commerce behind; far from it. Established families typically remained very active in trade, dealing not just in the sale of commodities produced on their estates but also in the importation and distribution of foreign merchandise. They frequently maintained a family member—not always the head—in the Mexico City Consulado. Commerce and agriculture were viewed as twin cornerstones of a long-term family fortune.

The wholesale traders of the capital actively pursued honors from their fellow merchants, the crown, the church, and local authorities. Many of the most successful served as prior or consul of the merchants' guild. Most of those who became officers of the Consulado were able to add several other honors; few who did not were able to. As to the military, wholesalers were quick to move into officer slots opened up in the new militia units created in the late colonial period. However, a great number of almaceneros did not actively pursue officer rank, but rather were quite satisfied to be common soldiers in the commercial regiment of the militia of the capital.

Only a few wholesalers received noble titles; some others became members of the military orders of Spain. Far fewer were designated familiars of the Inquisition, apparently due more to the distinguished lineage of their families and their achievements in other fields than to their accomplishments in commerce.

Many merchants became honorary regidores and alcaldes ordinarios of the city; this was common throughout Spanish America. But they shared these posts with roughly equal numbers of titled individuals and lawyers, most of whom represented established creole families. Uncommon was the merchant—and more uncommon the peninsular merchant—who gained a proprietary post on the city council of the capital.

The sons of wholesalers, who were of course creoles regardless of the status of their fathers, enjoyed the privilege of elite offspring, of having considerable discretion in their choice of careers. A significant portion followed their fathers into the world of trade. Others, although a distinct minority, chose one or another of the professions. A great many assumed supervisory posts in the now large and diversified family businesses. They almost always married women of equal station and thereby added even further to the family holdings and rank.

A number of daughters of wholesalers married up-and-coming peninsular merchants, sometimes their cousins, who were thereby absorbed into the greater family and trusted to watch over its interests. Far more merchants' daughters married into creole families which were the peers of their own. Some wed high-ranking government officials. Relatively few became nuns; more remained spinsters, more or less attached to the houses of married siblings.

Mexico City was more than a commercial-bureaucratic city; it supported a great number of manufacturing and processing plants.

These produced items mainly for the population of the greater metropolitan area; little if anything was marketed in the provinces, let alone abroad. Ownership or investment in these enterprises carried no social stigma. Members of the local elite participated in this field of the economy on a regular basis. No greater or lesser status accrued to the owners of these businesses; they were socially equal to any others in the society who had their wealth and backgrounds.

But this is not to say that these industries were very attractive investments. Many demanded heavy initial capital outlays and then forced their owners periodically into debt through borrowing to assemble the necessary raw materials. Labor was also often a problem. Work in these shops was certainly not inviting to most people; the owners therefore sometimes turned to convict labor or to other devices involving coercion to compel their labor force to remain with them.

As was the rule in commerce and agriculture, there was normally a separation between ownership and management in these industries, and company agreements were the device used to formalize the relationship between the two. Bakeries, slaughterhouses, and textile mills all utilized company arrangements to attract competent managers and increase investment from external sources. All these enterprises typically sold on credit and needed to acquire large amounts of raw materials. As a result, debt was endemic, and owners often contracted separate company agreements with individuals willing to insert additional capital into the business. Bakeries especially seemed to have difficulty in securing enough wheat. Owners, therefore, turned to a variety of methods, usually involving some sort of advance payment or loan to a producer, to ensure themselves a sufficient supply.

Despite the instability endemic to businesses in which debt was so common, some families maintained ownership of obrajes and other enterprises over generations. At times, sons or nephews served as operating managers; at other times, the family withdrew entirely from management by leasing out the business to an outside interest, who sometimes paid the entire lease price in advance.

Some items which were normally still produced in artisan shops were beginning to be turned out in larger shops in mass production. Shoes, hats, and other forms of apparel were manufactured in these establishments. It is not clear if the owners were themselves still masters in the craft or if there was any task specialization.

Finally, artisans by the thousands and in a grand variety of crafts prospered in the capital. There was considerable differentiation in the world of craft production. Some crafts were much more lucrative than others and carried much more status. Some required fine work, others brute labor. All maintained pronounced separation between masters (and proprietors), journeymen, and apprentices. All crafts were dependent on credit transactions, and no payment could be expected until the finished product was delivered.

Not all masters owned their own shops, but every artisan who owned a shop was a master. Some had more than a single shop and operated them through company agreements with other masters who acted as the managers. Some also formed partnerships with outside investors who were willing to put up the money they needed to expand their businesses. The successful masters of the most lucrative crafts lived in a manner quite similar to those of retail merchants and lower-level professionals. They were able to invest in moderate-sized estates, retail stores, and urban property. But masters of the lowest crafts lived at a subsistence level, with little opportunity to acquire wealth or property.

Journeymen in all the crafts endured low status and barely made a living wage. A reasonably comfortable existence required elevation at least to the master level. Apprentices typically entered into formal written contracts with their masters, which bound both parties to perform certain tasks and which inflicted liabilities if the stipulations were not met.

It is at the artisan level that we witness the large-scale infusion of castas and Indians into the urban economy. Despite regulations designed expressly to exclude them, members of these groups were able to enter every craft, even at the master level. On the other hand, Spaniards stayed in evidence in significant numbers down to the lower levels of the occupational scale. Thus, in a sense, the social spread of ethnic Spaniards was complete.

Certain themes and patterns in this work transcend individual chapters and manifest their general importance to the society and business world of late colonial Mexico City. Certainly one such theme is the centrality of the family in the organization of business. The definition of family at this time was generally quite extended, and whenever possible, businesses were run as family enterprises, with as many supervisory posts as possible held by family members. The interests of individual members were subordinated to the long-term benefit of the larger entity. Sons and nephews, formally or informally, apprenticed themselves in the professions of their fathers and uncles to prepare for eventual takeover of leadership positions. Family patriarchs earnestly endeavored to place all lesser members in positions which would promote the family interest and at least provide the occupant with a comfortable existence. Great effort was taken, though not always successfully, to avoid family splits and resentments, certainly any which might cause factions in the family to work against each other. A person's profession was often an inadequate indication of his true function, for many people practiced their occupations solely or predominantly on behalf of their families and even worked on their behalf in ways not directly related to their profession.

Few peninsulars in this society rose to positions of prominence. Whether compared to their own total numbers or to the number of creoles in each sector of the economy, most peninsulars never gained entrance into the elite. Many never aspired to do so, simply wishing to make a better life for themselves in the colony than they could have attained in Spain. Peninsulars dominated no sphere of the economy or any profession except for international trade. And even here some worked for the benefit of a larger, predominantly creole family into which they had been absorbed, while others aspired to do the same. Many of the least successful immigrants were forced into the countryside to find employment on ranchos and haciendas—a fate which most Hispanics sought to escape—and thus do not show up in the study of Mexico City or of provincial centers. Others who remained in the city never rose above manual labor or clerking.

Significant internal differentiation marked every occupation. Simply to designate a person's profession says little about his status or wealth in the late colonial world. Much closer examination is needed to ascertain his actual functions, family background, pattern of advancement, level of wealth, investments, marriage, and honors. There was no strict hierarchy of occupations, and in many cases a person in an unprepossessing calling could be both more prosperous and held in higher esteem than another person in a profession which seemed overall to carry more prestige.

Performance mattered in this economy, and the inept, even among the elite, were normally shuttled into sinecures which would not reflect badly on the family but which gave the occupant no real responsibility and also no opportunity to rise.

Children of the elite and of other established creole families enjoyed a wide option in career choices. And the choice was not simply between subsidized idleness and a career in one of the professions. These offspring made their careers in commerce, mining, agriculture, and any one of a number of supervisory posts in family businesses and outside of them. The economy was enormously sophisticated, containing a large number of responsible supervisory posts which are not readily lumped into one of the standard occupational groupings.

Certainly the society of the capital did not consist of a small elite, a miniscule middle level, and a massive lower class. Mexico City supported a very large and highly differentiated middle sector. It was predominantly, but not exclusively, Hispanic in composition, and embraced a wide variety of occupations, most but not all of which were nonmanual. There is no way in which the many retail merchants, functionaries, artisans, managers, and processors can be relegated to the lower class. They enjoyed a comfortable style of life, were able to invest in fields of the economy outside of their own specialties, and were honored within their own occupations (and often by the larger society as well). These people admired the elite way of life but well knew that neither they nor, probably, their children could aspire to that level. Some few, of course, did pass over the nebulous boundary into the elite, for upward and downward mobility existed throughout the society. But the great mass of people appreciated that they did not have the resources, occupy the positions, or enjoy the connections which would enable them to rise so high. They were quite proud of their own positions and achievements in life and did not live in frustration over not having risen to the pinnacle of society.

People at every level of society endeavored to diversify their investments, because all economic sectors suffered from unpredictable and sometimes violent downturns. The only way to protect oneself in this business climate was to move into as many fields of the economy as possible, presuming that all would not collapse at the same time.

Company agreements were the basic mechanism of business organization at every point in the economy. They were not restricted to the commercial world but rather permeated all spheres of production and distribution. This was possible because of the adaptability and wide variety of functions of this form of management. It separated ownership from daily supervision of enterprises, thus freeing the former to concern itself with other matters and enabling it to expand, whether within a single specialty or among different ones. Distinct agreements could be reached with the administrator of each branch or enterprise. The company also facilitated the entrance of capital from outside investors. Many potential financiers did not wish to settle for the level of return available through loan agreements; company contracts between the lender and the businessman enabled the former to gain a potentially far greater return on his money and the latter to obtain capital perhaps not otherwise available.

Agreements between ownership and management rewarded administrators for strong performances and punished them with a smaller return through their share of the profits for a poor one. The practice led to the creation of a large group of professional managers, most of whom aspired to become proprietors and whose income from company contracts might provide them with the means to do so. The company also acted as a mechanism for the training of relatives and other personnel in the ways of a specific business before they advanced to its head position.

Though many patterns and practices cut across the entire social spectrum of the business world, this cannot be attributed to the lower sectors' emulation or imitation of the elite. Rather, it signifies that every occupational group existed within the same economic setting and experienced virtually the same needs and requirements. For instance, there was no way that any enterprise, whatever its size, could operate without credit arrangements. And as every business was subject to precipitous downturns, diversification made sense at every economic level. Expansion and diversification of business was possible only when proprietors could separate themselves from daily supervision of their businesses and gain access to venture capital. Company contracts enabled them to do so. Every sector of society which engaged in business maintained a strong sense of family and aspired to place its members in advantageous posts; some used transferrable government positions, others membership in guilds, and still others influence with powerful individuals and institutions to secure advantages for their sons and nephews. Marriage was used by every group to cement beneficial affiliations and to transfer usable wealth or property whenever possible.

Certainly, many families of lower standing in the society sought affiliation of some sort with the elite. Such contacts could only redound to their benefit. But they did not slavishly copy its practices. Rather, people responded in like manner to pressures felt in common by every economically active element.

Despite the development of port cities and provincial centers in the eighteenth century and the loss of its official monopoly over international trade, Mexico City successfully maintained its dominance over most aspects of provincial commerce until the end of the colonial period. Merchants of the capital remained the primary financiers of mining ventures in the country and otherwise established commercial agreements with miners and provincial storekeepers which guaranteed their access to silver, a necessary component of their autonomy in international trade. Likewise, the merchants of the capital were able to circumvent regulations intended to lessen their control over the cochineal trade, continuing to finance provincial government officials who controlled much of the production in their districts.

Many of the great estate-owning families of the colony were citizens of Mexico City, and much of the marketing of raw materials and comestibles was directed through the capital and channelled by mercantile interests in that city. The merchants of the capital dominated the marketing of all goods, both foreign and domestic, within the city and within the greater Valley of Mexico—still in the late colonial period the major center of consumption in the country. As the cost of overland shipping remained so high, manufacturing and processing interests in Mexico City were not able to sell their domestically produced goods in the provinces. But for the same reason, provincial producers were unable to challenge the capital's domination of its hinterland. Mexico City—as the center of both the political and ecclesiastical bureaucracies of the colony—continued to attract the greatest number and the most qualified of professionals. Prominent provincial families regularly sent their sons to the capital for their higher education, and many of these new professionals chose to remain there, often representing their family's interests in the city or becoming officials in one or another of the city's bureaucracies.

Appendix

Priors and Consuls of the Consulado of New Spain, 1770–1826
M = Montañés Party Member   B = Basque Party Member
The order is always: Prior, Senior Consul, and Junior Consul

1770
Juan González Guerra   M
Antonio Barroso y Torrubia   B
Juan Bautista de Aldasoro   B
1771
Juan de Castañiza/Starting in April: B
Juan José Pérez Cano   B
Francisco del Rivero   M
Gabriel Gutiérrez de Terán   M
1772
Juan José Pérez Cano   B
Gabriel Gutiérrez de Teran   M
José de Cevallos   M
1773
Fernando González de Collantes   M
José de Cevallos   M
Francisco Bazo Ibáñez   B
1774
Fernando González de Collantes   M
Francisco Bazo Ibáñez   B
Joaquín Fabian de Memije   M

1775
Ambrosio de Meave	B
Joaquín Fabian de Memije	B
Pedro Alonso de Alles	M

1776
Ambrosio de Meave	B
Pedro Alonso de Alles	M
Juan Manuel González de Cosio	B

1777
Joaquín Dongo	M
José Joaquín de Ariscorreta	B
Pedro de Ayzinena	B

1778
Joaquín Dongo	M
José Joaquín de Ariscorreta	B
Pedro de Ayzinena	B

1779
Joaquín Dongo	M
Pedro de Ayzinena	B
José Martín Chávez	M

1780
Juan Bautista de Aldasoro	B
José Martín Chávez	M
Pedro Jiménez de la Plaza	M

1781
Antonio Barroso y Torrubia	B
Pablo Jiménez de la Plaza	M
Antonio de Bassoco	B

1782
Antonio Barroso y Torrubia	B
Antonio de Bassoco	B
Francisco Martínez Cabezón	M

1783
Francisco del Rivero	M
Francisco Martínez Cabezón	M
José Mariano de la Cotera, Marqués de Rivascacho	M

1784
Francisco del Rivero   M
Pablo Jiménez de la Plaza   M
Francisco Antonio de Rábago   B
1785
Gabriel Gutiérrez de Terán   M
Francisco Antonio de Rábago   B
Miguel Francisco Sánchez Hidalgo   B
1786
Gabriel Gutiérrez de Terán   M
Miguel Francisco Sánchez Hidalgo   B
Juan Antonio de Yermo   B
1787
Francisco Bazo Ibáñez   B
Juan Antonio de Yermo   B
Servando Gómez de la Cortina,   M
Conde de la Cortina
1788
Francisco Bazo Ibáñez   B
Servando Gómez de la Cortina,   M
Conde de la Cortina
Francisco Antonio de Pesquera   B
1789
José de Cevallos   M
Francisco Antonio de Pesquera   B
Francisco Ignacio de Iraeta   B
1790
José de Cevallos   M
Francisco Antonio de Iraeta   B
Sebastián de Eguía   B
1791
José Joaquín de Ariscorreta   B
Sebastián de Eguía   B
José de Orduña   M

1792
José Joaquín de Ariscorreta   B
José de Orduña   M
Miguel González Calderón   M
1793
Pedro Alonso de Alles,   M
Marqués de Santa Cruz de Inguanzo
Miguel González Calderón   M
Tomás Domingo de Acha   B
1794
Pedro Alonso de Alles,   M
Marqués de Santa Cruz de Inguanzo
Tomás Domingo de Acha   B
Francisco Sáenz de Santa María   M
1795
Antonio de Bassoco   B
Francisco Sáenz de Santa María   M
Rodrigo Sánchez   B
1796
Antonio de Bassoco   B
Rodrigo Sánchez   B
Matías Gutiérrez de Lanzas   M
1797
Antonio de Bassoco   B
Matías Gutiérrez de Lanzas   M
Juan Díaz González   B
1798
José Orduña   M
Juan Díaz González   M
José de los Heros   B
1799
Tomás Domingo de Acha   B
José de los Heros   B
Gaspar Martín Vicario   M

1800

Tomás Domingo de Acha	B
Gaspar Martín Vicario	M
Francisco de la Cotera	M

1801

Francisco Antonio de Pesquera	B
Francisco de la Cotera	M
Isidro Antonio de Icaza	B

1802

Francisco Antonio de Pesquera	B
Isidro Antonio de Icaza	B
Francisco de Chavarrí	B

1803

Sebastián de Eguía	B
Francisco de Chavarrí	B
Sebastián de Heras Soto	M

1804

Sebastián de Eguía	B
Sebastián de Heras Soto	M
Juan Ignacio González Vértiz	M

1805

Matías Gutiérrez de Lanzas	M
Juan Ignacio González Vértiz	M
Gabriel de Iturbe e Iraeta	B

1806

Francisco de la Cotera	M
Gabriel de Iturbe e Iraeta	B
Juan Fernando de Meoqui	B

1807

José Vicente de Olloqui	B
Juan Fernando de Meoqui	B
Juan Ignacio González Vértiz	M

1808

Juan Díaz González	B
José de la Cotera	M
José Ruiz de la Barcena	B

1809

Francisco Alonso de Terán	M
José Ruiz de la Barcena	B
Gabriel Joaquín de Yermo	B

1810

Francisco Alonso de Terán	M
Gabriel Joaquín de Yermo	B
Diego de Agreda	B

1811

Francisco de Chavarrí	B
Diego de Agreda	B
Lorenzo García Noriega	M

1812

Francisco de Chavarrí	B
Lorenzo García Noriega	M
Vicente Gómez de la Cortina, Conde de la Cortina	M

1813

Diego Fernández Peredo	M
Vicente Gómez de la Cortina, Conde de la Cortina	M
Tomás Ramón de Ibarrola	B

1814

Diego Fernández Peredo	M
Tomás Ramón de Ibarrola	B
Manuel de Urquiaga	B

1815

Diego de Agreda, Conde de la Casa de Agreda	B
Manuel de Urquiaga	B
Juan Marcos de Rada	M

1816

Diego de Agreda, Conde de la Casa de Agreda	B
Juan Marcos de Rada	M
Roque Pérez Gómez	M

1817

José Ruiz de la Barcena	B
Roque Pérez Gómez	M
José María de Echave	B

1818

José Ruiz de la Barcena	B
José María de Echave	B
Gregorio Sáenz de Sicilia	B

1819

Diego de Agreda,	B
Conde de la Casa de Agreda	
Gregorio Sáenz de Sicilia	B
Manuel Francisco Gutiérrez	M

1820

Antonio Velasco de la Torre	M
Manuel Francisco Gutiérrez	M
Pedro Marcos Gutiérrez	M

1821

Vicente Gómez de la Cortina,	M
Conde de la Cortina	
Pedro Marcos Gutiérrez	M
Martín Angel de Micháus	B

1822

José María de Echave	B
Martín Angel de Micháus	B
José Bernabé de Isita	M

1823

?
?
?

1824

José María de Echave	B
Francisco Cortina González	M
?	

1825
José María de Echave	B
Francisco Cortina González	M
José María de Urquiaga	B

1826
José María de Urquiaga	B
Gabriel Manuel de Iturbe	B
Juan García Castrillo	M

Abbreviations

AGN: Archivo General de la Nación
AHH: Archivo Histórico de Hacienda
AN: Archivo de Notarías del Departamento del
         Distrito Federal (México D.F.)
BN: Biblioteca Nacional
DM: *Diario de México*
GM: *Gazeta de México*
HAHR: *Hispanic American Historical Review*
JLAS: *Journal of Latin American Studies*

Notes

Preface

1. Ida Altman and James Lockhart, eds., *Provinces of Early Mexico*, Los Angeles: UCLA Latin American Center, 1976.

Chapter 1

1. Manuel Carrera Stampa, "La Ciudad de México a principios de siglo XIX," *Memorias de la Academia Mexicana de la Historia*, 26:2 (1967): 184–231; María Dolores Morales, "Estructura urbana y distribución de la propiedad en la Ciudad de México en 1813," *Historia Mexicana*, 25:3 (1976): 363–402; John E. Kicza, "The Pulque Trade in Late Colonial Mexico City," *The Americas*, 37:2 (October 1980): 193–221.

2. The population figures in Table 1 which are most worthy of confidence are those from 1790 and 1811, both being the results of actual censuses. The basis for the 1772 count is unknown; the number was given in the 1805 report from the Mexico City Consulado, which made no reference to its origins. A very interesting question is whether the 1790 and 1793 census figures are actually from the same count. The document supplying the 1790 data states very explicitly in its title (and this is substantiated by the statistical breakdowns included) that it is the summary of an actual census. It seems unlikely that the government only two or three years later carried out yet another census (the Revillagigedo census); yet every work that I have ever read has dated the Revillagigedo census of the capital from 1792 or 1793. Perhaps it was actually conducted in 1790 but not released until a few years later. The 1803 figure is the estimate

255

calculated by Humboldt by applying a rate-of-increase factor to the Revillagigedo census. The 1805 number is out of the Mexico City Consulado report; its basis is not given, but it seems to be an extrapolation of the 1790 census. The 1820 figure is from Fernando Navarro y Noriega, an official in Mexico City who paid close attention to population trends, and it is probably quite close to the actual number. The capital was hit by a virulent epidemic within a couple of years after the 1811 census, and the population dropped by some thousands of people as a consequence. By the middle of the decade, however, it was again on the rise.

3. John K. Chance, *Race and Class in Colonial Oaxaca* (Stanford: Stanford University Press, 1978); D. A. Brading and Celia Wu, "Population Growth and Crisis: León, 1720–1860," *JLAS*, 5:1 (1973): 1–36.

4. Morales, "Estructura urbana."

5. AGN, AHH, leg. 426, exp. 16, 1816.

6. Ibid.

7. See the map on p. 66 of Doris Ladd, *The Mexican Nobility at Independence 1780–1826* (Austin: University of Texas Press, 1976).

Chapter 2

1. This chapter is based on wills, business contracts, powers of attorney, dowry agreements, and related material located in the Archivo de Notarías del Departamento del Distrito Federal, on court cases, membership lists, and census material found in various ramos of the Archivo General de la Nación, on the two newspapers of late colonial Mexico City, on membership lists of the *Colegio de Abogados*, artisan guilds, and other organizations, on population summaries and the *Guías de forasteros* found in the Biblioteca National, on published manuscripts and documents from the time, and on the substantial research, published and unpublished, which has emerged on colonial social history in the past two decades.

2. BN, "Estado reducido."

3. See L. N. McAlister, "Social Structure and Social Change in New Spain," *HAHR*, 43:3 (August 1963): 349–370; William B. Taylor and John K. Chance, "Estate and Class in a Colonial City—Oaxaca in 1792," *Comparative Studies in Society and History*, 19:4 (October 1977): 454–487; Chance's book *Race and Class in Colonial Oaxaca* (Stanford: Stanford University Press, 1978); and Dennis N. Valdés, "The Decline of the *Sociedad de Castas* in Mexico City" (Ph.D. diss., University of Michigan, 1978) for discussions of the workings of social race in colonial Mexico.

4. Ladd, *The Mexican Nobility*, pp. 20–21.

5. Only those peninsular immigrants sponsored by uncles and cousins who were wholesale merchants in Mexico (not counting government and church officials) could expect to be placed in promising employment situations, and even then many of them never ascended very far or even at all. See Chapter 6.

6. See Chapter 9.

7. Christon I. Archer, *The Army in Bourbon Mexico, 1760–1810* (Albuquerque: University of New Mexico Press, 1977), pp. 210–215.

8. The related questions of the size of the families being examined and the wealth of the greater clan versus that of individuals within it are obviously crucial. The families, as discussed in the text, endeavored to define their membership as broadly as possible, but as a consequence, some members were clearly of secondary status. I regard a family's wealth and property as being that which it assembled and managed as a collective unit, often in a very integrated fashion. Quite understandably, some families were wealthier and more extensive than others. These could subdivide and thereby create separate but related families, all derived from the same ancestry and now operating their holdings primarily as independent entities.

9. Brian R. Hamnett, *Politics and Trade in Southern Mexico 1750–1821* (Cambridge: Cambridge University Press, 1971), pp. 5–8; William B. Taylor, *Landlord and Peasant in Colonial Oaxaca* (Stanford: Stanford University Press, 1972), pp. 199–201.

10. Reinhard Liehr, *Ayuntamiento y oligarquía en Puebla, 1787–1810* (Mexico: SepSetentas, 1976), vol. I, pp. 22 and 45–47.

11. Alexander von Humboldt, "Tablas geográficas políticas del reino de Nueva España," in Enrique Florescano and Isabel Gil, eds., *Descripciones económicas generales de Nueva España, 1784–1817* (Mexico: SEPINAH, 1973), p. 153. The Intendancy of Veracruz in 1803 had a population less than that of nine of the twelve intendancies of Mexico. The Intendancy of Mexico had nine times its population, and Mexico City alone had approximately the population of all of Veracruz.

12. D. A. Brading, *Miners and Merchants in Bourbon Mexico 1763–1810* (Cambridge: Cambridge University Press, 1971), Chapters 8 and 9 passim.

13. Richard Lindley, "Kinship and Credit in the Structure of Guadalajara's Oligarchy 1800–1830" (Ph.D. diss., University of Texas at Austin, 1976), pp. 49–50 and 63.

14. See Chapter 7.

15. Eduardo Báez Macías, ed., "Planos y censos de la Ciudad de México, 1753," *Boletín del Archivo General de la Nación*, 8:3–4 (1967): 487–1115; AGN, Padrones, vols. 53–77, 1811.

16. Ladd, *The Mexican Nobility*, Table 7, p. 28 and John Tutino, "Creole Mexico: Spanish Elites, Haciendas, and Indian Towns, 1750–1810" (Ph.D. diss., University of Texas at Austin, 1976), p. 24.

17. Tutino, "Creole Mexico," p. 21; D. A. Brading, *Haciendas and Ranchos in the Mexican Bajío: León 1700–1860* (Cambridge: Cambridge University Press, 1978), p. 23.

18. See Chapter 7.

19. Charles H. Harris III, *A Mexican Family Empire*, (Austin: University of Texas Press, 1975), p. 79.

20. Charles Gibson, *The Aztecs Under Spanish Rule* (Stanford: Stanford University Press, 1964), pp. 328–329.

21. Kicza, "The Pulque Trade," p. 202.

22. Enrique Florescano, *Precios del maíz y crisis agrícolas en México (1708–1810)* (Mexico: El Colegio de Mexico, 1969), p. 92.

23. Kicza, "The Pulque Trade," pp. 203–207.

24. Brading, *Haciendas and Ranchos*, p. 11; Tutino, "Creole Mexico," p. 165.

25. Lindley, "Kinship and Credit," pp. 140–145.

26. AN, Juan Manuel Pozo, April 4, 1810; Tutino, "Creole Mexico," p. 129. For vertical integration in mining, see Brading, *Miners and Merchants*, p. 149 and P. J. Bakewell, *Silver Mining and Society in Colonial Mexico, Zacatecas 1546–1700* (Cambridge: Cambridge University Press, 1971), pp. 115–118, 125, and 137.

27. Harris, *A Mexican Family Empire*, p. 115; Tutino, "Creole Mexico," p. 269. The planters of yet another American colonial society—the tobacco growers of the eighteenth-century Chesapeake—have also been traditionally described as disdainful toward commerce, but recent research has disclosed that they also acted as commodity traders and as distributors of imported goods for smaller upland farmers. See Aubrey Land, "Economic Base and Social Structure: The Northern Chesapeake in the Eighteenth Century," in Stanley N. Katz, ed., *Colonial America: Essays in Politics and Social Development* (Boston: Little, Brown and Company, 1975), pp. 345–359, especially pp. 352–355. The commercial and manufacturing investments of São Paulo coffee growers is covered in Warren Dean, *The Industrialization of São Paulo 1880–1945* (Austin: University of Texas Press, 1969), Chapter III.

28. Ibid.

29. See Chapter 6. While technically independent agents, a number of Consulado traders were subordinated to or sponsored by more powerful merchant firms from which they had derived. Virtually all of these Creole families belonged to this dominant group.

30. Ibid.

31. For one such case, see AN, Félix Fernando Zamorano y Barrera, Dec. 24, 1804.

32. See Chapter 7.

33. Considerable information about the 1802 collapse of the previously mighty trading house of Oteiza y Vértiz and its repercussions on a number of smaller firms is available in AGN, Consulado, leg. 183, exp. 3.

34. Brading, *Miners and Merchants*, pp. 169–170.

35. Brading, *Haciendas and Ranchos*, pp. 115–118.

36. These statements are based on a preliminary examination of the entrance records to the Mexico City Colegio de Abogados in the period 1761–1821 and on a much closer study of a number of individual legal careers. The name and rank of specific clerics in the capital are located in the *Guía de forasteros* for each year. The social position of a number of them was determined from notarial and judicial records as well as from census and membership lists.

37. John E. Kicza, "Business and Society in Late Colonial Mexico City" (Ph.D. diss., University of California, Los Angeles, 1979), pp. 290–294.

38. AN, Zamorano y Barrera, Aug. 6, 1808; AGN, Consulado, leg. 161, exp. 9, f. 1, July 8, 1805 and leg. 184, exp. 1, Oct. 22, 1802; Guillermo S. Fernández de Recas, *Aspirantes Americanos a Cargos del Santo Oficio* (Mexico: Librería de M. Porrúa, 1956), p. 181.

39. Kicza, "Business and Society," pp. 342–347.

40. Felix Osores, *Noticias biobibliográficas de alumnos distinguidos del Colegio de San Pedro, San Pablo, y San Ildefonso de México* I, (Mexico: Viuda de C. Bouret, 1908), p. 106; AGN, Hospital de Jesús, leg. 350, exp. 12, Oct. 23, 1784; José Mariano Beristáin de Souza *Biblioteca hispanoamericana septentrional*, VI, (Mexico, 1816), p. 350.

41. *Gazetas de México*, Feb. 14, 1786; Jan. 30, 1787; Nov. 20, 1787; Feb. 5, 1793; and Aug. 29, 1804; Lucas Alamán, *Historia de Méjico* III, (Mexico: Imprenta de J.R. Lara, 1850), p. 52; Walter Howe, *The Mining Guild of New Spain and its Tribunal General, 1770–1821* (Cambridge: Harvard University Press, 1949), p. 88.

42. For a preliminary view of overall creole participation in the central

government of the colony, see Linda Arnold, "Social, Economic, and Political Status in the Mexico City Central Bureaucracy: 1808–1822," in Elsa Cecilia Frost, Michael C. Meyer, and Josefina Zoraida Vázquez, eds., *Labor and Laborers through Mexican History* (Tucson: University of Arizona Press, 1979), pp. 281–310; and Kicza, "Business and Society," pp. 381–417.

43. The inheritance laws of Castile applied in colonial Mexico. They are briefly summarized in Brading, *Miners and Merchants*, pp. 102–103.

44. Ladd, *The Mexican Nobility*, pp. 64–67.

45. An accurate guide to those in colonial Mexico who entered the different noble orders and at what time is provided by Guillermo Lohmann Villena, *Los Americanos en los Ordenes Nobiliarios 1519–1900*, 2 vols. (Madrid: Instituto Gonzalo Fernández de Oviedo, 1947).

46. Information on these families is available in Fernández de Recas, *Aspirantes americanos*.

47. AN, Joaquín Barrientos, April 16, 1788.

48. Brading, *Miners and Merchants*, passim., especially the genealogical chart on page 348.

49. Ladd, *The Mexican Nobility*, pp. 200–202.

50. A discussion of the extensive kinship and marital ties maintained by two creole families in the Mexico City Consulado in the late colonial era is found in Chapter 7.

51. Brading, *Miners and Merchants*, Appendices 1–4; Ladd, *The Mexican Nobility*, Appendix F.

52. For information on the number of unwed adults in this society and their residential patterns, see Table 3 and the censuses of the city for 1753 and 1811.

53. See Chapter 7.

54. These writings include Christiana Borchart de Moreno, "Los Miembros del Consulado de la Ciudad de México en la Epoca de Carlos III," *Jahrbuch für Geschichte von Staat, Wirtschaft, und Gesellschaft Lateinamericas*, 14 (1977): 134–160; Brading, *Miners and Merchants*, *Haciendas and Ranchos*; and "Government and Elite in Late Colonial Mexico," *HAHR*, 53:3 (August 1973): pp. 389–414; Kicza, "Business and Society"; Ladd, *The Mexican Nobility*; Lindley, "Kinship and Credit"; and Tutino, "Creole Mexico."

55. The topic of the honors received by international merchants in late colonial Mexico is explored in Chapter 7.

Chapter 3

1. Allan Christelow, "Great Britain and the Trade from Cádiz and Lisbon to Spanish America and Brazil, 1759–1783," *HAHR*, 27:1 (February 1947): 20–21.

2. James C. LaForce Jr., *The Development of the Spanish Textile Industry, 1750–1800* (Berkeley: University of California Press, 1965), pp. 2–3.

3. Lerdo de Tejada, *Comercio esterior*, Appendix 14.

4. Humboldt, *Ensayo político*, p. 499.

5. Ibid., p. 316.

6. Lists are not available before 1809. There is every indication that in the context of these documents, voting membership was equal to full membership.

7. AGN, Consulado, leg. 102, exp. 4, f. 3, Nov. 6, 1821.

8. AGN, Consulado, leg. 102, exp. 6, f. 31, Jan. 5, 1826.

9. Robert S. Smith, "The Institution of the Consulado in New Spain," *HAHR*, 24:1 (February 1944): 82.

10. AN, Barrientos, March 18, 1791.

11. AN, Barrientos, Jan. 27, 1792 and Pozo, Feb. 24, 1810 are representative examples. The notarial files of Pozo are replete with such cases.

12. AN, Pozo, May 23, 1797, June 14, 1800, May 21, 1803, May 27, 1805, and March 13, 1806 are merely a few examples of this very common practice.

13. AN, Pozo, April 2, 1800.

14. Bernard Bailyn, *The New England Merchants in the Seventeenth Century* (New York: Harper and Row, 1964), p. 100.

15. Brading, *Miners and Merchants*, p. 97.

16. AN, José Antonio Burillo, Jan. 8, 1788; Pozo, July 14, 1791.

17. AGN, Consulado, leg. 37, exp. 10, f. 1, Oct. 27, 1795.

18. AGN, Consulado, leg. 75, exp. 7, f. 1. See also Consulado, leg. 26, exp. 4, for an unsuccessful undertaking from 1803 where a Mexico City resident shipped leather and other goods to his cousin, a merchant of Cádiz, for an equal share of any profits.

19. AGN, Consulado, leg. 23, exp. 8, f. 3.

20. Miguel Capilla and Antonio Matilla Tascón, *Los Cinco Gremios Mayores de Madrid: Estudio Crítico-Histórico* (Madrid, 1957), pp. 288–289.

21. AGN, Consulado, leg. 198, exp. 14, f. 1, June 15, 1790 and leg. 125, exp. 7, f. 1, Jan. 2, 1799.

22. Some examples are AN, Pozo, Sept. 15, 1800 and Dec. 13, 1809; Burillo, Aug. 22, 1799; Barrientos, Jan. 12, 1814.

23. AN, José Antonio Troncoso, Oct. 16, 1783.

24. AN, Pozo, Oct. 21, 1801.

25. AN, Pozo, Feb. 20, 1800.

26. AN, Pozo, March 31, 1802.

27. AN, Pozo, July 15, 1802.

28. A good example is provided in AGN, Consulado, leg. 60, exp. 14, Jan. 23, 1802.

29. William L. Schurz, *The Manila Galleon* (New York: E.P. Dutton and Co., 1959), p. 189.

30. AGN, Consulado, leg. 86, exp. 9.

31. AN, José María de Torija, Jan. 23, 1788; Mariano Cadena, Feb. 6, 1792.

32. AN, Pozo, Jan. 14, 1805.

33. AN, Pozo, Jan. 11, 1796; AGN, Consulado, leg. 164, exp. 11, f. 1, Jan. 30, 1801.

34. AN, Pozo, April 2, 1797.

35. AGN, Consulado, leg. 161, exp. 11, f. 1, April 15, 1803.

36. AGN, Consulado, leg. 142, exp. 3, f. 11, Jan. 30, 1783.

37. Leslie K. Lewis, "Colonial Texcoco: A Province in the Valley of Mexico, 1570–1630" (Ph.D. diss., University of California, Los Angeles, 1977), pp. 115–116.

38. AGN, Consulado, leg. 53, exp. 13, f. 1, Jan. 17, 1809 and leg. 139, exp. 14, f. 1, Feb. 18, 1805.

39. AGN, Industria y Comercio, leg. 8, exp. 3.

40. Ibid.

41. AGN, Consulado, leg. 87, exp. 16, f. 3, Feb. 27, 1812.

42. AN, Pozo, May 25, 1809.

43. AN, Pozo, Feb. 28, 1789 and Feb. 3, 1795.

44. AN, Pozo, June 9, 1798; AGN, Consulado, leg. 87, exp. 16, f. 3, Feb. 27, 1812.

45. Hamnett, *Politics and Trade*, chapter 1.

46. AGN, Consulado, leg. 41, exp. 6, Sept. 28, 1804 shows that Spanish firms also stayed active in the importation of Mexican sugar.

47. AN, Francisco Javier Benítez, Sept. 30, 1797; Tomás Hidalgo de los Reyes, Feb. 20, 1799.

48. AGN, Consulado, leg. 185, exp. 3, f. 1, Nov. 6, 1803.

49. AN, Pozo, Feb. 12, 1805.

50. Much material on this bankruptcy is contained in AGN, Consulado, leg. 185, exp. 3.

51. AN, Pozo, Jan. 11, 1804.

52. AN, Pozo, Feb. 17, 1804.

53. AGN, Consulado, leg. 23, exp. 26, f. 2, May 9, 1823.

54. AN, Burillo, Sept. 27, 1787; Pozo, May 21, 1811; AGN, Consulado, leg. 198, exp. 17, f. 1 and leg. 42, exp. 1, f. 1, Sept. 15, 1802.

Chapter 4

1. Some examples of these companies are: AN, Barrientos, April 20, 1797; Burillo, May 5, 1808; Torija, Dec. 22, 1784; Tomás Hidalgo de los Reyes, June 1, 1810; AGN, Consulado, leg. 145, exp. 11, f. 1, July 22, 1807, leg. 160, exp. 5, f. 1, April 29, 1809, leg. 244, exp. 2, f. 1, July 11, 1780.

2. AN, Pozo, Feb. 28, 1805.

3. AN, Pozo, Feb. 15, 1800.

4. AGN, Consulado, leg. 228, exp. 2, Dec. 2, 1777.

5. AGN, Consulado, leg. 120, exp. 2.

6. AN, Pozo, Oct. 26, 1789.

7. AN, Torija, May 12, 1787, April 24, 1790, Dec. 17, 1790, April 27, 1787.

8. Some examples of these different types are contained in: AGN, Consulado, leg. 143, exp. 2, f. 29, April 15, 1794, leg. 211, exp. 2, f. 1, Oct. 19, 1798, leg. 89, exp. 2, f. 1, Nov. 17, 1813, leg. 25, exp. 17, f. 1, May 22, 1805, leg. 25, exp. 7, f. 1, leg. 188, exp. 9, f. 1, Oct. 24, 1801, leg. 93, exp. 7, f. 5, April 22, 1814, leg. 221, exp. 10, f. 1, Dec. 1, 1789, leg. 149, exp. 2, f. 1, April 15, 1807, leg. 192, exp. 17, f. 1, July 23, 1800; Civil, leg. 951, exp. 17, f. 1, Dec. 1, 1789.

9. AGN, Consulado, leg. 75, exp. 14, f. 6, July 17, 1807.

10. AN, Pozo, July 6, 1787; AGN, Consulado, leg. 188, exp. 7, f. 1, Dec. 5, 1801.

11. AN, Pozo, July 17, 1790.

12. AN, Tomás Hidalgo de los Reyes, Feb. 20, 1799; Pozo, July 6, 1787; AGN, Consulado, leg. 188, exp. 7, f. 1, Dec. 5, 1801.

13. AN, Torija, March 12, 1789 and March 14, 1789.

14. AN, Pozo, Oct. 8, 1801.

15. AN, Barrientos, March 18, 1791.

16. AN, Pozo, Jan. 10, 1807 and March 15, 1811; Manuel de Puertas, Jan. 24, 1782; AGN, Consulado, leg. 229, exp. 4, f. 72; Civil, leg. 966, exp. 7, ff. 1–20, March 9, 1785.

17. AN, Tomás Hidalgo de los Reyes, March 5, 1807 and April 19, 1792.

18. AGN, Minería, leg. 24, exp. 1, f. 3, March 10, 1781.

19. AN, Pozo, Feb. 28, 1789. Other examples can be found in Pozo, Feb. 6, 1809 and Vicente Hidalgo de los Reyes, Oct. 12, 1805.

20. Harris, *A Mexican Family Empire*, pp. 100, 106, and 108–109, describes the character of commercial arrangements between the Sánchez Navarro family and several Mexico City trading houses.

21. AGN, Consulado, leg. 118, exp. 13, Sept. 30, 1817.

22. AN, Pozo, Jan. 16, 1805 and footnotes #21 and 23.

23. AGN, Consulado, leg. 87, exp. 5, f. 16, Dec. 17, 1811; AN, Pozo, April 28, 1801.

24. Ward Barrett, "Morelos and Its Sugar Industry in the Late Eighteenth Century" in Altman and Lockhart, eds., *Provinces*, p. 162.

25. AGN, Consulado, leg. 41, exp. 5, f. 7, April 11, 1804 and leg. 186, exp. 4, f. 3, Feb. 10, 1804.

26. AGN, Consulado, leg. 127, exp. 15, f. 18, March 6, 1790 and leg. 73, exp. 3, f. 1, Jan. 31, 1805.

27. AGN, Consulado, leg. 42, exp. 6, f. 1, April 3, 1802.

28. AGN, Consulado, leg. 53, exp. 5, ff. 1–4, May 4, 1808 and leg. 34, exp. 1, f. 11, Aug. 19, 1817.

29. AGN, Consulado, leg. 157, exp. 9, f. 1, Feb. 8, 1806, leg. 191, exp. 5, f. 1, Nov. 18, 1796, and leg. 214, exp. 1, f. 3, Jan. 19, 1799.

30. Hamnett, *Politics and Trade*, Chapter 1.

31. Ibid., Chapter 6.

32. Appendix 8 in Hamnett's book is used to argue the takeover of the cochineal trade by Veracruz, but to me it indicates the continuing healthy presence of Mexico City traders.

33. Hamnett, *Politics and Trade*, pp. 67–71.

34.. AN, Pozo, Feb. 4, 1799.

35. AN, Pozo, July 18, 1799.

36. AN, Barrientos, Nov. 19, 1803.

37. AN, Torija, Jan. 2, 1787.

38. AGN, Consulado, leg. 60, exp. 12, f. 1, March 9, 1807; AN, Barrientos, March 16, 1802. In his will, Manuel Aranda states that he owes money from his business to the subdelegado of Tetelco, the site of his *aguardiente* distillery.

39. AN, Torija, Oct. 26, 1787.

40. AGN, Consulado, leg. 98, exp. 2, f. 1, Sept. 27, 1815.

41. Lockhart, *Spanish Peru*, pp. 84–85. These itinerant traders were termed *tratantes* in early colonial Peru and still in late colonial Oaxaca. See Chance, *Race and Class*, pp. 142 and 168.

42. AGN, Consulado, leg. 88, exp. 10, f. 4, July 9, 1810 and AN, Pozo, Oct. 24, 1785 and Nov. 7, 1800 offer examples of large sales on credit.
43. AGN, Consulado, leg. 86, exp. 7, f. 1, Jan. 13, 1812.
44. AGN, Consulado, leg. 122, exp. 2.

Chapter 5

1. *Comerciante* was the general term used for identification by every person who owned a commercial establishment of whatever size. *Mercader* was a formal term not used in normal conversation. The Consulado referred to itself as the *Colegio de Mercaderes*. *Almacenero* was used, but not very commonly. Wholesalers did not insist on being so addressed; in fact, some of the more prominent did not even refer to themselves as such.
2. AGN, Consulado, leg. 91, exp. 11, f. 1, Oct. 30, 1795 and leg. 224, exp. 2, f. 1, July 11, 1780; AN, Pozo, Aug. 8, 1803.
3. Ibid., and AN, Torija, Dec. 22, 1784 and Dec. 24, 1784.
4. AGN, Consulado, leg. 244, exp. 2, July 11, 1780.
5. AN, Torija, Dec. 22, 1784 and Dec. 24, 1784.
6. AN, Torija, Jan. 28, 1788.
7. AGN, Consulado, leg. 166, exp. 8, f. 30, June 4, 1804.
8. AN, Pozo, Aug. 8, 1803.
9. AGN, Consulado, leg. 91, exp. 11.
10. AN, Pozo, Dec. 16, 1801.
11. AGN, Consulado, leg. 93, exp. 2
12. AGN, Consulado, leg. 145, exp. 6, f. 1, Jan. 20, 1807 and leg. 161, exp. 8, f. 1, Dec. 2, 1805; AN, Pozo, May 27, 1805.
13. AGN, Consulado, leg. 188, exp. 15, f. 1, Nov. 6, 1799; AN, Pozo, May 16, 1792, Oct. 31, 1793, May 1, 1795, July 1, 1795, Jan. 14, 1797, and Feb. 4, 1799.
14. AN, Torija, Feb. 3, 1789.
15. AN, Barrientos, April 5, 1794, April 28, 1794, and May 21, 1794.
16. AN, Pozo, May 2, 1798.
17. AN, Pozo, Aug. 11, 1785, July 17, 1787, July 7, 1791, April 2, 1800, and Sept. 23, 1801.
18. AGN, Consulado, leg. 91, exp. 11.
19. AGN, Consulado, leg. 78, exp. 14, f. 1, June 25, 1810; AN, Burillo, Feb. 13, 1809, Aug. 12, 1790, and Jan. 21, 1799.
20. AN, Tomás Hidalgo de los Reyes, Jan. 31, 1814.

21. AN, Pozo, Dec. 5, 1809.
22. AN, Pozo, Jan. 4, 1810.
23. AN, Burillo, July 18, 1788.
24. AN, Pozo, April 29, 1786.
25. AN, Burillo, Feb. 26, 1794. Examples of similar companies are: Burillo, Nov. 15, 1792 and Pozo, Aug. 19, 1794.
26. AN, Barrientos, Oct. 22, 1800; Burrillo, Feb. 27, 1790.
27. AN, Burillo, April 25, 1789; Pozo, Feb. 23, 1801.
28. AN, Barrientos, Sept. 10, 1791; Pozo, Feb. 23, 1801.
29. BN, ms. 1320, "Reglamento para el gobierno y direccion de las tiendas de pulpería," 1810, p. 2.
30. AGN, Consulado, leg. 11, exp. 16, Dec. 17, 1823; AN, Pozo, Nov. 5, 1784, March 5, 1785, July 20, 1786, Feb. 6, 1801, and Feb. 28, 1805.
31. AN, Pozo, Oct. 14, 1785 and March 15, 1792.
32. AGN, Abastos y Panaderías, leg. 4, exp. 2, Feb. 12, 1795.
33. GM, Nov. 12, 1795; AN, Burillo, Aug. 25, 1804; AGN, Consulado, leg. 37, exp. 6, f. 1, Oct. 21, 1802.
34. For the 1796 survey, officials went from door to door canvassing these establishments. The owner, though identified, was rarely present. Rather, the administrator would respond to the questions. Several women stated that they worked for their mothers who owned the stores.
35. AGN, Civil, leg. 978, exp. 1, f. 1, July 20, 1795; Consulado, leg. 200, exp. 5, ff. 1–6, June 30, 1797.
36. DM, Dec. 12, 1814; AN, Barrientos, June 5, 1812; Francisco de la Torre, Aug. 20, 1821.
37. AN, de la Torre, Aug. 20, 1821; Pozo, Oct. 24, 1785.
38. AGN, Consulado, leg. 200, exp. 3, May 22, 1800 and leg. 161, exp. 3, June 7, 1805.
39. AGN, Consulado, leg. 223, exp. 2, Nov. 28, 1793.
40. AGN, Consulado, leg. 127, exp. 1, Sept. 2, 1786.
41. AGN, Consulado, leg. 127, exp. 6, f. 13, Sept. 26, 1789. Other examples of owner–manager companies are: Consulado, leg. 221, exp. 5, Feb. 3, 1789, leg. 53, exp. 15, f. 7, June 19, 1809, and leg. 127, exp. 16, March 15, 1790.
42. AGN, Consulado, leg. 160, exp. 11, Nov. 26, 1802 and leg. 160, exp. 12, July 1, 1805.
43. DM, Jan. 9, 1811.
44. BN, ms. 1320, "Reglamento," p. 2.
45. For distilleries see: AGN, Consulado, leg. 67, exp. 10, f. 3, Jan.

28, 1811; AN, Barrientos, March 16, 1802 and July 16, 1808. For rural estates see: Tomás Hidalgo de los Reyes, June 1, 1810. For other stores see: Puertas, April 11, 1786 and Tomás Hidalgo de los Reyes, June 1, 1810.

46. AGN, Consulado, leg. 67, exp. 10, f. 3, Jan. 28, 1811, leg. 14, exp. 9, f. 1, Sept. 24, 1804, leg. 88, exp. 8, f. 2, April 24, 1813, leg. 188, exp. 3, f. 1, May 21, 1800, leg. 25, exp. 12, f. 1, Oct. 26, 1804, leg. 68, exp. 4, f. 1, June 20, 1808, leg. 54, exp. 1, ff. 10–13, May 16, 1809.

47. AGN, Consulado, leg. 100, exp. 8, f. 10, Dec. 14, 1798 and leg. 25, exp. 12, f. 1, Oct. 20, 1804.

48. AN, Tomás Hidalgo de los Reyes, June 1, 1810.

49. AGN, Consulado, leg. 54, exp. 1, ff. 10–13, May 6, 1809.

50. AGN, Consulado, leg. 14, exp. 9, f. 1, Sept. 24, 1804.

51. AGN, Consulado, leg. 38, exp. 3, f. 2, Oct. 8, 1805.

52. AGN, Protomedicato, leg. 2, exp. 3, f. 2v, July 18, 1787.

53. AGN, Padrones, leg. 52, Dec. 1811.

54. AGN, Padrones, leg. 80, 1796; AN, Torija, Nov. 8, 1783.

55. AGN, Padrones, leg. 80, 1796.

56. Ibid.

57. AN, Burillo, Aug. 27, 1784.

58. AN, Pozo, Dec. 20, 1785.

59. AN, Burillo, May 23, 1800 and Nov. 15, 1800.

60. AN, Burillo, Jan. 11, 1798 and Jan. 24, 1799.

61. AN, Burillo, July 1, 1782.

62. AN, Burillo, Aug. 27, 1784.

63. AN, Burillo, Jan. 2, 1805 and Sept. 17, 1807.

64. AN, Pozo, June 6, 1800, Feb. 15, 1800, Feb. 6, 1801, and July 25, 1801. In 1799 Isita rented five pulquerías and sublet them to another party. In 1808 he rented two pulquerías belonging to a sister of the Conde de Regla.

65. AN, Torija, June 7, 1783 and Jan. 18, 1785.

66. *Jacal* is the Mexican-Spanish derivation of the Nahuatl word "xacalli," meaning crude or temporary structure. See Luis Cabrera, *Diccionario de Aztequismos*, (México, 1974), p. 84.

67. AGN, Policía, leg. 15, exp. 1.

68. Most of the information found in this section about the retail pulque trade comes from an extensive *informe* prepared for the viceroy in 1784 and found in: "Informe sobre pulquerías y tabernas el año de 1784," *Boletín del Archivo General de la Nación*, primera serie, 18:2 (1947): 189–236; 18:3 (1947): 363–405.

69. See Ricardo Beller N. and Patricia Cowan de Beller, *Curso de Náhuatl moderno: Náhuatl de la Huasteca* II (México, 1979), p. 210, where a tangerine is called an *otonlalax* ("Otomi orange").

70. From Nahuatl *tlahchiqui*, "to scrape the heart of the maguey to extract the juice." See Fray Andrés de Molina, *Vocabulario el lengua castellana y mexicana y mexicana y castellana* (México, 1970), Nahuatl to Spanish section, f. 32v, entry "ichiqui."

71. AN, Pozo, Oct. 21, 1793.

72. AN, de la Torre, Aug. 20, 1821.

73. AGN, AHH, leg. 491, exp. 52, ff. 1–7, Dec. 3, 1796.

74. AN, Pozo, Jan. 23, 1790.

75. AGN, Consulado, leg. 149, exp. 8, f. 1.

76. AN, Barrientos, Feb. 13, 1789.

77. AGN, Consulado, leg. 90, exp. 1, f. 4, July 27, 1813.

78. AGN, Consulado, leg. 155, exp. 1, f. 1, Feb. 13, 1813.

79. AGN, Consulado, leg. 87, exp. 6, May 4, 1812.

Chapter 6

1. DM, Aug. 3, 1806 and Sept. 15, 1806. Other examples are DM, Oct. 7, 1805, Dec. 21, 1805, Feb. 9, 1806, and May 23, 1806.

2. Francisco Tovar advertised for a post in a tienda or a vinatería which would pay him 300 pesos or a half-share of the profits. See DM, March 3, 1806.

3. AGN, Consulado, leg. 25, exp. 8, Jan. 4, 1805.

4. AN, Zamorano y Barrera, Nov. 3, 1794 and Aug. 3, 1797.

5. AN, Burillo, Aug. 6, 1792, Oct. 17, 1796, Oct. 18, 1797, Dec. 9, 1799, Feb. 8, 1808, and May 25, 1810.

6. Lucas Alamán, *Historia de Méjico*, I (Mexico: J.R. Lara, 1849), pp. 8–9; Brading, *Miners and Merchants*, pp. 109–112.

7. AN, Pozo, March 8, 1793 and April 2, 1800; Barrientos, Nov. 2, 1790 and June 18, 1798; AGN, Consulado, leg. 145, exp. 5, Aug. 21, 1807.

8. AN, Pozo, May 12, 1802.

9. AN, Pozo, April 19, 1797.

10. AGN, Consulado, leg. 161, exp. 8, f. 1, Dec. 2, 1805.

11. AN, Pozo, April 13, 1801.

12. AN, Pozo, June 9, 1798.

13. AN, Pozo, March 22, 1791, June 14, 1800, Oct. 19, 1801, April 3, 1803, May 27, 1805, Jan. 2, 1807, Feb. 3, 1814, and Oct. 16, 1815. An-

other example of a merchant helping aspiring relatives who were not in line to inherit from him is contained in AN, Pozo, Sept. 6, 1797.

14. AN, Burrillo, Aug. 26, 1784, Jan. 14, 1792, Jan. 16, 1793, and Dec. 30, 1793. Other merchants who began their careers in the provinces usually started out in mining centers.

15. AGN, Consulado, leg. 44, exp. 8 and 9; AN, Burillo, Jan. 27, 1789.

16. AN, Torija, Jan. 6, 1784; Burillo, Oct. 12, 1785.

17. AGN, Consulado, leg. 161, exp. 9, f. 1, July 8, 1805.

18. AN, Pozo, April 10, 1786, July 4, 1787, Aug. 3, 1792, Aug. 27, 1793, April 9, 1795, and Oct. 17, 1796; Burillo, Aug. 29, 1794.

19. AN, Barrientos, Sept. 10, 1798.

20. AN, Torija, Sept. 27, 1781.

21. AN, Torija, June 2, 1781, June 4, 1782, and June 23, 1788.

22. Ladd, *The Mexican Nobility*, p. 206.

23. AGN, Consulado, leg. 216, exp. 1; AN, Burillo, April 13, 1796.

24. AN, Burillo, Oct. 18, 1804. He owed his own son over 51,000 pesos.

Chapter 7

1. AN, Zamorano y Barrera, Dec. 24, 1804.

2. See the chart in Ladd, *The Mexican Nobility*, p. 16, for a good example of the extent to which elite intermarriage could extend.

3. Brading, *Miners and Merchants*, Appendix I.

4. AN, Pozo, Feb. 17, 1815; Burillo, March 15, 1798.

5. AN, Burillo, Jan. 7, 1781.

6. AN, Burillo, Nov. 29, 1800; de la Torre, Aug. 19, 1809.

7. AN, Pozo, Feb. 17, 1815.

8. AN, Pozo, Jan. 3, 1806.

9. AN, Pozo, Sept. 5, 1794.

10. AN, Pozo, June 27, 1815.

11. Ibid.

12. AN, Pozo, Jan. 2, 1796.

13. AGN, Tierras, leg. 1288, exp. 4, f. 34, March 21, 1797; AN, Burillo, June 28, 1799.

14. AGN, Consulado, leg. 229, exp. 5, Oct. 4, 1799.

15. AN, Pozo, Nov. 5, 1784.

16. AN, Pozo, June 6, 1800, Feb. 15, 1800, and Feb. 6, 1801.

17. AN, Pozo, Feb. 28, 1805.

18. AN, Pozo, Oct. 27, 1807.

19. In his book on the Sánchez Navarro family, Charles H. Harris III repeatedly notes the family's recurrent commercial economy, not only in marketing its own commodities, but also in the trade of items shipped in to supply the population of surrounding towns.

20. AN, Pozo, May 7, 1800.

21. GN, Jan. 11, 1799 and March 13, 1802; AN, Barrientos, July 3, 1799.

22. AGN, Consulado, leg. 53, exp. 8, July 5, 1809; AN, Pozo, Feb. 6, 1805 and May 10, 1805.

23. Archer, *The Army in Bourbon Mexico*, pp. 212–213, Table 18.

24. AGN, AHH, leg. 130, exp. 26, 1807.

25. The *Comisarios Ordenadores Honorarios de Ejército* were: Juan Díaz González, Pedro González Noriega, Fernando de Hermosa y Miranda, and Manuel Fernández Sáenz de Santa María.

26. AN, Pozo, Nov. 4, 1801.

27. AGN, Padrones, leg. 53, Dec. 1811.

28. AN, Pozo, June 29, 1786, Dec. 9, 1801, June 30, 1814; Burillo, June 19, 1802.

29. AN, Burillo, Jan. 2, 1805.

30. AN, Burillo, June 26, 1800.

31. AGN, Consulado, leg. 216, exp. 3, May 31, 1796.

32. AGN, Consulado, leg. 164, exp. 12, f. 2, Oct. 15, 1801; AN, Pozo, Oct. 10, 1805 and Nov. 12, 1805.

Chapter 8

1. AGN, Abastos y Panaderías, leg. 4, exp. 4, May 5, 1793.

2. AGN, Tierras, leg. 1207, exp. 2, Oct. 30, 1790.

3. DM, Dec. 6, 1805, suplemento, pp. 289–292.

4. DM, Nov. 24, 1805.

5. AN, Pozo, May 2, 1807.

6. AN, Pozo, May 16, 1791.

7. AN, Burillo, April 23, 1785.

8. AN, Pozo, Dec. 10, 1790.

9. AGN, Consulado, leg. 160, exp. 7, f. 7, 1805.

10. AGN, Civil, leg. 985, exp. 10, f. 3, July 18, 1791.

11. AN, Tomás Hidalgo de los Reyes, Aug. 29, 1797.

12. AN, Puertas, March 12, 1789.

13. AN, Tomás Hidalgo de los Reyes, Oct. 30, 1804.

14. AN, de la Torre, July 14, 1814.

15. AN, Vicente de los Reyes, Oct. 3, 1807.

16. AN, Pozo, Oct. 1, 1791.

17. AN, Barrientos, Aug. 8, 1805 and March 9, 1809.

18. AN, Pozo, April 3, 1787.

19. AN, Torija, March 10, 1787 and Jan. 30, 1788; Barrientos, Oct. 8, 1790.

20. AN, San Martín, March 18, 1791.

21. AN, Pozo, June 12, 1793.

22. AN, Pozo, Feb. 16, 1792.

23. AN, de la Torre, March 28, 1805 and July 3, 1805.

24. AN, Torija, Dec. 20, 1781.

25. AN, Barrientos, Aug. 1, 1799.

26. Alexander von Humboldt, "Tablas geográficas políticas," in Florescano and Gil, *Descripciones económicas*, p. 152.

27. See Ward Barrett, "The Meat Supply of Colonial Cuernavaca," *Annals of the Association of American Geographers*, 64:4 (December 1974): 525–540 for a description of the system in another colonial city.

28. AN, Puertas, March 5, 1782.

29. AN, Burillo, June 2, 1797.

30. GM, Feb. 8, 1800.

31. AN, Vicente Hidalgo de los Reyes, Feb. 7, 1807.

32. AN, Burillo, April 16, 1806.

33. AN, Burillo, April 16, 1806 and Feb. 18, 1804; Torija, May 26, 1790; DM, Nov. 20, 1808.

34. AN, Pozo, May 7, 1800.

35. AN, Burillo, May 10, 1796.

36. AN, Tomás Hidalgo de los Reyes, Nov. 11, 1811.

37. AN, Burillo, Nov. 18, 1795.

38. AGN, Civil, leg. 1628, exp. 1, f. 35, 1798.

39. GM, June 19, 1787.

40. AN, Torija, June 22, 1785; Pozo, Nov. 14, 1785.

41. AGN, Civil, leg. 987, unpaginated, Sept. 2, 1807.

42. AN, Tomás Hidalgo de los Reyes, June 14, 1794 and Aug. 2, 1794.

43. AN, Tomás Hidalgo de los Reyes, April 5, 1797, July 20, 1797, Oct. 11, 1797, and Dec. 8, 1797.

44. AN, Pozo, Sept. 12, 1777.

45. AN, Torija, June 22, 1785.

46. AN, Torija, July 23, 1785; Pozo, Oct. 14, 1785.

47. AN, Tomás Hidalgo de los Reyes, March 27, 1806.

48. AN, Pozo, April 4, 1810.

49. AN, Tomás Hidalgo de los Reyes, Sept. 14, 1793.

50. AN, Pozo, Sept. 19, 1801.

51. AN, Pozo, May 18, 1810.
52. AN, Burillo, May 27, 1801; AGN, Padrones, 54, Dec. 1811; DM, Dec. 3, 1805.
53. AN, Tomás Hidalgo de los Reyes, Nov. 23, 1804.
54. AN, Barrientos, July 20, 1791.
55. With the coming of Independence, investment in processing and manufacturing continued, but now increased direct investment came from foreign sources, especially from British businessmen. Marshall and Manning were the Mexican agents of the Baring Brothers bank of England, a major lender to the new government, and formed themselves into a commercial company with branches in Mexico City and Veracruz. While the investments of such parties in mining, commerce, and government bonds are well known, their participation in manufacturing is less appreciated. In 1825 Guillermo Skinner Marshall, speaking for himself and his absent partner Roberto Manning, agreed to the separation of Justino Tuaillon (Twayne?) from their company in a brewery in the city. The two remaining partners gave Tuaillon 2,000 pesos for his share in the company, and he agreed to remain working in the brewery for another two months at the salary of 100 pesos a month. He further agreed not to found his own brewery in either the city or the State of Mexico and to admit Manning and Marshall as half partners if he established one in the state of Guanajuato. See AN, Benítez, Feb. 21, 1825 and Barbara A. Tenenbaum, "Merchants, Money, and Mischief. The British in Mexico, 1821–1862," *The Americas*, 35:3 (January 1979): 318–320.

Chapter 9

1. AN, Tomás Hidalgo de los Reyes, May 30, 1808.
2. AN, Barrientos, April 23, 1795.
3. AN, Burillo, Jan. 23, 1795.
4. AN, Tomás Hidalgo de los Reyes, July 15, 1808.
5. AN, Burillo, June 30, 1784.
6. AN, Tomás Hidalgo de los Reyes, Jan. 21, 1795. For similar companies involving goldsmiths, see: AN, Tomás Hidalgo de los Reyes, Sept. 22, 1804 and Burillo, Feb. 4, 1801.
7. AN, Tomás Hidalgo de los Reyes, Jan. 27, 1791.
8. AN, Pozo, July 20, 1809.
9. AN, Tomás Hidalgo de los Reyes, March 30, 1798.
10. DM, Feb. 2, 1810.
11. AN, Barrientos, Jan. 19, 1791.
12. AN, Pozo, Sept. 4, 1809.

13. AN, Torija, April 27, 1787; Pozo, Sept. 19, 1798.
14. AN, Torija, July 29, 1785.
15. AGN, Civil, leg. 973, exp. 3, f. 4, Oct. 16, 1783.
16. AN, Burillo, April 28, 1801.
17. DM, Oct. 10, 1815.
18. AGN, Civil, leg. 1784, exp. 8, f. 1, Dec. 19, 1800.
19. DM, Oct. 28, 1805.
20. AN, Burillo, March 18, 1795.
21. AN, Burillo, April 28, 1801.
22. AGN, Consulado, leg. 37, exp. 6, Oct. 21, 1802.
23. AGN, Industria y Comercio, leg 5, exp. 7, Feb. 23, 1793.
24. AGN, Industria y Comercio, leg. 5, exp. 8, Dec. 29, 1792.
25. The protocols of the notaries José Antonio Troncoso and Tomás Hidalgo de los Reyes are replete with these contracts.
26. AGN, Consulado, leg. 76, exp. 5, f. 4, no date.
27. AGN, Civil, leg. 829, exp. 2, f. 1, Dec. 1, 1806; AN, Tomás Hidalgo de los Reyes, March 29, 1813.
28. AN, Vicente Hidalgo de los Reyes, July 14, 1806.
29. AN, Burillo, May 7, 1782.
30. AN, Pozo, May 10, 1805.
31. AN, Benítez, July 7, 1812.
32. AGN, Civil, leg. 829, exp. 2, f. 1, Dec. 1, 1806.
33. AN, Barrientos, May 4, 1785; AGN, Civil, leg. 862, exp. 6, Feb. 14, 1785 and leg. 951, exp. 3, no date.
34. AGN, Civil, leg. 43, exp. 9, 1801.
35. AGN, Consulado, leg. 183, exp. 12, Aug. 23, 1802.
36. AN, Tomás Hidalgo de los Reyes, April 22, 1807.
37. AN, Tomás Hidalgo de los Reyes, June 21, 1808.
38. AN, Tomás Hidalgo de los Reyes, April 18, 1810.
39. AN, Pozo, March 17, 1789.
40. AN, Burillo, Feb. 28, 1800.
41. AN, Burillo, Jan. 30, 1793.
42. AN, Tomás Hidalgo de los Reyes, April 22, 1800.
43. AN, Pozo, May 8, 1787.
44. AGN, Industria y Comercio, leg. 21, exp. 4, 1796.
45. AGN, Industria y Comercio, leg. 18, 1805.
46. AN, Torija, Jan. 15, 1783.
47. AN, Pozo, June 28, 1792.
48. AN, Tomás Hidalgo de los Reyes, Jan. 27, 1791.
49. GM, Nov. 11, 1799.
50. AGN, AHH, leg. 491, exp. 32, f. 6, 1795.

51. AN, Pozo, June 30, 1801.
52. AN, Tomás Hidalgo de los Reyes, Sept. 23, 1793.
53. AN, Barrientos, March 18, 1784; GM, June 12, 1799.
54. AN, Burillo, Jan. 14, 1792.
55. AN, Burillo, July 19, 1788; Torija, May 25, 1789.

Conclusion

1. Several scholars have recognized the regularity with which merchants purchased rural estates early in their careers (because they constituted economically rational investments) and how on the other hand established elite families, who were commonly identified with agricultural interests, maintained a healthy activity in commerce. This, of course, draws into question the accuracy of dividing the colonial elite into an "agricultural sector" and a "mercantile sector." For Central Mexico, see Tutino, "Creole Mexico," pp. 17–23; for León, see Brading, *Haciendas and Ranchos*, pp. 115 and 118; for Guadalajara, see Richard B. Lindley, "Kinship and Credit," p. 89 and Eric Van Young, *Hacienda and Market in Eighteenth-Century Mexico* (Berkeley: University of California Press, 1981), pp. 149–160; for Northern Mexico, see Harris, *A Mexican Family Empire*, pp. 94–95.

Glossary

accesoría: a niche or a room on the first floor of a building usually used as a small store

alcalde del crimen (or *de corte*): criminal judge of the royal court

alcalde mayor: chief magistrate of a district

alcalde ordinario: a municipal judge

almacenero: a wholesale trader

apoderado: a person with another's power of attorney

arras: an amount of money put up by a groom to guarantee the maintenance of his bride

asesor: legal advisor

audiencia: the royal court

bodega: a storeroom

cabildo: the city council

cajero: a commercial employee or apprentice

capellanía: a chaplaincy

casa de vecindad: a roominghouse

casta: person neither a Spaniard nor an Indian

catedrático: a university professor with a permanent chair

cofradía: a religious sodality

colegio de abogados: the lawyers' guild

conductor de plata: a silver shipper

consulado: the merchants' guild

corredor de commercio: a commercial agent

cuartel: a physical division of the city

dependencias activas: funds loaned out

dependencias pasivas: funds borrowed

depósito irregular: a loan, typically stated to be for a set number of years at 5 percent simple annual interest

escribano: a notary

esperas: a legal device to give a debtor a period of time free from harassment from his creditors

estanquillo: a small stand which sold products of the tobacco monopoly

factor: a business agent, usually representing the government

fiador: a guarantor of payment

275

fiscal: a government prosecutor

hacienda de beneficio: an ore refinery

libranza: a bill of exchange

mayorazgo: an entailed estate

mesón: an inn

obra pía: a pious endowment

obraje: a textile mill

oidor: civil judge of the royal court

prendas: pawned goods

procurador: an attorney who represents clients before a court

protomedicato: the governmental board which licensed medical practitioners

regimiento: a seat on the city council

viandante: an itinerant trader

Bibliography

Previous Writings on Mexico City

The historical literature on colonial Mexico City is surprisingly sparse, and few indeed are the writings that deal with the city's social structure and dynamics. Interestingly, the first to do so considered not one of the upper strata but perhaps the very lowest. In the chapter on Mexico City in his classic work *The Aztecs Under Spanish Rule*, Charles Gibson accurately described certain aspects of Indian life in the capital. Derived from governmental reports, regulations, official letters, and chronicles, the chapter concentrated on the operation of the Indian government and markets of the city, yet Gibson also offered some astute observations about the character of Indian society in an urban setting. He recognized, for example, that Indians eventually penetrated every guild despite regulations explicitly designed to exclude them, and that Indians and persons of mixed descent continued to dwell independently throughout the city even after action was taken to exclude them from the central district after the riots of 1692.

The work of Gibson notwithstanding, the systematic study of colonial Mexico City society must be dated from the 1971 publication of D. A. Brading's *Miners and Merchants in Bourbon Mexico 1763–1810*. In the second part of this three-part book and in a subsequent article on elite recruitment and composition, Brading pointed out many salient behavioral characteristics of the urban elite, especially its members involved in international trade. Brading was the first to describe the "nephew syndrome," where a nephew or cousin, often an immigrant from Spain, was recruited into the family business and frequently succeeded to its director-ship, sealing his status through marriage to his predecessor's widow or daughter. The economic function of matrimony, the composi-tion of the elite, and the diversification of investment carried out by successful merchants are among the other themes developed in this book. But perhaps more important than any single pattern of behavior described by Brading is the fact that he was the first to recognize and elaborate upon the existence of social and economic patterns that cut across the lives of individuals and particular fam-ilies to entire sectors of the society and—as we shall see in the body of the present work—sometimes across the larger urban so-ciety. Brading's book also argues the indispensability of studying not just the individual but the larger family, for the careers and economic activities of many people only make sense in that con-text. And, expanding upon this latter point, Brading revealed how family history can best be understood over generations. Many dy-namic factors and patterns of behavior are disclosed only when dif-ferent families are examined over the course of at least several lives.

Brading's research concentrated on a relatively small group of wholesale merchants, and his information and findings on other sectors of this society largely reflect that group's interests and per-spectives. Doris Ladd, in her dissertation and subsequent book, expanded upon this base and considered the entire Mexican titled nobility in the final years of the colonial period and the very first of the national. Ladd's work too is distinguished by its discovery of previously unrecognized social patterns and its utilization of multigenerational family portraits.

Benefiting from a diversity of original sources, Ladd was able to reveal the number of economic interests maintained by leading families and the variety of professions open to members of this group. She recognized the importance of estate ownership to the long-term financial survival of elite families. She also made clear that neither commerce nor any other enterprise, large or small, was outside of the purview of the elite solely because of risk or its potentially demeaning qualities.

Given the nature of Ladd's study, it is understandable that she should stress the titled nobility's domination of the Mexico City elite. I would not dispute that these families were among the highest elite, but they were joined there by a number of untitled families who maintained social and economic parity with them.

In a 1976 dissertation, John Tutino carried our knowledge of the upper strata of Mexico City society yet further by studying rural estate owners of the capital and by examining their internal differentiation, relationships with each other, with smaller farmers, and with Indian towns, and their participation in other fields of the economy. He demonstrated that the great estate owners emerged from an assortment of backgrounds and had no corporate image of themselves as an interest group. Rather, this group was composed of heads of various kinds of families, holding rural estates within a diversified and sometimes integrated portfolio of economic interests which was normally managed for the betterment of the greater family rather than of specific individuals.

Dennis N. Valdés examined eighteenth-century Mexico City society in a quite different fashion in his 1978 dissertation. Applying aggregate analysis to the 1753 and 1811 censuses of the capital and supplementing these findings with illustrative case studies drawn from judicial proceedings, Valdes investigated the workings—and the breakdown—of the caste system in the late colonial period and showed how ethnic groups fit into the larger social scheme. By concentrating primarily on groups, however defined, and entire districts in Mexico City, Valdes was prevented from displaying the interplay of ethnic, occupational, and social factors in determining an individual's status or how persons in different or the same classifications perceived and dealt with each other. Overall, his investigations constitute a useful approach to the study of popular sectors in urban society, while his conclusions are congruent with those of this and the previously discussed works.

While the above-cited studies have already appeared, another project, not yet completed, is worthy of mention. Under the supervision of Alejandra Moreno Toscano, present director of the Mexican National Archives, a group of researchers is analyzing Mexico City censuses from the late colonial and early national periods to uncover quantitative changes in the employment, ethnicity, and residential patterns of the capital's citizenry. While the works discussed previously and the one before you all contain a number of tables and have a quite important statistical component, they uniformly generate their statistics from the study of individual lives and careers. The Moreno Toscano project, however, will not concentrate on specific people or families nor investigate their change through time, but will transfer every case into figures suitable for statistical analysis.

This work is based primarily on three bodies of documents: the notarial archives of Mexico City, the court cases contained in various sections of the Mexican national archives—especially the records of the merchants' court—and lists and manuscripts found in the Mexican national library. Of the three, the notarial archives are far and away the most valuable. The Archivo de Notarías del Departamento del Distrito Federal (Mexico, D.F.) contains the collected extant documentation of all licensed notaries for the city throughout its history. For the greater part of the colonial period, the holdings are surprisingly complete. In the late colonial period, it is uncommon for even a single year of a notary's protocols to be missing.

These records embrace a great variety of personal and business activities. The most comprehensive, and normally the most personal, of documents are the wills. These frequently offer excellent summaries of a person's family and business history, quickly revealing to the investigator the extent to which these two aspects of an individual's life intermingled. The one document oftentimes gives information on three generations of a single family. The business life of the individual is further illuminated by the number of company contracts and sales and purchase agreements which appear. These are especially helpful in pointing out the ancillary business activities of a person, activities not normally subsumed under the occupational title which the subject has adopted. Powers of attorney can be occasionally frustrating, for many of them were given to professional agents. While that itself is worthy of note, the practice does not reveal the personal connections which so often characterized business understandings.

No other form of documentation rivals wills for giving accurate and comprehensive information about families. Nonetheless, business agreements and contracts often make indirect reference to marital and blood ties which are useful in figuring out the family connections which riddled the business world. Dowry and arras receipts and acknowledgements of inheritances are beneficial in the sorting out of family relationships and in the understanding of when and how actual transfer of property and money occurred in a marriage.

The Archivo General de la Nación (National Archive) is the greatest single repository of documents relating to the life of the Mexican nation. However, only a few branches contained material which bears on the present study. By far the most important of these was "Consulado," the section containing the records of the merchants' guild. Most of these documents pertain directly to individual court cases involving sales of merchandise and payment for them. These revealed the normal forms of business organization, how merchants of different rank and in different locations dealt with each other, and what were standard business procedures, especially regarding use of personnel, separation of ownership and management, and credit and payment arrangements. (I myself examined some hundreds of cases, each of which was indexed and which referred to a Mexico City merchant between 1770 and the court's demise in 1826.) This material is also valuable for showing the commercial activity of individuals and groups not usually associated with this field of enterprise and the business activity of merchants outside of commerce itself.

Other sections in the AGN were very helpful. "Civil" contains some excellent material on business and property disputes. "Padrones" has the 1811 census of the city in very readable form. Other sections do not necessarily have an abundance of pertinent material, but do have specific lists or documents which reveal business and social practices among sectors of the population which are not easily studied.

The Biblioteca Nacional (National Library) has a good number of very useful lists and manuscripts. These lists are especially illuminating about the holders of offices in the government, the church, and educational institutions. This library has a nearly complete holding of the *Guías de forasteros* from its beginning in 1761 until well into the national period. Other manuscripts detail membership in various guilds and professional organizations. Here too is to be found the most complete holding of publications dating from the late colonial period.

The Hemeroteca Nacional (National Periodical Collection) has a nearly complete run of the *Diario de México* and the *Gazeta de México*, the two newspapers—the first daily and the second weekly—of late colonial Mexico City. Both contained a number of interesting articles which gave little information that was directly useful; however, both also had personal and situation-wanted sections which were most revealing about the existence and condition of such groups as newly arrived immigrants from Spain, domestics, clerks, and unskilled laborers. The newspaper remains largely untapped as a source of social history.

Finally, the elaboration of this study was aided considerably by published books which trace the genealogy of individual families, the careers of colonial writers, the lives of distinguished graduates of a school, and the like. While such works cannot by themselves reconstruct the life or career patterns of a professional or social group, they are of pronounced usefulness in helping to thread together the strands of a person's life.

Archival Materials Consulted

Archivo de Notarías del Departamento del Distrito Federal (Mexico D.F.)

Joaquín Barrientos, 1782–1815.
Francisco Javier Benítez, 1794–1825.
José Antonio Burillo, 1781–1809.
Mariano Cadena, 1780–1793.
Francisco Calapiz, 1789–1800.
José María de Castro, 1803–1816.
Manuel Domingo Chavero, 1780–1796.
Andrés Delgado Camargo, 1784.
Tomás Hidalgo de los Reyes, 1790–1814.
Vicente Hidalgo de los Reyes, 1804–1811.
Juan Manuel Pozo, 1784–1815.
Manuel de Puertas, 1782–1789.
José Rodríquez Gallardo, 1804–1809.
Ignacio de San Martín, 1787–1791.

José María de Torija, 1780–1790.
Francisco de la Torre, 1804–1823.
José Antonio Troncoso, 1783–1789.
Félix Fernando Zamorano y Barrera, 1803–1808.
Archivo General de la Nación
  Ramos de:
    Abastos y Panaderías.
    Archivo Histórico de Hacienda.
    Ayuntamientos.
    Civil.
    Consulado.
    Escribanos.
    Historia.
    Hospital de Jesús.
    Industria y Comercio.
    Inquisición.
    Minería.
    Padrones.
Biblioteca Nacional
  Manual y Guía de Forasteros, 1761–1833.
  Manuscritos.
Hemeroteca Nacional
  Diario de México, 1805–1813.
  Gazeta de México, 1784–1821.

Published Documents

Báez Macías, Eduardo, ed. "Planos y censos de la Ciudad de México, 1753," *Boletín del Archivo General de la Nación*, 8:3–4 (1967): 487–1115.
Castro Santa Anna, José Manuel de. "Diario de sucesos notables," in *Documentos para la Historia de México*, primera serie, v. 4–6, México: Imprenta de J. R. Navarro, 1854.
Fernández de Recas, Guillermo S. *Grados de Licenciados Maestros y Doctores en Artes, Leyes, Teología y Todas Facultades de la Real y Pontificia Universidad de México*. México: UNAM, 1963.
———. *Aspirantes Americanos a Cargos del Santo Oficio*. México: Librería de M. Porrúa, 1956.
Florescano, Enrique and Isabel Gil, eds. *Descripciones económicas generales de Nueva España, 1784–1817*. México: SEPINAH, 1973.
Gómez, José. "Diario curioso de México," in *Documentos para la Historia*

de México, primera serie, v. 7, México: Imprenta de J. R. Navarro, 1854.

"Informe sobre pulquerías y tabernas el año de 1784," *Boletín del Archivo General de la Nación*, 18:2–3 (1947): 189–236 and 363–405.

Lerdo de Tejada, Miguel M. *Comercio esterior de México desde la Conquista hasta Hoy*. México: Rafael, 1853.

México dividida en Cuarteles Mayores y Menores. México: Manuel Antonio Valdés, 1811.

"Notable Carta reservada del Segundo Conde de Revillagigedo," *Boletín del Archivo General de la Nación*, primera serie, 1:2, 2:1, and 2:2 (1930–1931): 190–211, 41–49, and 196–211.

Conde de Revillagigedo. *Informe sobre las Misiones, 1793, e Instrucción reservada al Marqués de Branciforte, 1794*. México: Editorial Jus, 1966.

Serano, Francisco. *Noticias de México*. 3 vols., México: Secretaría de Obras y Servicio, 1974.

Scholarly Works Consulted

Alamán, Lucas. *Historia de Méjico*. 5 vols., México: Imprenta de J. R. Lara, 1849–1852.

Andrade, Vicente de P. "Los Oidores de Nueva España," *Boletín Bibliográfico Mexicano*, (May–June 1956): 16–25.

Anna, Timothy E. *The Fall of Royal Government in Mexico City*. Lincoln: University of Nebraska Press, 1978.

Archer, Christon I. *The Army in Bourbon Mexico, 1760–1810*. Albuquerque: University of New Mexico Press, 1977.

Arcila Farías, Eduardo. *Comercio entre Venezuela y México en los Siglos XVII y XVIII*. México: El Colegio de México, 1950.

———. *Reformas económicas del siglo XVIII en Nueva España*. 2 vols., México: SEPSETENTAS, 1974.

Arnold, Linda. "Bureaucracy and Bureaucrats in Mexico City: 1808–1824," M.A. thesis, University of Texas at Austin, 1975.

———. "Social, Economic, and Political Status in the Mexico City Central Bureaucracy: 1808–1822," in Elsa Cecilia Frost, Michael C. Meyer, and Josefina Zoraida Vázquez, eds., *Labor and Laborers through Mexican History*. Tucson: University of Arizona Press, 1979.

Arrom, Silvia M. *La Mujer Mexicana ante el Divorcio Eclesiástico (1800–1857)*. México: SEPSETENTAS, 1976.

———. "Women and the Family in Mexico City, 1800–1857," Ph.D. diss., Stanford University, 1978.

Arroniz, Marcos. *Manual de Biografía Mejicana*. Paris: Rosa, 1857.

Atienza, Julio de. *Títulos Nobiliarios Hispanoamericanos*. Madrid: M. Aguilar, 1947.

Bailyn, Bernard. *The New England Merchants in the Seventeenth Century*. New York: Harper and Row, 1964.

Barbier, Jacques A., "Elites and Cadres in Bourbon Chile," *Hispanic American Historical Review*, 52:3 (August 1972): 416–35.

Barrett, Ward. "The Meat Supply of Colonial Cuernavaca," *Annals of the Association of American Geographers*, 64:4 (December 1974): 525–40.

————. "Morelos and its Sugar Industry in the Late Eighteenth Century," in Ida Altman and James Lockhart, eds., *Provinces of Early Mexico*, Los Angeles: University of California Press, 1976.

Bazant, Jan. *Cinco Haciendas Mexicanas*. México: El Colegio de México, 1975.

Beristáin de Souza, José Mariano. *Biblioteca Hispanoamericana Septentrional*. 3 vols., México: A. Valdés, 1816–1821.

Borchart de Moreno, Christiana. "Los Miembros del Consulado de la Ciudad de México en la Epoca de Carlos III," *Jahrbuch für Geschichte von Staat, Wirtschaft, und Gesellschaft Lateinamericas*, 14 (1977): 134–160.

Brading, D. A. *Haciendas and Ranchos in the Mexican Bajío, León 1700–1860*. Cambridge: Cambridge University Press, 1978.

————. *Miners and Merchants in Bourbon Mexico 1763–1810*. Cambridge: Cambridge University Press, 1971.

————. "Los Españoles en México hacia 1792," *Historia Mexicana*, 23:1 (July–Sept. 1973): 126–44.

Brown, Jonathan C. *A Socioeconomic History of Argentina, 1776–1860*. Cambridge: Cambridge University Press, 1979.

Burkholder, Mark A. "From Creole to Peninsular: The Transformation of the Audiencia of Lima," *Hispanic American Historical Review*, 52:3 (August 1972): 395–415.

————. *Politics of a Colonial Career*. Albuquerque: University of New Mexico Press, 1981.

Burkholder, M. A. and D. S. Chandler. "Creole Appointments and the Sale of Audiencia Positions in the Spanish Empire Under the Early Bourbons, 1701–1750," *Journal of Latin American Studies*, 4:2 (November 1972): 187–206.

————. *From Impotence to Authority*. Columbia: University of Missouri Press, 1977.

Calderón de la Barca, Fanny. *Life in Mexico*, edited by Howard T. Fisher and Marion Hall Fisher, Garden City: Doubleday and Co. Inc., 1970.

Capella, Miguel and Antonio Matilla Tascón. *Los Cinco Gremios Mayores de Madrid: Estudio crítico-histórico*. Madrid, 1957.

Calderón Quijano, José Antonio. *Los Virreyes de Nueva España en el Reinado de Carlos III.* 2 vols., Seville: Escuela Gráfica Salesiana, Publicaciones de Escuela de Estudios Hispano-Americanos de Sevilla, 1968.

Carreño, Alberto María. *La Real y Pontificia Universidad de México, 1536–1865.* México: UNAM, 1961.

Carrera Stampa, Manuel. "La Ciudad de México a principios del siglo XIX," *Memorias de la Academia Mexicana de la Historia*, 26:2 (1967): 184–231.

————. "Las Ferias Novohispanas," *Historia Mexicana*, 2:3 (January–March 1953): 319–42.

————. *Los Gremios Mexicanos: La Organizacion Gremial en Nueva España, 1521–1861.* México: Ibero Americana, 1954.

————. "Planos de la Ciudad de México," *Boletín de la Sociedad Mexicana de Geografía y Estadística*, 67:2–3 (March–June 1949).

————. "Plano de la Ciudad de México 1737," *Memorias de la Academia Mexicana de la Historia*, 15:4 (October–December 1956): 363–98.

Chance, John K. *Race and Class in Colonial Oaxaca.* Stanford: Stanford University Press, 1978.

Chávez Orozco, Luis. *Historia de México (1808–1836).* México: Editorial Patria, 1947.

————. *La Educación pública elemental el la Ciudad de México durante el siglo XVIII.* México: Secretaría de Educacion Pública, 1936.

————. "El Cultivo de Café en México, Sus Origenes," in *Documentos para la Historia Económica de México*, México: Banco Nacional de Crédito Agrícola y Ganadero, 1954.

Christelow, Allan. "Great Britain and the Trade from Cádiz and Lisbon to Spanish America and Brazil, 1759–1783," *Hispanic American Historical Review*, 27:1 (February 1947): 2–29.

Cooper, Donald B. *Epidemic Disease in Mexico City 1761–1813.* Austin: University of Texas Press, 1965.

Cuenca Esteban, Javier. "Statistics of Spain's Colonial Trade, 1792–1820: Consular Duties, Cargo Inventories, and Balances of Trade," *Hispanic American Historical Review*, 61:3 (August 1981): 381–428.

Davies, Keith A. "Tendencias demográficas urbanas durante el siglo XIX en México," *Historia Mexicana*, 21:3 (January–March 1972): 481–524.

Dean, Warren. *The Industrialization of São Paulo 1880–1945.* Austin: University of Texas Press, 1969.

Diccionario Universal de Historia y de Geografía. 10 vols., Mexico: Imprenta de F. Escalante y Cía., 1855–1856.

Esquível Obregón, Toribio. *Biografía de don Francisco Javier de Gamboa.* México: Talleres Gráficos Laguna, 1941.

Flores Caballero, Romeo. *Counterrevolution.* Lincoln: University of Nebraska Press, 1974.

Flores Marín, Carlos. *Casas virreinales en la Ciudad de México.* México: Fondo de Cultura Económica, 1970.

Florescano, Enrique. *Precios de Maíz y crisis agrícolas en México (1708–1810).* México: El Colegio de México, 1969.

———. "El Problema Agrario en los últimos años del Virreinato, 1800–1821," *Historia Mexicana,* 20:4 (April–June 1971): 477–510.

Ganster, Paul B. "A Social History of the Secular Clergy of Lima during the Middle Decades of the Eighteenth Century," Ph.D. diss., University of California, Los Angeles, 1974.

García Martínez, Bernardo. "El Sistema monetario de los últimos años del Período Novohispano," *Historia Mexicana,* 17:3 (January–March 1968): 349–60.

Gibson, Charles. *The Aztecs Under Spanish Rule.* Stanford: Stanford University Press, 1964.

González Obregón, Luis. *La Vida de México en 1810.* México: Secretaría de Obras y Servicio, 1975.

———. *Las Calles de México.* México: Ediciones Botas, 1944.

———. *México Viejo.* México: Secretaría de Fomento, 1895.

Gortari, Hira de, and Guillermo Palacios. "El Comercio Novohispano a través de Veracruz (1802–1810)," *Historia Mexicana,* 17:3 (January–March 1968), 427–54.

Greenleaf, Richard E. "The Obraje in the late Mexican Colony," *The Americans,* 22:3 (January 1967): 227–50.

Hamnett, Brian R. *Politics and Trade in Southern Mexico, 1750–1812.* Cambridge: Cambridge University Press, 1971.

Hardy, Robert William Hale. *Travels in the Interior of Mexico in 1825, 1826, 1827, and 1828.* London: H. Colburn and R. Bentley, 1829.

Harris III, Charles H. *A Mexican Family Empire.* Austin: University of Texas Press, 1975.

Hoberman, Louisa Schell. "Merchants in Seventeenth-Century Mexico City: A Preliminary Portrait," *Hispanic American Historical Review,* 57:3 (August 1977): 479–503.

Howe, Walter. *The Mining Guild of New Spain and its Tribunal General 1770–1821.* Cambridge: Harvard University Press, 1949.

Humboldt, Alejandro de. *Ensayo Político sobre el Reino de la Nueva España.* México: Editorial Porrúa, 1973.

Hunt, Marta Espejo-Ponce. "Colonial Yucatán: Town and Region in the Seventeenth Century," Ph.D. diss., University of California, Los Angeles, 1974.

Katz, Stanley N. *Colonial America: Essays in Politics and Social Develop-ment.* Boston: Little, Brown and Company, 1975.

Kicza, John E. "Business and Society in Late Colonial Mexico City," Ph.D. diss., University of California, Los Angeles, 1979.

————. "The Pulque Trade of Late Colonial Mexico City," *The Americas,* 37:2 (October 1980): 193–221.

Ladd, Doris M. *The Mexican Nobility at Independence, 1780–1826.* Austin: University of Texas Press, 1976.

LaForce Jr., James C. *The Development of the Spanish Textile Industry, 1750–1800.* Berkeley: University of California Press, 1965.

Lafuente Ferrari, Enrique. *El Virrey Iturrigaray y los orígenes de la Indepen-dencia de Méjico.* Madrid: Instituto Gonzalo Fernández de Oviedo, 1941.

Lerner, Victoria. "Consideraciones sobre la población de la Nueva Es-paña (1793–1810)," *Historia Mexicana,* 17:3 (January–March 1968), 327–48.

Lewis, Leslie K. "Colonial Texcoco: A Province in the Valley of Mexico, 1570–1630," Ph.D. diss., University of California, Los Angeles, 1977.

Liehr, Reinhard. *Ayuntamiento y oligarquía en Puebla, 1787–1810.* 2 vols., México: SEPSETENTAS, 1976.

Lindley Richard B. "Kinship and Credit in the Structure of Guadalajara's Oligarchy 1800–1830," Ph.D. diss., University of Texas at Austin, 1976.

Lockhart, James. *Spanish Peru, 1532–1560: A Colonial Society.* Madison: University of Wisconsin Press, 1968.

Lohmann Villena, Guillermo. *Los Americanos en las Ordenes Nobiliarias 1529–1900.* 2 vols., Madrid: Instituto Gonzalo Fernández de Oviedo, 1947.

————. *Los Ministros de la Audiencia de Lima en el Reinado de los Borbones (1700–1821).* Seville: Universidad de Sevilla, 1974.

López Sarrelangue, Delfina E., "Población Indígena de la Nueva España en el siglo XVIII," *Historia Mexicana,* 12:4 (April–June 1963): 516–30.

Lynch, John. *The Spanish American Revolutions, 1808–1826.* New York: Norton, 1973.

MacLachlan, Colin M. and Jaime E. Rodríguez O. *The Forging of the Cos-mic Race.* Berkeley: University of California Press, 1980.

Maniau, Joaquín. *Compendio de la historia de la Real Hacienda de Nueva Es-paña escrito en el año de 1794.* México: Secretaría de Industria y Comer-cio, 1914.

Marroqui, José María. *La Ciudad de México.* 2 vols., México: J. Aguilar Vera y Cía., 1900.

Martínez, María del Carmen Calvento. "Intereses particulares y política de abastecimiento en México: el Reglamento del Gremio de Panaderos, 1770," *Revista de Indias*, 35:143–44 (January–June 1976): 159–211.

Martínez Cosío, Leopoldo. *Los Caballeros de las Ordenes Militares en México*. México: Editorial Santiago, 1946.

de la Maza, Francisco. *La Ciudad de México en el siglo XVII*. México: Fondo de Cultura Económica, 1968.

McAlister, L. N. "Social Structure and Social Change in New Spain," *Hispanic American Historical Review*, 43:3 (August 1963): 349–70.

Millares Carlo, Agustín, and José Ignacio Mantecón. "El Archivo de Notarías del Departamento del Distrito Federal (Mexico, D.F.)," *Revista de Historia de América*, 17 (June 1944): 69–118.

Mora, José María Luis. *México y sus Revoluciones*. 3 vols., México: Editorial Porrúa, 1965.

Morales, María Dolores. "Estructura urbana y distribución de la propiedad en la Ciudad de México en 1813," *Historia Mexicana*, 25:3 (January–March 1976): 363–402.

Moreno Toscano, Alejandra, "Cambios en los patrones de urbanización en México, 1810–1910," *Historia Mexicana*, 22:2 (October–December 1972): 160–87.

Moreno Toscano, Alejandra, and Carlos Aguirre Anaya. "Migrations to Mexico City in the Nineteenth Century," *Journal of Interamerican Studies and World Affairs*, 17:1 (February 1975): 27–42.

Obregón Jr., Gonzalo. *El Real Colegio de San Ignacio de México (Las Vizcaínas)*. México: El Colegio de México, 1949.

Ocampo, Javier. *Las Ideas de un Día*. México: El Colegio de México, 1969.

Orozco y Berra, Manuel. *Historia de la Ciudad de México*. México: SEP-SETENTAS, 1973.

―――. *Memoria para el Plano de la Ciudad de México*. México: Imprenta de S. White, 1867.

Ortiz de la Tabla, Javier. *Comercio exterior de Veracruz, 1778–1821*. Seville: Escuela de Estudios Hispanos-Americanos, 1978.

Osores, Félix. *Noticias biobibliográficos de alumnos distinguidos del Colegio de San Pedro, San Pablo, y San Ildefonso de México*. México: Viuda de C. Bouret, 1908.

Poinsett, Joel R. *Notes on Mexico*. London: P. Miller, 1825.

Ramírez Flórez, José. *El Real Consulado de Guadalajara*. Guadalajara: Banco Refaccionario de Jalisco, 1952.

Rees, Peter. *Transportes y Comercio entre México y Veracruz 1519–1910*. México: SEPSETENTAS, 1976.

Restrepo Sáenz, José María. *Biografías de los Mandatarios y Ministros de la Real Hacienda (1617–1819)*. Bogota: Editorial Cromos, 1952.

Rice, Jacqueline A. "The Porfirian Political Elite: Life Patterns of the Delegates to the 1892 Union Liberal Convention," Ph.D. diss., University of California, Los Angeles, 1979.

Romero de Terreros, Manuel. *Antiguas Haciendas de México*. Mexico: Editorial Patria, 1956.

Romero de Terreros, Manuel. *Residencias coloniales de México*. México: Impresora de la Secretaría de Hacienda, 1918.

Rubio-Argüelles, Angeles. "Zúñiga, Impresor del siglo XVIII en México," *Las Ciencias*, 22:3 (1957): 507–61.

Rydford, John. *Foreign Interest in the Independence of New Spain*. Durham: Duke University Press, 1935.

Schurz, William L. *The Manila Galleon*. New York: E.P. Dutton and Co., 1959.

Sims, Harold D. *La Expulsión de los Españoles de México (1828–1832)*. México: Fondo de Cultura Económica, 1974.

Smith, Robert S. "Sales Taxes in New Spain, 1575–1770," *Hispanic American Historical Review*, 28:1 (February 1948): 2–37.

———. "Shipping in the Port of Veracruz, 1790–1821," *Hispanic American Historical Review*, 23:1 (February 1943): 5–20.

———. "The Institution of the Consulado in New Spain," *Hispanic American Historical Review*, 24:1 (February 1944): 61–83.

Socolow, Susan M. *The Merchants of Buenos Aires, 1778–1810: Family and Commerce*. Cambridge: Cambridge University Press, 1978.

Spell, J. R. "The Historical and Social Background of El Periquillo Sarniento," *Hispanic American Historical Review*, 36:4 (November 1956): 447–70.

Stein, Stanley J. "Bureaucracy and Business in the Spanish Empire, 1759–1804: Failure of a Bourbon Reform in Mexico and Peru," *Hispanic American Historical Review*, 61:1 (February 1981): 2–28.

Tanck Estrada, Dorothy. *La Educación Ilustrada (1786–1836)*. México: El Colegio de México, 1977.

Tenebaum, Barbara A. "Merchants, Money, and Mischief. The British in Mexico, 1821–1862," *The Americas*, 35:3 (January 1979): 317–39.

Tayloe, Edward Thornton. *The Journal and Correspondence of.* Edited by C. Harvey Gardiner, Chapel Hill: University of North Carolina Press, 1959.

Taylor, William B. *Landlord and Peasant in Colonial Oaxaca*. Stanford: Stanford University Press, 1972.

Taylor, William B. and John K. Chance. "Estate and Class in a Colonial

City—Oaxaca in 1792," *Comparative Studies in Society and History*, 19:4 (October 1977): 454–87.

Títulos de Indias, Catálogo XX del Archivo General de Simancas. Valladolid, 1954.

Toussaint, Manuel, Federico Gómez de Orozco, and Justino Fernández. "Planos de la Ciudad de México, siglos XVI and XVII," *XVI Congreso Internactional de Planificacion y de la Habitacion*, Mexico, 1938.

Tutino, John M. "Creole Mexico: Spanish Elites, Haciendas, and Indian Towns, 1750–1810," Ph.D. diss., University of Texas at Austin, 1976.

Valdés, Dennis N. "The Decline of the *Sociedad de Castas* in Mexico City," Ph.D. diss., University of Michigan, 1978.

Van Young, Eric J. *Hacienda and Market in Eighteenth-Century Mexico.* Berkeley: University of California Press, 1981.

Villaseñor y Sánchez, José Antonio de. *Theatro Americano.* 2 vols., Mexico: Imprenta de la Viuda de J. Bernardo Hogal, 1746.

Villoro, Luis. *La Revolución de Independencia.* México: UNAM, 1953.

Walker, Geoffrey J. *Spanish Politics and Imperial Trade, 1700–1789.* Bloomington: Indiana University Press, 1979.

Ward, H. G. *Mexico in 1827.* 2 vols., London: H. Colburn, 1828.

Zavala, Lorenzo de. *Ensayo Histórico de las Revoluciones de Mégico desde 1808 hasta 1830.* 2 vols., Paris: Imprenta de P. Dupont et G. Laguionie, 1831.

Index

Abad, José Nicolás: marriage-age
difference with wife, 166
Abasto, 196
Academics, 29
Acapulco, 66, 67, 70, 74, 98, 150,
152, 230
Acha, Juan José de: honors received, 174
Acha: Tomás Domingo de: honors received, 174
Accessorías, 114
Adalid, Diego, 151
Adalid, Francisco Antonio: bankruptcy of, 181; mentioned, 151
Adalid, Ignacio: owner of *pulque*
ranchos, 181; owner of *pulquería*, 122
Adalid, José: honors received, 174;
in the cabildo, 35; mine shareholder, 89; owner of *pulquería*,
122; rental of *pulquerías*, 124;
uncle of Francisco Antonio, 151
Adalid family, 333
Agreda, Diego de: dowry received, 163; honors received,
174; marriages, 70, 143–44,
182; supplier to artisans, 215;

ties to Spanish merchant house,
62
Agriculture, 165, 179, 227, 238
Aguadores: guild membership, 211
Aguardiente, 264
Aguayo, Marqués de, 19, 38, 151
Aguirre y Viana, Guillermo, 125
Agujereros: guild membership, 210
Alacena, 8
Alamillo, Ventura, 212
Albañiles: guild membership, 211
Albia, Angel, 222
Alcalde de barrio, 168
Alcaldes, 34, 36
Alcaldes mayores, 93
Alcaldes ordinarios: merchants as,
178; mentioned, 201, 217, 237
Alcántara, Order of: given to
merchants, 177; mentioned, 34
Alcedo, Matías, 114
Aldana, Joaquín de: activities as
provincial trader, 78–79; com-
pany in store, 80; owner of bak-
ery, 191; owner of estates, 168
Algarín, José, 220–21
Algodoneros: guild membership,
209

Alles, José Alonso de: honors received, 174
Alles, Pedro Alonso de: bondsman of *subdelegado*, 94–95; honors received, 174; use of relatives in business, 142–43. *See also* Inguanzo, Marqués de
Almacén, 8
Almaceneros: as militia officers, 177; as suppliers to artisans, 213; mentioned 179, 193, 237. *See also* International merchants; International traders; Merchants; Wholesalers
Alonso de Terán, Antonio: honors received, 174; mentioned, 140, 158
Alonso de Terán, Francisco: honors received, 174; kinship ties in Consulado, 140; mentioned, 158
Alonso de Terán family, 177
Alvarez, Ignacio, 203
Amecameca, 224
Angulo Guardamino, Lorenzo de: honors received, 174; lieutenant colonel, 173; mine shareholder, 89; sells stores to *cajeros*, 105
Antepara, Juan Lorenzo de, 69
Apan, 96
Apartado, Marqués de: family remains in commerce, 170; mentioned, 26, 69
Apecechea, Juan José de, 87
Apprentices: misbehavior by, 201; mentioned, 212, 217–18, 223, 239
Aranda, Manuel: business with *subdelegado*, 264
Arangoiti, Bernabé de, 145
Arangoiti, Bernardino de: com-

mercial company with uncle, 65; mentioned, 144
Arangoiti, Francisco de, 145
Arangoiti, Juan Manuel de, 144
Aránzazu, Nuestra Señora de, 59
Architects, 212. *See also Arquitectos*
Arechaga, Juan de, 193–94
Ariscorreta, José Joaquín de: cacao importer, 70; honors received, 174; mentioned, 225–26
Aristegui, Miguel de, 191–92
Arizaga, José Francisco, 221
Arizpe, 79, 81, 108
Arquitectos: guild membership, 210. *See also* Architects
Arras, 162–64, 197, 221
Arredondo, Juan de, 193
Arte de la Seda: guild membership, 209
Arte de leer: guild membership, 209
Artisans, 170, 172, 177, 195, 239, 241
Assayer, 208
Asturias, 197
Attorneys. *See* Lawyers
Audiencia: *alcalde del crimen* of, 160; Mexico, 37, 38, 182; *oidor* of, 160; mentioned, 29, 52, 181, 192
Avila, José Mariano de, 213–14
Ayuntamiento of Mexico City: merchants in, 178–79; mentioned, 182. *See also* Cabildo
Ayusto, Francisco, 222–23
Azucarería, 8
Azucarero, 91

Bajío, 20, 173
Bakeries: purchased by wholesalers, 170; mentioned, 111, 238. *See also Panaderías*

Bakery owners: limits of wealth and status, 191
Balbontín, José Manuel: honors received, 174
Banineli, Antonio, 218
Barandiarán, Martín de, 126
Baratillo, 130
Barberi family, 33
Barberos: guild membership, 211
Barcelona, 48
Barcena, Fernando de la: use of family in store, 141–42
Barcena, Juan de la, 141
Barcena, Patricio de la, 141–42
Barcena é Izquierdo, Fernando, 141
Baring Brothers, 272
Barreda, Bartolomé, 213
Barreda, José Manuel de, 194–95
Bartomeu, Isidro, 62
Basabe, Pedro, 62–63
Basque party, 51–52, 53, 159
Bassoco, Antonio de: commercial company with nephew, 65; honorary accountant of the military, 179; honors received, 174; mine shareholder, 89; sets up nephews in business, 144–45; mentioned, 71
Bassoco, José María de: honors received, 174; mentioned, 145
Basurto, José, 78–79
Bateojas: guild membership, 209
Baz, José Bernardo: China tade, 67–68; honors received, 174
Beato, Santos, 131
Benavente, José María de: contracts to buy wheat for bakery, 195
Berazueta, Pedro José de, 191–92
Bergechín, Juan, 222

Beristáin, José Antonio, 118
Bernal, José María: owner of ceramics shop, 216; mentioned, 215
Berrio y Saldívar, Miguel de, 38
Berruecos, José Vicente, 118
Betancurt, María Josefa, 130
Beye de Cisneros, Ignacio: cabildo member, 35
Beye de Cisneros famiy, 29, 333
Bilbao, 66, 152, 171
Blacks, 5
Blacksmiths, 219–22
Blancas, José de, 218–19
Bolado Regato, Manuel: merchant as mineowner, 87
Bolaños, 17, 88
Bolío, Juan, 125
Bondsmen, 20, 59–60, 80, 95, 97, 104, 171
Bordadores: guild membership, 209
Borunda, Mariano, 190
Botello, Joaquín, 222–23
Botica, 112
Boticarios: guild membership, 211
Bourbon reforms, 55, 93
Brazil, 45
Buendía, José, 225
Buenvecino, Estéban: cacao importer, 70; mentioned, 69
Bureaucrats. *See* Government officials
Busce, Domingo, 131
Bulnes Villar, Juan Alonso de: honors received, 174
Bustillo, Vicente, 114, 117

Cabildo, 34, 18
Cacahuaterías, 107, 110. *See also* *Pulperías*
Cacao, 45, 62, 65, 230

Cacique, 205
Cádiz, 45, 46, 48, 49, 62, 65, 109, 146, 261
Cajeros; definition of the term, 135–36; mentioned, 78, 79, 85, 103, 104, 105, 108, 137, 138, 139, 141, 146, 147, 216, 235
Cajones, 6, 8, 105, 106, 107–9, 111, 112, 118, 120, 138, 145, 167, 168, 225
Calatrava, Order of: given to merchants, 177; mentioned, 34
Calderón, Eduardo, 214
Calderos: guild membership, 210
Calo, Leonardo María: merchant investing in bakery, 193
Canteros: guild membership, 211
Cañeros: guild membership, 211
Capellanías, 57, 58, 200
Caracas: cacao from, 68, 69; mentioned, 65
Cargadores: guild membership, 211
Carlos III, Order of: given to merchants, 177; mentioned, 34, 181
Carpinteros: guild membership, 210; mentioned, 208
Carriage-maker: company with merchant, 171. *See also Carroceros*; Coachmakers
Carriers, 212
Carrocerías, 218
Carroceros: guild membership, 210
Casa Flores, Conde de: marriage of, 38
Casal, Alvaro del, 192
Casanueva, Baltasar de: dowry received, 163
Casasola, Francisco, 58
Caso, Mariano de, 197
Caso, Pedro de: diversified invest-
ments, 120–21; merchant investing in bakery, 193
Castañiza, Domingo de: capital at marriage, 163
Castañiza, Marqués de: family remains in commerce, 170; mentioned, 26, 145
Castañiza family, 144
Castas: in cigarette factory, 205; in guilds, 208; mentioned, 4, 239
Castile, 260
Castilla, Mariscal de: in the cabildo, 36
Castillo, Juan José de, 192
Castillo, Manuel del, 219
Castro, Pedro, 214
Castro, Tomás, 114
Catalonia, 146
Catorce, 83, 85
Ceramics shop, 216
Cererías, 8, 138
Cereros: guild membership, 210
Cervantes, Antonio, 212
Cervantes y Padilla, Juan María de: in the cabildo, 36
Cervantes y Padilla family, 19, 33
Ceuta, 212
Cevallos, Francisco Antonio, 58
Cevallos, José de: marriage into González Calderón family, 181; mentioned, 155
Cevallos, José Antonio, 58
Chalco, 20, 168, 199
Charles III, 46, 55
Chavarrí, Francisco de: dowry received, 161, 163; honors received, 174
China trade, 75. *See also* Manila Galleon
Church: elite entrance into, 39–40
Cigarrerías, 129, 130

Cinco Gremios Mayores de Madrid, 62–63
City Council, 196. *See also* Ayuntamiento; Cabildo
Clerics, 195
Coachmakers, 207, 208, 212, 218–19. *See also Carroceros*
Coachrentals, 219
Cobián, Juan Antonio: company in Parián store, 104–5; honors received, 174
Cobián de los Ríos, José Pasqual: honors received, 174
Cocheros: guild membership, 211
Cochineal: amount shipped to Spain, 72; commerce in, 45; mentioned, 71, 94, 230, 243, 264
Coffee growers of São Paulo, 258
Cofradías: popularity among merchants, 180; real-estate ownership, 5; mentioned, 59, 224
Coheteros: guild memberhsip, 210
Colegio de Abogados, 28, 29, 259
Colegio de Mercaderes, 264
Colima, 88
Colla, Joaquín de: colonel of merchants' regiment, 173; honors received, 174
Comerciante, 264
Commerce: among colonial American planters, 258; lack of specialization, 60; use of relatives, 65–66; mentioned, 165, 227, 228, 238
Commercial houses: nature of, 64–65. *See also* Trading houses
Commodity trading: in Mexico City, 89–93; with Spain, 261; 61, 146, 232–33
Companies: among saddlemakers,

225; among tailors, 222–23; between owners and managers, 78, 79, 190; commercial, 52, 65; common in managing plants and mills, 238; importance of, 152–54, 242; in Manila Galleon, 67; in mines, 85; in Parián store, 22; in provincial trade, 77–81; in retail stores, 98, 105, 233; reasons for their frequency, 135; their role in commerce, 234; to gain capital, 57; with partners in Spain, 66
Confiteros: guild membership, 211
Consulado: abolition of, 54–55; chief notary of, 149; creole membership in, 25, 38; elite family representation, 170; kin group operating in, 147–48; marriage as a means of entrance, 182; monopoly over the China trade, 66; of Mexico City, 18, 25, 26, 37, 38, 41, 91, 104, 125, 140, 145, 146, 148, 149, 236, 255, 260; militia regiment, 15; officer of, 177; politics, 52; presence of intermarried families, 235–36; mentioned, 17, 29, 51, 54, 64, 92, 98, 105, 113, 120, 132, 138, 143, 144, 145, 148, 150, 155, 158, 181, 192, 229, 237, 264, 265
Convents, 191, 196
Coppersmithery, 213, 216
Cordoneros: guild membership, 209
Corredores de comercio: place in militia, 177; mentioned, 132–33
Correspondence accounts, 56, 231
Cortés, Bárbara, 194
Cortés, Juan Julio, 125

Cortina, Conde de la: family remains in commerce, 170
Cortina González, Francisco: honors received, 174
Cortina González, Joaquín: honors received, 174
Cotera, Domingo de la, 194
Cotera, José Mariano de la; honors received, 174
Cotton, 187
Council of the Indies, 37, 124, 160
Coyoacán, 204–15
Credit: among artisans, 214–15, 239; as mechanism to control provincial trade, 84; importance of, 55; in commerce, 64; in operation of bakeries, 192–94; mentioned, 19, 230–31
Creoles: in commerce, 25; mentioned, 4
Cuautla Amilpas, 77, 79, 96
Cuernavaca, 89, 90, 167, 168, 225
Cuerpo de Comerciantes Pulperos, 111
Cuevas, Bernardino, 225
Cuevas y Aguirre family, 33
Curtidores: guild membership, 210

Danz y Freire, Juan, 120
Delgado y Sotomayor, Josefa, 130
Delinquent youths: incarceration in *obrajes*, 201
Dependencias activas, 55
Depósitos irregulares, 56
Desa, Bruno, 198
Díaz González, Juan: honors received, 174; mentioned, 270
Dies, Ventura Pablo: cacao importer, 70
Doradores: guild membership, 210
Dowries: among bakery owners,

195; among blacksmiths, 221–22; among silversmiths, 212–13; of merchants' daughters, 182; mentioned, 144, 161–64, 197, 213, 224. *See also* Marriages
Durán de Otero, Manuel, 200–201
Durango, 83, 144, 145

Ecce Homo, 58
Echave, José María de: dowry received, 161, 163; honors received, 175; second marriage, 160; mentioned, 159
Echegaráy, Ignacio José de, 218
Echeveste, Juan Manuel, 194
Economic diversification: common at all social levels, 241–42; mentioned, 27, 30, 169–70
Elías, Juan José de: loan to tobacco monopoly administrator, 95–96; mine shareholder, 89
Elite families: economic diversification, 169–70; in the ayuntamiento, 178
Elorreaga, Francisco Emeterio: sells wheat to bakery, 195; mentioned, 58
Elosúa Abarrategui, Pedro: merchant who rents out quarry, 204–5
Empedradores: guild membership, 211
Enderica, Manuel, 195
England, 45, 46, 47
English merchants, 71
Enríquez, Pedro José: rents a mill, 197
Entails, 32, 169
Escobillería, 224–25
Escultores: guild membership, 211

Espaderos: guild membership, 211
Esperas, 113, 132
Espinos de los Monteros, Francisco Ramón, 108
Espinosa y Segura, José, 225
Esquível y Vargas, Antonio José, 117
Estanquillos, 129, 130
Estate ownership: by merchants, 19–20, 41; mentioned, 19, 20, 31, 37, 42
Estates: acquisition and leasing by tanners, 225; diversification of, 20–21; division of after death, 167; leasing, 22, 166–67; owners' activities, 24; profitability, 21; transfer of wealth, 22
Europe, 143

Fagoaga, José Juan de: cacao importer, 69, 70; in the cabildo, 35
Fagoaga, José Luis de: invests in provincial store, 81
Fagoaga, José Mariano de: in the cabildo, 36
Fagoaga, Juan Bautista de: mineowner, 87
Fagoaga family, 37. *See also* Apartado, Marqués de
Familiar of Inquisition: appointment of merchants, 178
Federal District, 55
Fernández, José, 215
Fernández, Juan Domingo, 74
Fernández de Celís, Diego, 214
Fernández de Cevallos, Diego, 58
Fernández de Córdoba family, 33
Fernández de Jáuregui family, 203
Fernández de Madrid, Diego: *oidor*, 37
Fernández de Madrid family, 33

Fernández de Peredo, Diego: company in silver-shipping firm, 74; honors received, 175
Fernández de Peredo, Juan: mine shareholder, 89
Fernández de Peredo, Manuel: company in his slaughterhouse, 198–99
Fernández de Sierra, Doctor Miguel, 212
Fernández Sáenz de Santa María, Manuel: honors received, 175; marriage-age difference with wife, 166; mentioned, 270
Fernando VII, 179
Fiadores. See Bondsmen
Fleet system, 46, 61
Foncerrada family, 33
Fonda, 130
Fonderos: guild membership, 211
Frago, Antonio del, 147
Frago, Manuel de: company with store manager, 138–39
Fragoso, Lugarda María Ana: *pulquería* owner, 122
Franciscans, 193
Franciscans, Third Order of, 59
Free Port system, 47–48
Frenero, José Mariano, 218
Frías, José Saturnino, 221–22
Fuero: eligibility for, 173
Fundidores: guild membership, 210

Gach, Estéban, 81
Galindo Gutiérrez, María, 132
Gallardo, Miguel, 219
Gamboa, Francisco Javier: *oidor*, 37
García, Francisco, 37
García, Juan José, 136

García, Santiago: mine shareholder, 89
García Bravo, Diego: cacao importer, 70
García de Aguirre, Licenciado Mariano: invests in coachrenting business, 219
García de la Carrera, Mariana: owner of bakery, 194
García Díaz, Bartolomé, 215
García González de Noriega, Lorenzo: honors received, 175
García Herreros, Manuel: commodity trading with Spain, 66; financier of mining company, 87; honors received, 175; merchant as mineowner, 88; mine shareholder, 89; nephew of Francisco Martínez Cabezón; mentioned, 71
García Jove, Doctor José Ignacio: *pulquería* owner, 122, 123; rental of *pulquerías*, 124
García Noriega, Lorenzo: owner of sugar estate, 91
García Sáenz, Ignacio: bondsman of *subdelegado*, 94; capital at marriage, 163; honors received, 175; managing partner of company, 106
García Trujillo, Juan: cacao importer, 70
Garrido, Félix Clemente: dowry received, 163
Gazeta de México, 74
Goldworkers, 207, 208
Gómez Campos, José: company in store, 106; financier of mining expedition, 88; honors received, 175, 179; mining supplier, 86; ownership of stores run as companies, 103–4; sales to provincial clients, 82–83; supplier to artisans, 215
Gómez de Barreda, Diego: honors received, 175; mentioned, 95
Gómez de Cervantes, Ignacio Leonel: in the cabildo, 36
Gómez de Cervantes family, 33
Gómez de la Cortina, Servando: honors received, 175
Gómez de la Cortina, Vicente: honors received, 175
Gómez de Leís, Mateo Julián: dowry received, 161, 163; ties to Spanish merchant house, 62
Gómez Rodríguez de Pedroso, Antonia: *pulquería* owner, 122
Góngora, José Ignacio, 225
González, Jose, 109
González Alonso, Antonio: honors received, 175; mentioned, 104
González Calderón, Bárbara: marriage to José de Cevallos, 181; mentioned, 155
González Calderón, Francisco José: careers of children, 181; mentioned, 155
González Calderón, José: career as ecclesiastic, 181
González Calderon, José María, 155
González Calderón, Miguel: career as merchant, 181; mentioned, 155
González Calderón, Tomás: career as jurist, 181; *oidor*, 37
González Calderón family: genealogy of, 156–57; in commerce, 170; mill ownership, 24; untitled, 177; mentioned, 26, 33, 38

González Castañeda, José: in the cabildo, 35
González Castañeda family, 33
González de Collantes, Fernando: cacao importer, 70
González Guerra, Antonio Vicente, 158
González Guerra, Francisco, 155–58
González Guerra, Juan Ignacio: honors received, 175; mentioned, 158
González Guerra family: genealogy of, 156–57; in commerce, 170; untitled, 177; mentioned, 26, 33
González Maldonado, Francisco Ignacio: *oidor*, 37
González Maldonado, Doctor Luis Gonzaga: in the cabildo, 35, 37; rental of *pulquería*, 125
González Maldonado family, 33
González Noriega, Pedro: honors received, 175; mentioned, 270
González Noriega family: in commerce, 170
González Vértiz, Juan Ignacio: honors received, 175; mentioned, 158–59
González Vértiz family, 26, 33
González y Obín, Bartolomé, 197
Gorráez family, 33
Government officials: creoles as, 38; marriages of children, 236; role in commerce, 232; mentioned, 29, 36, 207, 219, 237, 257
Government service, 42, 165, 227
Goya, Manuel Ramón de: mine shareholder, 89
Goycoechea, Ramón de, 85

Grain, 187
Grocery stores, 110–15. *See also Cacahuaterías; Pulperias; Tiendas; Mestizas*
Grooms, 212
Guadalajara, 16, 17, 22, 75, 182
Guanajuato, 16, 17, 169, 272
Guardiola, Marqués de: family remains in commerce, 170; mentioned, 26
Guardiola, Marquesa de, 155
Guatemala City, 68
Guayaquil: cacao from, 68, 69; mentioned, 62, 70, 152
Guerrero family, 33
Guilds: membership in, 209–11
Guilez, Juan Manuel, 131
Gutiérrez, Pedro Marcos: marriage-age difference with wife, 166
Gutiérrez de la Iguera, Justo, 120
Gutiérrez de Terán, Damián, 140, 158
Gutiérrez de Terán, Gabriel: honors received, 175; mentioned, 140, 158
Gutiérrez de Terán, María Ignacia, 140
Gutiérrez de Terán, María Rafaela: marriage of, 38
Gutiérrez de Terán, María Teresa, 158
Gutiérrez de Terán family: geneology of, 156–57
Guzmán, José, 213

Haberdashery, 66
Hacendados, 232. *See also* Estate owners
Havana: cacao from, 68; mentioned, 65, 73, 225

Heras, Francisco Javier de: honors received, 175; mentioned, 148

Heras, José de, 147

Heras, Manuel de, 147–48

Heras Soto, Ignacio de, 148

Heras Soto, Manuel de: honors received, 175; trained in Spain, 148

Heras Soto, Sebastián de: entailment of his wealth, 169; export of commodities, 73; honors received, 175; marriage-age difference with wife, 166; mine shareholder, 89; use of relatives in business, 147–48; mentioned, 26

Hermosa y Miranda, Fernando: company with postal administrator, 96; dowry received, 163; honors received, 175; marriage-age difference with wife, 166; mentioned, 270

Hernández, José, 119

Herradores: guild membership, 210

Herrera y Rivero, Vicente: marriage of, 160

Herreros: guild membership, 210

Hidalgo, Manuel Joaquín de: company in *vinatería*, 131

Hidalgo Revolt, 61

Hiladores de Seda: guild membership, 209

Honorary army commisary: title given to merchants, 179

Honorary *regidores*: merchants as, 178; mentioned, 34, 36

Horcasitas, Francisco Antonio de: dowry received, 163; mentioned, 180

Horcasitas, Manuel José de: dowry received, 163; honors received, 175, 179; marriage into Montezuma family, 180

Hortigosa, Miguel Alonso de: cacao importer, 70

Hourat, Jorge (Diego José García): dowry received, 163; mentioned, 146–47

Huautla, 87

Hurtado, José Manuel: marriage-age difference with wife, 166

Ibáñez de Rivero, Antonio: dowry received, 163

Ibarrola, Francisco Javier de, 148

Ibarrola, Ignacio José de, 148

Ibarrola, José Mélchor de: sons in commerce, 148–49

Ibarrola, Luis Gonzaga de, 28–29, 149

Ibarrola, Tomás Ramón de: honors received, 175

Ibarrola family: in commerce, 170; mentioned, 26, 33

Icaza, Agustín de: cacao importer, 70

Icaza, Antonio de: honors received, 175; mentioned, 158

Icaza, Isidro Antonio de: dowry received, 163; honors received, 175; in the cabildo, 35; mentioned, 158–59, 161

Icaza, José Gabriel de, 158–59

Icaza, José Mariano de, 158–59

Icaza, Mariano José de, 158–59

Icaza é Iraeta, Antonio: marriage of, 161

Icaza family: genealogy of, 156–57; in commerce, 170; untitled, 177; mentioned, 26, 33

Icedo, Julián de, 58

Iglesias, Francisco de: diversified

investments, 171; honors received, 175, 179; mentioned, 219
Independence, 230, 272
Indians: in cigar factory, 205; in guilds, 208; workers in *panaderías*, 189; workers in slaughterhouses, 196; mentioned, 4–5, 190, 204, 239
Indigo, 73
Infante, José Manuel: company in a *pulpería*, 216; mentioned, 214
Inguanzo, Marqués de: in the cabildo, 35. *See also* Alles, Pedro Alonso de
Inns, 221
Inquisition: familiars, 237; mentioned, 34, 58, 114
Intendancy system, 160–61
International traders: cabildo officeholding, 34; division of trading houses, 23; elite families as, 25; response to challenge from provincial cities, 75; mentioned, 229. *See also Almaceneros*; Merchants; Wholesalers
Iraeta, Francisco Ignacio de: honors received, 175; leasing of estate, 167; mentioned, 158
Iraeta é Icaza, Antonio: marriage of, 38
Iraeta family: genealogy of, 156–57; mentioned, 33
Irapuato, 83
Isita, José Bernabé de, 126
Iturbe é Iraeta, Gabriel de: honors received, 175; mentioned, 158
Iturbe é Iraeta, Gabriel Manuel de, 158–59
Iturbe family, 26
Iturriaza, Francisco Javier de: supplier to an *obraje*, 202

Jala, Conde de: daughter's marriage, 181; family remains in commerce, 170; ownership of *pulquerías*, 121; mentioned, 26, 151
Jalapa, 150
Jalapa fair, 55, 61
Jaral de Berrio, Marqués de: in the cabildo, 35
Jaral de Berrio, Marquesa de, 38
Jarcieros: guild membership, 209
Jicayán, 94
Jiménez, Antonio María: dependency on credit sales at bakery, 192
Jiménez del Arenal, Manuel, 81
Journeymen, 208, 212, 216–17, 223, 224, 239
Juzgado de Capellanías, 200

Kelly, Juan: partnership in *cajón*, 109

Lacayos: guild membership, 211
Ladrón de Guevara, Baltasar: *oidor*, 37
La Fraga, Pedro, 195
La Guaira, 65
Lara, José Vicente de, 58
Lawyers: from mercantile families, 181; in the cabildo, 178; mentioned, 20, 28, 29, 169, 182, 205, 219
Lawyers' guild, 149. *See also* Colegio de Abogados
Leguinzábal, Manuel de: cacao importer, 70
León, 85
Libranzas, 85
Librerías, 8
Listoneros: guild membership, 209

Llampallas, Silvestre: career as *viandante*, 98; loan to a *subdelegado*, 95

Llano Velasco y Chavarrí, Manuel: company with brother, 65

Llano y Urresti, Francisco Javier de: cacao importer, 70; mentioned, 69

Llanos Vergara, Juan Antonio: cacao importer, 70

Llanos y Váldez, Doctor Andrés Ambrosio de, 194

Llantada Ibarra, Manuel de: cacao importer, 70

Locerías, 8

Loceros: guild membership, 210

López, José Agustín, 225

López del Diestro, Juan Francisco: company with brother, 65

López de León, Francisco, 118

López de Ortuño, María Isabel: *pulquería* owner, 122

López Frías, Licenciado José Antonio, 214–15

López Herrero, Antonio, 141

López Herrero, Gaspar, 141

López Herrero, Juan Antonio, 141–42

Lugo y Terreros, Miguel Francisco de: in the cabildo, 35

Lugo y Terreros family, 33

Luyando, Luis María de: in the cabildo, 35

Luyando, Manuel de: in the cabildo, 35

Luyando family, 19, 22

Machón, José Antonio, 204

Maderería, 8

Málaga, 48

Managers: their social position, 234

Maniau y Torquemada, Francisco: honors received, 175; in the cabildo, 35; mentioned, 150

Maniau y Torquemada, Ildefonso José, 150

Maniau y Torquemada family, 26, 33

Manila, 45, 67, 68, 143, 152

Manila Galleon, 230. *See also* China trade

Manning, Roberto, 272

Manso Cevallos, Manuel, 58

Manufacturers, 213

Manufacturing plants, 237

Maque, Antonio, 192

Maracaibo: cacao from, 68, 69

Marín, Pedro, 103

Márquez, José Rafael, 117

Martel, Miguel María, 212–13

Marriage: among blacksmiths, 221–22; among journeymen; among merchants, 236; among silversmiths, 212–13; mentioned, 26, 33

Martínez, Juan de Dios: supplier to blacksmiths, 220–21

Martínez Barenque, José: honors received, 175; marriage-age difference with wife, 166

Martínez Cabezón, Blas, 143

Martínez Cabezón, Francisco: aid to relatives in commerce, 143–44; cacao importer, 69, 70; China trade, 70; dowry received, 163; honors received, 176, 179; marriage of daughter, 182; ship owner, 70; supplier to mining company, 88

Martínez Cabezón y Sau, María Ignacia, 144

Martínez de Soto, Antonio, 108

Master artisans, 212, 223, 239
Matos y Rivera, José de: cacao importer, 70
Mayorazgos. See Entails
Mayordomos: merchants as, 180; of *panaderías*, 190
Meat, 187
Meca, José Franco, 58
Medina y Torres, Juan María de, 38
Mendoza, Gerónimo de: rental of sugar estate, 167
Menoyo, Manuel de: wheat merchant, 194
Meoqui, Juan Fernando: mine shareholder, 89
Meoqui, Juan Tomás: cacao importer, 70
Mercader, 264
Mercerías, 8, 112
Merchant houses: ability to dominate provincial commerce, 82, 84
Merchants: agreements with officials, 232; as mayordomos of charities, 180; as moneyborrowers, 56; as *regidores*, 178; access to silver, 231, 243; daughters' marriages, 181–82; dowries received, 163; marriage patterns, 236; membership in *cofradías*, 180; ownership of estates, 146, 236; pursuit of honors, 236–37; mentioned, 169, 207. *See also* Retailers; Wholesalers
Mero, Josefa de: marriage to Angel Pedro de Puyade, 167
Mero family, 162
Mestizos: as goldworkers, 208; workers in *panaderías*, 189; mentioned, 4–5, 190

Mexico, 51, 52, 56, 62, 144, 179, 183, 260
Mexico City: cabildo, 34; commercial rivalry with Veracruz, 63–64; meat consumption, 196; population of, 1, 2–3, 14, 63, 257; mentioned, 16, 17, 20, 24, 25, 33, 36, 45, 50, 55, 62, 63, 64, 69, 73, 78, 79, 90, 92, 93, 94, 97, 98, 101, 108, 121, 126, 146, 152, 168, 181, 187, 200, 207, 219, 227, 229, 230, 237, 239, 240, 241, 243, 244, 264
Micháus y Aspiros, Martín Angel de: dowry received, 163; honors received, 176; marriage-age difference with wife, 166; owner of sugar estate, 91; owner of tannery, 171; sergeant major of merchants' regiment, 173; silver shipper, 73; supplier to tanners, 225; mentioned, 74
Mier de Terán, Gregorio, 140
Mier y Trespalacio, Cosmé de, 160
Mill ownership, 27
Mills: flour, 24; textile, 24; mentioned, 113. *See also Obrajes*
Millers, 203–4
Mimiaga, Ignacio Tomás de: in the cabildo, 35
Mimiaga, José Mariano de: in the cabildo, 35
Mimiaga family, 33
Miners, 231, 232, 243
Mines: owned in partnership by merchants, 167; mentioned, 32, 169, 170, 171
Mining: division of ownership, 233; merchants in, 56; vertical integration of, 258; mentioned, 42, 165, 179, 227, 228

Miravalle, Conde de: in the cabildo, 35
Mixed bloods, 204
Money-lending: by merchants, 57; mentioned, 171–72
Monroy Guerrero y Luyando, Manuel: in the cabildo, 35
Montalvo y Cuesta, María Antonia: owner of *pulpería*, 216
Montañés party, 51–52, 53, 140, 158
Montesa, Order of, 34
Montenegro, José, 138–39
Monterde, José, 213–14
Montero, José, 124
Montezuma family: marriage with merchant, 180
Mora, Antonio: intendant of Oaxaca, 38
Mora y Peysal, Antonia, 161
Mujeres Hiladores de Seda: guild membership, 209
Mulattoes: as goldworkers, 208; workers in *panaderías*, 189; mentioned, 5
Moreu, Tomás, 192
Músicos: guild membership, 211

Navarre, 146
Navarro, Juan, 126–27
Navarro y Noriega, Fernando, 47
New Spain: population of, 47; production of precious metals, 47; mentioned, 48, 50, 55, 65, 91. *See also* Mexico
Noble titles, 42, 229, 237
Non–Spaniards, 207, 208
Noriega, Francisco, 131
Noriega, Licenciado Francisco de: editor of paper, 203

Noriega Cortina, Manuel: honors received, 176
Noriega y Escandón, Nicolás: marriage-age difference with wife, 166
Notaries, 108
Nuns, 182, 237. *See also* Convents

Oaxaca, 71, 93, 94, 98, 106, 264
Obando family, 33
Obras pías, 58, 150
Obrajeros: guild membership, 209
Obrajes: in Mexico City, 91; workers, 212; mentioned, 200, 201, 202, 223, 238
Ojalateros: guild membership, 209
Ojeda, Juan José de, 198
Olloqui, José Vicente de: marriage of, 149
Oqueli, Raymundo, 125
Ordóñez, Manuel de, 220
Orduña, Francisco, 193
Orihuela, Antonio de, 199
Orihuela, María Magdalena, 197
Orozco, Francisco, 214
Ortega, José Aniceto: company with *subdelegado*, 95
Oteiza, Juan José de: cleric and editor, 203; mentioned, 194–95
Oteiza y Vértiz trading house: collapse of, 259; mentioned, 73
Otero, Mariana de, 202
Otero y Araujo, Manuel de: complains about workers, 200–201; purchase of *obraje*, 201–2
Otumba, 96

Pachuca, 169
Paint factory: owned by merchant, 171
Paint manufacturers, 203

Palacio y Romaña, José, 140, 149
Palacio y Romaña, Lucas, 140
Palacio y Romaña, Manuel, 140
Palacios, Joaquín: partnership in
  pulpería, 114; mentioned, 117
Palma, José Tomás, 202
Panaderías: ownership of, 187;
  workforce, 188–90; men-
  tioned, 78, 145, 168. *See also*
  Bakeries
Parián, 6, 18, 102, 104, 138, 142,
  148, 225
Partnerships. *See* Companies
Pasamaneros: guild membership,
  209
Pasarín, Tomás, 95
Pastor Morales, Bruno: honors received, 176; mentioned, 146
Patriarchalism: in family organiza-
  tion, 31–32; mentioned, 30, 39,
  240
Pátzcuaro, 83
Paz y Pérez, Ignacio de: managing
  partner in bakery, 191
Peluqueros: guild membership, 211
Peninsulars: absorption into the
  elite, 164–65; as artisans, 208;
  as merchants, 257; as silversmiths, 212; domination of international trade, 25, 40, 140–
  41, 150–52; population, 2, 4;
  mentioned, 108, 125, 126, 148,
  149, 155, 166, 173, 182–83,
  190, 196, 197, 235, 237, 240
Peña, José Leandro de la, 216
Peñasco, Conde de: family remains in commerce, 170; marriage of, 150; mentioned, 26
Peredo y Cevallos trading house:
  loans made by, 57, 58
Pérez Chacón, José, 117

Pérez de Elizalde, Gabriel: mine
  shareholder, 89
Pérez de Tagle, José, 119
Pérez Galvez, Antonio de: colonel
  of cavalry, 173; honors received,
  176
Pérez Gómez, Roque: honors re-
  ceived, 176; inheritance, 163
Pérez Hernández, José Lucas, 193
Peru, 68, 181, 264
Pharmacists, 212
Picazo, Miguel, 214
Pila, Julián, 203
Piñeda, Rafael, 119
Plan of Iguala, 54
Plateros: guild membership, 209
Portal de Flores, 6–8
Portal de Mercaderes, 6, 105
Portugal, 45
Prado Alegre, Marquesa de, 124
Prado y Zúñiga, Manuel de: in the
  cabildo, 35
Prebend, 108, 181
Presa de Jalpa, Conde de: in the
  cabildo, 35
Priests: from mercantile families,
  181; real-estate ownership, 5;
  mentioned, 29, 30, 169, 225
Printers, 203
Prieto, Félix: owner of bakery
  with brother, 194
Prieto, Francisco, 220–21
Prieto, Manuel, 219
Procurador, 201, 218
Professionals: cabildo officehold-
  ing, 34; mentioned, 207, 219,
  239, 244
Professions, 28–30, 212
Protomedicato, 212
Provincial commerce: domination
  by Mexico City, 243

Provincial elite, 16, 17
Provincial storekeepers, 81–85
Puebla, 16, 200
Puesto, 8, 130
Pulperías: companies in, 111; supplied by bakeries, 187–88; mentioned, 107, 110, 111, 112, 114, 115, 116, 117, 118, 120, 121, 130, 224
Pulque: production of, 21–22; mentioned, 23, 120, 160, 168
Pulque ranchos, 20, 22, 181
Pulque trade, 78, 121–29, 168, 234
Pulquerías: leasing of, 23; ownership of 22, 122–23; mentioned, 9, 31, 120, 168, 234
Puyade, Angel Pedro de: dowry received, 162, 163; honorary intendant, 179; leases an estate, 167; ownership of sugar estates, 167
Puyade family, 33

Querétaro, 148, 200
Quito, audiencia of, 160

Rábago, Conde de: ties to Spanish merchant houses, 62
Rábago, Domingo de, 38, 160
Rábago, Francisco Antonio de: honors received, 176
Rada, Juan Marcos de: honors received, 176
Razo, Juan, 200
Regency of the Mexican Empire, 54
Regidores: merchants as, 178; mentioned, 34, 36, 195, 219, 237
Regla, Conde de: family remains in commerce, 170; ownership of

pulquerías, 121; mentioned, 26, 160
Reparaz, Conde de, 146
Retail commerce: as investment by silversmiths, 216
Retailers: owners of landed estates, 108, 110, 111, 121; mentioned, 195, 212, 213, 233, 239, 241. *See also* Merchants; Storeowners
Revillagigedo census, 255–56
Reyes, Juan: profits as store manager, 80; mentioned, 79
Río, Francisco Antonio del: dowry received, 163; purchase of estate, 167
Rios Mantilla, José de los: cacao importer, 70
Rivas Cacho, Marqués de: mine shareholder, 89; mentioned, 26
Rivero, Francisco del: honors received, 176
Rodallega, José María: enters bankruptcy, 215
Rodríguez, Ana María: *pulquería* owner, 122
Rodríguez de Velasco, Antonio: in the cabildo, 35
Rodríguez de Velasco, José: in the cabildo, 35
Rodríguez de Velasco family, 33
Rodríguez Pablo Fernández, María Josefa, 160
Rodríguez Piniellos y Gómez, María Josefa: *pulquería* owner, 122
Rojas, José de, 130
Roldán, José, 219
Romero Caamaño, Joaquín: gets free coach as *regidor*, 219; sells wheat to bakery, 195

Romero de Terreros, María Do-
lores: *pulquería* owner, 122;
mentioned, 160
Romero de Terreros, María Igna-
cia: *pulquería* owner, 122
Romero de Terreros family: as
pulque producer, 168
Rosales, Ramón, 118
Rosales de Velasco, Doctor José
Maximiliano, 212–13
Rosario, 108
Royal mint, 160
Rubio y Benito, Mateo, 104
Ruiz, Acensio, 214, 224
Ruiz de la Barcena, José: honors
received, 176; invests in slaugh-
terhouses, 170
Rural estates: owned by mer-
chants, 236, 274; mentioned,
228. *See also* Estates; Estate
ownership

Saddlemakers, 207, 225
Sáenz de Escobosa, Francisco:
honors received, 176
Sáenz de Santa María, Agustín,
202
Sagarraga, José, 58
Saldaña, María Josefa: rents an
obraje, 202
Salinas, Marqués de: in the
cabildo, 35; mentioned, 19
Salvat, Jaime: dowry received,
163; mentioned, 161
Sámano, Fernando, 214
San Agustín de las Cuevas, 219
San Julián, Pedro Pablo de, 193
San Luis Potosí, 123, 150, 168
San Miguel el Grande, 225
San Román, Marquesa de: mar-
riage of, 38

Sánchez, Rodrigo: agent for
Conde de Tepa, 125
Sánchez de Almazán, Ramón:
rents his estate, 216
Sánchez de Espinosa, Joaquín: in
the cabildo, 35
Sánchez de Espinosa, José: ar-
ranges a company for his chil-
dren, 106; becomes a priest,
106; dowry received, 163; hon-
ors received, 176; *pulquería*
owner, 122; son of government
official, 150
Sánchez de Espinosa, José Ma-
riano: in the cabildo, 36
Sánchez de Espinosa family, 26, 33
Sánchez de la Concha, Mateo: ties
to Spanish merchant house, 62
Sánchez de Tagle, Francisco Man-
uel: in the cabildo, 35
Sánchez de Tagle family, 33, 37
Sánchez de Vargas family, 219
Sánchez Hidalgo, Doctor Ignacio
María, 149
Sánchez Hidalgo, José Joaquín: in
the cabildo, 35
Sánchez Hidalgo, José María, 149
Sánchez Hidalgo, José Miguel:
honors received, 176
Sánchez Hidalgo, María de
Guadalupe, 149
Sánchez Hidalgo, Miguel Fran-
cisco: careers of children,
149–50
Sánchez Hidalgo family, 26, 33,
181
Sánchez Navarro family: in com-
merce, 270; mentioned, 264
Sánchez Recuenco, Antonio,
223–24
Sandoval y Rojas, Josefa de, 194

Santa María, Spain, 63
Santander, 48, 66, 73, 140, 148, 152
Santiago, Conde de, 19, 34, 160, 197
Santiago, Order of: given to merchants, 177, mentioned, 38
São Paulo, 258
Sastres: guild membership, 209. *See also* Tailors
Sayaleros: guild membership, 209
Sederías, 8, 7
Segura, María Manuela, 119
Selva Nevada, Marqués de: in the cabildo, 36; seek to buy an *obraje*, 202
Semillerías, 8, 112, 138
Seven Years War, 45, 48, 61
Sevilla, Bachiller Juan José Nicholás de: invests in coachmaking company, 218–19
Seville, 221
Sierra, Francisco Antonio de la, 58
Sierra, Manuel de la, 58
Sierra de Pinos, 85, 95
Sierra Urunuela, Juan de: honors received, 176; merchant as mineowner, 88; mine shareholder, 89
Silk-spinners, 223
Silleros: guild membership. *See also* Saddlemakers
Silver, 229, 230, 243
Silver shipping, 73–75, 231
Silversmiths: companies among, 213–14; diversification of investments, 215–16; mentioned, 207, 208, 212, 213, 214, 217–18, 224
Skinner Marshall, Guillermo, 272
Slaughterhouses: social charac-
teristics of owners, 197; mentioned, 196, 197, 198, 238. *See also Tocinerías*
Slaves, 216
Soberón y Corral, Francisco de: dowry received, 163; honors received, 176; marriage-age difference with wife, 166
Social mobility, 5, 14
Sola, Pedro Vicente de: managing partner in a *cajón*, 106
Sombrereros: guild membership, 209
Somera, Antonio: company in his *tocinerías*, 170
Somoano Alonso, Simón de: dowry received, 163; mentioned, 104, 160
Soriano, Gertrudis: owner of *tienda mestiza*, 192
Spain: as commodity market, 71; effect of wars with England, 73; granting of monopolies, 46–47; mentioned, 25, 30, 37, 45, 48, 49, 50, 52, 61, 62, 63, 65, 66, 72, 124, 144, 179, 180, 183, 203, 222, 229, 237, 240
Spaniards: in cigar factory, 205; mentioned, 208, 239
Spanish America, 143
State of Mexico, 55
Storeowners: as mining investors, 168–69; as owners of rural estates, 68. *See also* Merchants; Retailers
Sugar: acquisition of, 72; amount shipped to Spain, 72; commerce in, 45, 66, 71, 91; mentioned, 90, 168, 230, 233, 262
Sugar estates, 167
Subdelegados, 93, 94, 106, 143

Tabasco: cacao from, 68, 69; mentioned, 197
Tailors, 208, 225–26. *See also* Sastres
Teachers, 212
Tejedores de Seda de lo Angusto: guild membership, 209
Tenochtitlán: *pulquería* owner, 122; mentioned, 124, 125
Teotihuacán, 78, 168
Tepa, Conde de: marriage of, 160; *pulquería* owner, 122; rental of *pulquerías*, 124–25
Teposcolula, 95, 98, 143
Tercer orden de San Francisco. *See* Franciscans, Third Order of
Teruel, Felipe Antonio de: in the cabildo, 35
Teruel family, 19, 33
Tetelco, 264
Textile mills, 31, 238. *See also* Mills; *Obrajes*
Tezontle, 204, 205
Theran, Pedro: cacao importer, 70
Tienda, 8, 138, 268
Tienda de algodones, 138
Tiendas mestizas, 80, 107, 110, 112, 118, 120, 138, 168, 171
Tintoreros: guild membership, 209
Tiradores de oro: guild membership, 210
Tithes, 50
Titled families, 33, 34
Tlachique, 129
Tlapalería, 8
Tobacco monopoly, 147, 205
Tocinerías, 170, 196, 197, 198. *See also* Slaughterhouses
Toluca, 77, 79, 168, 195
Tonaleros: guild membership, 210

Toro, Antonio Mariano: managing partner of store, 141–42
Torre Calderón, José de la: *pulquería* owner, 123
Torre y Albornoz, Simón María de la: marriage-age difference with wife, 166
Tovar, Francisco, 268
Trading houses, 32. *See also* Commercial houses; Merchant houses
Tratantes, 264. *See also* Viandantes
Trejo, Leonardo, 136
Troytinas, Pedro, 119
Tuaillon, Justino, 272
Turin, 203

Uluapa, Marqués de: in the cabildo, 35
Urquiaga, Manuel de: marriage-age difference with wife, 166
Urrutia, Cayetano, 220
Uscola, Capitán Antonio de: company in silver-shipping firm, 74

Valcárcel, Domingo, 160
Valiente, Roque: affiliated with brother in Cádiz, 62; marriage-age difference with wife, 166
Valladolid, 83, 95, 146, 168, 215
Valle, Juan del: *pulquería* owner, 122
Valle, Manuel del: marriage-age difference with wife, 166
Valle Ameno, Marqués de: as *pulque* producer, 168
Valle de la Colina, Marqués del, 38
Valle de Orizaba, Conde del: in the cabildo, 35; mentioned, 19, 38

Valley of Mexico, 167, 168, 187
Vargas, Domingo de, 225
Vázquez, José María, 193
Vázquez, Juan Antonio, 74
Vázquez, María Guadalupe, 74
Vega, Manuel de la, 221
Velasco de la Torre y Mora, Antonio: marriages of children, 182
Velasco de la Torre y Mora, Antonio (son): marriage into landed family, 182
Velázquez de la Cadena, Juan Manuel: in the cabildo, 35
Velázquez de la Cadena family, 33
Velería, 8
Veleros: guild membership, 210
Vélez de Escalante, Estéban: investment in urban properties, 172; marriage-age difference with wife, 166
Vendors, 205
Venezuela, 68, 144
Vera, José, 215
Veracruz: population of, 63, 257; role in cochineal trade, 94; shipping volume, 48; mentioned, 16, 17, 58, 61, 62, 63, 64, 71, 73, 74, 75, 144, 152, 230, 264
Verástegui, Ildefonsa, 213
Vertical integration of business, 23–24, 30, 31, 228
Vértiz, Pedro de: as silver shipper, 73
Vértiz family: in commerce, 170
Viana, Francisco de. *See* Tepa, Conde de
Viandante, 83, 96–99, 106, 113, 145, 232. *See also Tratantes*
Viceroy Iturrigaray: gives order affecting *panaderías*, 189–90; mentioned, 173

Vico, Conti and Company, 63
Vidal, Vicente Francisco: mine shareholder, 89
Vidrería, 8
Villar, José de, 109
Villaurrutia family, 33, 37
Villaverde, Francisco Antonio: *pulquería* owner, 122
Vinaterías, 8, 9, 112, 118–21, 131, 138, 220, 224, 268
Vivanco, Antonio de: mine shareholder, 89
Vivanco, Marqués de: family remains in commerce, 170; ownership of *pulquerías*, 121, 122; rental of *pulquerías*, 124; mentioned, 26

Wars of Independence: effect on city-council makeup, 178–79; mentioned, 55, 56, 69
Water drawers, 212
Weavers: guild membership, 224; mentioned, 223–24
Wholesalers: access to honors, 173–79; age at marriage, 165; as commodity traders, 91, 232–33; as mining investors, 27, 88, 89; as money-lenders, 84–85; as owners of different types of stores, 102–3, 106–7; as partners of government officials, 93–96; careers of children, 180–82; economic diversification, 166–68; giving of *arras*, 162; investors in small stores, 233; investors in urban property, 172; mechanisms to obtain silver, 85–89; need for silver, 55–56; ownership of landed estates, 164; purchase of bakeries,

170; receiving noble titles, 177; rental of landed estates, 142; response to trade reforms, 61; suppliers to *hacendados* and miners, 232; mentioned, 17, 18, 31, 45, 51, 166, 181, 203. *See also Almaceneros*; Merchants
Women: as storeowners, 111, 121, 129–30; as weavers, 223–24; ownership of bakeries, 187; restricted from bakeries, 190; mentioned, 213, 266
Wool, 187

Xochimilco, 192

Yermo, Gabriel Joaquín de: honors received, 176

Yermo, Gabriel Patricio de: honors received, 176

Zacatecas, 79, 149, 169
Zacualpan, 83, 86
Zapateros: guild memberhsip, 210
Zapotlán el Grande, 83
Zavala, Antonio de: cacao importer, 70
Zayas, Antonio, 98
Zúñiga y Ontiveros, Felipe de, 203
Zúñiga y Ontiveros, Mariano José de: publisher and businessman, 203
Zurrandores:: guild membership, 210